Pharisees, Scribes and Sadducees in Palestinian Society

A Sociological Approach

by

Anthony J. Saldarini

Michael Glazier
Wilmington, Delaware

For Maureen

First published in 1988 by Michael Glazier, Inc., 1935 West Fourth Street, Wilmington, Delaware 19805.

Copyright ©1988 by Michael Glazier, Inc. All rights reserved.

Library of Congress of Cataloging-in-Publication Data

Saldarini, Anthony J.
    Pharisees, scribes and Sadducees in Palestinian
society.

    Includes index.
    1. Pharisees.   2. Scribes, Jewish.   3. Sadducees.
4. Social classes—Palestine.   5. Bible. N.T.—Criticism,
interpretation, etc.   I. Title.
BM175.P4S24   1988   305.6'96'033   88-31060
ISBN 0-89453-744-X

Typography by Phyllis Boyd LeVane.
Printed in the United States of America.

Table of Contents

Abbreviations in the Notes

Ant.	Josephus' Jewish Antiquities
b.	Babylonian Talmud (followed by the name of the tractate)
BJS	Brown Judaic Series
CBQ	Catholic Biblical Quarterly
CBQMS	Catholic Biblical Quarterly Monograph Series
HDR	Harvard Dissertations in Religion
HTR	Harvard Theological Review
HUCA	Hebrew Union College Annual
IDB	Interpreter's Dictionary of the Bible
IDBS	Interpreter's Dictionary of the Bible, Supplementary Volume
IESS	International Encyclopedia of Social Sciences
JAAR	Journal of the American Academy of Religion
JBL	Journal of Biblical Literature
JJS	Journal of Jewish Studies
JQR	Jewish Quarterly Review
JSJ	Journal for the Study of Judaism
JTS	Journal of Theological Studies
m.	Mishnah (followed by the name of the tractate)

NTS	New Testament Studies
NovTest	Novum Testamentum
p.	Palestinian Talmud (followed by the name of the tractate)
RSR	Religious Studies Review
SBLDS	Society of Biblical Literature Dissertation Series
SJLA	Studies in Judaism in Late Antiquity
SPB	Studia Post-Biblica
SNTSMS	Society for New Testament Studies Monograph Series
t.	Tosefta (followed by the name of the tractate)
VT	Vetus Testamentum
War	Josephus' Jewish War
ZAW	Zeitschrift für die alttestamentliche Wissenschaft
ZNW	Zeitschrift für die neuestestamentliche Wissenschaft

Chronology

Year(s)	Events
198 B.C.E.	Antiochus III the Great, Seleucid ruler in Syria gains effective control of Palestine from Egypt.
175-164	Antiochus IV Epiphanes is Seleucid ruler in Syria.
168-164	Seleucid persecution in Judea, desecration of the Temple, revolt under the Maccabees. Rededication of the Temple under Judas Maccabee.
161	Judas Maccabee killed.
152	Jonathan Maccabee named high priest by Alexander Balas.
150-134?	Founding of the Essene community at Qumran.
142	Jonathan killed and succeeded by his brother Simon. Demetrius relieves Simon of obligation to pay tribute.
141	Simon conquers the Akra.
140	Simon acclaimed as high priest by the nation.
134	Simon killed.
134-104	John Hyrcanus, Simon's son, is high priest and ruler.
103-76	Alexander Jannaeus is high priest and king.
76-67	Alexandra, Alexander Jannaeus' wife, is queen. Hyrcanus is high priest.
63	Ptolemy and the Romans conquer Jerusalem and Palestine. Hyrcanus continues as high priest.
40	Parthian invasion of Palestine. Herod appointed king by the Roman Senate.
37-4	Herod is king in Palestine.

31 B.C.E.- 14 C.E.	Caesar Augustus is Roman Emperor.
4 B.C.E.- 6 C.E.	Archelaus rules Judea.
4 B.C.E.- 39 C.E.	Herod Antipas rules Galilee.
6-41	Roman prefects rule in Judea and Samaria.
14-38	Tiberius is Roman Emperor.
26-36	Pontius Pilate is Roman prefect. Death of Jesus.
41	Emperor Gaius Caligula threatens to place a statue of himself in the Temple.
41-44	Agrippa I rules in Judea and Samaria. 38-40: Galilee and areas to the north.
44-66	Roman procurators rule in Judea and Samaria.
66-70	War against Rome.
70	Destruction of Jerusalem and the Temple.
70-200	Tannaitic period of rabbinic activity.
200	Editing of the Mishnah under Rabbi Judah the Prince.

Part I

PALESTINIAN SOCIETY

1

The Problem of Jewish Groups in Palestine

Recent research on the Pharisees has paradoxically made them and their role in Palestinian society more obscure and difficult to describe. Scholars have pictured the Pharisees as a sect within Judaism, a powerful religious leadership group, a political leadership group, a learned scholarly group, a lay movement in competition with the priesthood, a group of middle-class urban artisans or some combination of these. The Sadducees have usually been identified as coterminous with the Jewish governing class, including the chief priests, high officials and rich families in Jerusalem. The scribes are described as a middle class professional class. In most historical reconstructions of Jewish society the categories used to describe these groups, such as sect, school, upper class, lay leadership, etc. are ill defined or misused and not integrated into an understanding of the overall structure and functioning of society.

The proliferation of hypotheses about the Pharisees shows how poorly they are understood. Bits of evidence are often taken out of context, harmonized with each other and used as building blocks for very improbable structures. Though Josephus says that the Sadducees were drawn from the upper class, he does *not* say that all of the upper class were Sadducees, contrary to the claims of most treatments of them. The scribes appear as a cohesive group only in the New Testament. Elsewhere scribes fill a variety of social roles, from high officials to lowly copyists. In general, because Josephus names the three leading Jewish "schools of thought" as the Pharisees, Sadducees and Essenes and because the Pharisees, scribes and Sadducees appear in the New Testament as opponents of Jesus, the importance and roles of these groups in Jewish society are vastly overemphasized.

Most reconstructions of the Pharisees and Sadducees use their beliefs (as recorded in Josephus' summaries) as the generative and defining characteristics of the group. But their social identity is more broadly based on political, economic, and social factors and interests with which their religious beliefs are inextricably joined. This study will broaden the inquiry into the Pharisees, scribes and Sadducees by asking questions such as: what social classes did the Pharisees, scribes and Sadducees come from? What social statuses did they enjoy in Jewish society? What political involvement did they have at different stages of their history? What kind and degree of authority or influence did they have with the people and with the other Jewish leadership groups? How important were they among the many classes, groups and forces at work in Jewish society? What degree of direct political power did they exercise? What was their goal for themselves and for Jewish society? What kind of program did they propose for Jewish society? These questions concerning their place in society will throw some light on the more internal questions, such as: How large was their membership and what kind of organization did they have? How was membership defined? What beliefs, ideas and rules governed their communal involvement? The use of sociological method in conjunction with literary and historical analysis will allow a systematic and controlled reading of the evidence in its proper setting. Those questions which cannot be answered will demonstrate the limits of our knowledge and prevent facile generalizations.

The Pharisees, scribes and Sadducees as a variety of Jew, as thinkers and as leaders must be seen as part of Palestinian Jewish society and accurately located and described in relationship with other Jewish leaders and social movements from 200 B.C.E. to 100 C.E. Jewish leaders included the high priest, the chief priests, elders and notables who were probably the recognized heads of prominent families at the local and national level. These leaders were assisted by several groups whom Gerhard Lenski identifies as retainers (see ch. 3). Retainers included the bureaucrats, soldiers and functionaries associated with the Hasmoneans, the Herods and the Romans as well as the Temple servants and officers associated with the chief priests. It is among the retainers that we shall find the scribes and most of the Pharisees. The Sadducees were members of the governing class, according to Josephus, but we know little more of their roles in society.

RELIGION IN ANCIENT SOCIETY

Because modern sociology and political theory usually separate religion from political society, a special word needs to be said about the place of religion and specialized religious functionaries and groups in ancient society. The modern separation of church and state and the stress on individual, private faith commitment as the foundation of religion were unknown in antiquity. In traditional society, including the Roman empire and Jewish Palestinian society, religion was embedded in the political and social fabric of the community. Religious belief and practice were part of the family, ethnic and territorial groups into which people were born. People did not choose their religion, nor did most social units or groups have members with different religions. Religion was integral to everything else and inseparable from it. People might worship new gods in addition to the old ones and engage in additional cultic practices, but they remained what they were culturally and socially. Radical conversion to another religion and rejection of one's inherited beliefs and behavior meant (and still mean today in such societies) separation and alienation from family and hereditary social group. Thus, involvement with religion is in itself political and social involvement in the broad sense of those terms. Consequently, the Pharisees and Sadducees should not be seen as sects withdrawn from society with no political impact. In fact, the Qumran community, living by the Dead Sea, were part of Jewish society and quite likely had a political impact. They were not completely cut off from Jewish society since the area was inhabited, contained defensive installations and presumably paid taxes to the Hasmoneans and Romans. To be a Jew was to be part of Jewish society, which included culture, behavior, cult, identity with people and land, etc. Those who disagreed with the Temple authorities, like the Qumran community, were still within the social boundaries of Judaism and an influence to be reckoned with.

Though religion was embedded in political society in a way it is not today, those with cultic or religious functions could form separate power centers in political society. In larger societies complex religious organizations and specialized religious roles developed and were institutionalized among the leaders.[1] Consequently, the identity between the entire community and the religious sphere which is common in patrimonial societies is partly absent in more complex societies and so competition could arise among groups within a religion.[2] This autonomous religious sphere is severely limited, especially compared with modern religion. Though the leadership, sects, orders, groups, etc. of a religion can achieve a real independence, the whole religious community's identity is still tied to local community identity.[3] As will be seen, the Pharisees, scribes and Sadducees seem to fit in such a framework.

Groups with a strong religious base could acquire independence and power within society by a stress on universal values and ideology and by relatively open membership. Such groups, separate from the traditional territorial and status hierarchy, could be conservative in support of the regime, and so be politically valuable for central political leaders, or promote a critical stance toward society, based on moral and symbolic appeals to the people.[4] Such a relatively independent religious establishment is firmly political and typically tries to dominate society through the establishment of a canon of sacred books, schools to interpret the texts, educational organizations to spread knowledge, and the fostering of a total world view. In a complex society which spawns such groups, such as Judaism during the Greco-Roman period, the 'little traditions' of local groups and families are gradually integrated into the 'great tradition' of the

[1]S. N. Eisenstadt, *The Political Systems of Empires: The Rise and Fall of Historical Societies* (Glencoe/New York: Free Press/Collier-Macmillan, 1963), 50.

[2]Eisenstadt, *Empires,* 61.

[3]Eisenstadt, *Empires,* 61-62 and 65.

[4]Eisenstadt, *Empires,* 62-65.

larger society.[5] The conflicts among various groups reflected in the post-exilic sections of the Bible and in the stories of social and religious conflict in Josephus bespeak the struggle to direct and control Jewish society by numerous groups, of whom the Pharisees, scribes and Sadducees are just a few.

PREVIOUS STUDIES OF THE PHARISEES

No attempt will be made to review all the previous studies of the Pharisees, the divergent methods used and the welter of conclusions proposed.[6] Earlier studies by Christians suffered from the tendency to read the polemical account of the Pharisees, scribes and Sadducees in the New Testament as history and then use it to interpret the rabbinic sources, a tendency which still persists in some New Testament scholarship.[7] Many Christian scholars and handbooks are still influenced by the biased picture of Judaism developed by Schürer and perpetuated in numerous introductions and summaries.[8] Though many recent studies have clarified aspects of Judaism in the second Temple period, the Pharisees, scribes and Sadducees remain obscure because of the paucity of evidence and the biases of the sources.

Most presentations of the Pharisees have sought to overcome the slim second Temple evidence by an appeal to the abundance of rabbinic literature, even though these sources date from later

[5]Eisenstadt, *Empires,* 65.

[6]See a brief review and references to other literature in Gary G. Porton, Ch. 2, "Diversity in Postbiblical Judaism," pp. 69-72 and Anthony J. Saldarini, Ch. 17, "Reconstructions of Rabbinic Judaism," pp. 457-460 in *Early Judaism and Its Modern Interpreters,* eds. Robert A. Kraft and George W. E. Nickelsburg (Atlanta: Scholars, 1986). Select authors will be cited as necessary. Many of the positions on the Pharisees and Sadducees are summarized in the annotated bibliography on Josephus by Louis Feldman, *Josephus and Modern Scholarship* (Berlin/New York: deGruyter, 1984) 542-580. Literature on the scribes and Sadducees will be treated in Part Three.

[7]See the extensive review of Christian bias in its evaluation of Judaism in E. P. Sanders, *Paul and Palestinian Judaism* (Philadelphia: Fortress, 1977) 33-238. Other literature is reviewed in Anthony J. Saldarini, "Judaism and the New Testament," in *The New Testament and Its Modern Interpreters,* eds. Eldon J. Epp and George MacRae (Atlanta: Scholars, forthcoming).

[8]See Shaye J. D. Cohen, "The Political and Social History of the Jews in Greco-Roman Antiquity: The State of the Question," Ch. 1 in *Early Judaism,* 34-37, for an evaluation of the influence of Schürer.

centuries and do not purport to be historical.[9] Such a naive reading of rabbinic literature as a first-century source is based on the presuppositions that 1. rabbis of the second and third centuries are a later form of Pharisees; 2. there was little change over time in their way of life (even after the destruction of the Temple); 3. accounts of second Temple events and institutions recounted one to six centuries later are both informed and unbiased; and 4. rabbinic literature, which does not attempt to present a history of Pharisaism, gives enough information for an adequate understanding of the Pharisees.

Each of these presuppositions is either wrong or misused in reconstructing the Pharisees. 1. It is very likely that the pre-70 Pharisees contributed to the emergence of the post-70 rabbis, but evidence is not abundant.[10] The tannaitic authors of the earliest rabbinic sources did not identify themselves as Pharisees[11] and many other components of the Jewish community and tradition besides Pharisaism contributed to the form Judaism took in the centuries after the destruction of the Temple. 2. Even granted some kind of continuity between the Pharisees and rabbis, the loss of the Temple, of the Jerusalem leadership and of the clear political identity which went with them caused major adjustments to the Jewish understanding of the world as well as its symbolic system, behavioral patterns and values. 3.

---

[9]This is true of recent surveys, such as *Compendia Rerum Iudaicarum ad Novum Testamentum. Section 1. The Jewish People in the First Century,* ed. S. Safrai, et al., vols. 1-2 (Philadelphia: Fortress, 1974, 1976) and E. Schürer, revised by G. Vermes et al., *The History of the Jewish People in the Age of Jesus Christ (175 B. C.-A. D. 135),* Vol 2. (Edinburgh: Clark, 1979) 381-414. It is common in various introductions and popularizations as well as in scholarly monographs.

[10]Shaye J. D. Cohen, "The Significance of Yavneh: Pharisees, Rabbis, and the End of Jewish Sectarianism," *HUCA* 55 (1984) 36-41, reviews the evidence and argues for its cumulative strength.

[11]Cohen, "Yavneh," 37. In the article (pp. 27-53) he offers a theory that after the destruction of the Temple the rabbis encouraged debate within schools and discouraged the formation of "sects" in order to ensure the survival of Judaism. For this reason they were reluctant to identify themselves as Pharisees. The theory has two problems. First, the lack of sects is better explained sociologically. Sects depend upon the presence of a powerful, established body against which to react; after the destruction of the Temple leadership, such a body was lacking. Second, the talmuds record mainly the disputes of the rabbinic movement which was a long time in gaining control of Jewish society. The absence of sects in rabbinic literature does not prove that there were none. Even after it did gain control in the mid and late talmudic period, various sect-like movements and protests against talmudic control emerged.

More importantly, rabbinic literature (Mishnah, Tosefta, the two Talmuds and the midrashic collections) and the traditions collected there are enormously varied in genre, purpose, date and origin. Many traditions about the Pharisees, Sadducees and other second Temple institutions, laws, events and people bear the clear marks of later interests and outlooks. Even rules for festivals and sacrifices in the Temple cannot be surely related to the first century because they reflect later scholars' views of how things ought to have been. 4. Finally, even if some reliable traditions can be isolated, they are strikingly incomplete and reflect the rabbinic authors' lack of interest in history.[12] In sum, contrary to the approach used in many histories and studies, the rabbinic sources will not be used as the core body of evidence for the Pharisees and Sadducees. Rather, each source will be presented and critically assessed separately in order to determine the historical reliability of its claims.

Two recent, major studies of the Pharisees by Jacob Neusner and Ellis Rivkin have provided sophisticated approaches to the rabbinic evidence along with extensive and serious interpretations of Josephus and the New Testament.[13] Each will be considered in more detail in chapter ten. For the present it is enough to note that, though Rivkin tries to control his reading of rabbinic literature by using as a control group texts which speak of Pharisees and Sadducees together, he then uses his control group to read rabbinic texts from different sources and periods as one body of reliable historical evidence.[14] Further, he imagines the Pharisees as scholars who wrested control of Judaism from the established authorities, a very unlikely hypothesis, as will be seen below, and as the creators of an

[12]See ch. 10 for a more detailed assessment of the rabbinic evidence concerning the Pharisees and Sadducees.

[13]Jacob Neusner, *The Rabbinic Traditions about the Pharisees before 70* (Leiden: Brill, 1971), 3 vols.; Ellis Rivkin, "Defining the Pharisees: The Tannaitic Sources," *HUCA* 40-41 (1969-70) 205-249 and *A Hidden Revolution: The Pharisees' Search for the Kingdom Within* (Nashville: Abingdon, 1978). Neusner has also written many essays on the Pharisees and rabbis. One particularly convenient collection is *Formative Judaism: Religious, Historical and Literary Studies. Third Series. Torah, Pharisees, and Rabbis* (BJS 46; Chico: Scholars, 1983).

[14]Rivkin bases much of his case on a relatively uncritical reading of Josephus, as well, an aspect of his work which will not be explicitly dealt with in this study. See the critical review by Shaye J. D. Cohen in *JBL* 99 (1980) 627-629.

internalized form of Judaism, a very modern sounding ideology indeed.[15] Neusner's interpretation of the Mishnah and of the texts about the pre-70 sages is historically critical in a way similar to contemporary studies of the Bible. His elucidation of legal themes of interest to the Pharisees is fundamental, but his characterization of them as a non-political sect (in some of his work) is based on a misunderstanding of how religion was part of the social and political scene in the first century. His work will be used extensively, but put in a different sociological context.

The Plan of This Study

The sparse evidence for the Pharisees, scribes and Sadducees must be set in a larger historical and sociological context in order to be interpreted correctly. To picture the Pharisees, Sadducees and Essenes as the only or as the dominant groups in first century Judaism, as many treatments implicitly do, is to underestimate the diversity of Judaism in the first century and misunderstand the social structure of the Roman empire. Though it is impossible within the limits of this study to describe all aspects of the society of the empire or of Jewish Palestine, major aspects of that society will be sketched.[16] An attempt will be made to situate the Pharisees, scribes and Sadducees within the whole of society and to show their roles and contributions to it.

Part One describes certain aspects of Palestinian society within its larger context in the Empire. After this introductory chapter,

---

[15]See the summary and critique of his way of reconstructing history by D. Ellenson, "Ellis Rivkin and the Problems of Pharisaic History: A Study in Historiography," *JAAR* 43 (1975) 787-802.

[16]New Testament scholars interested in the origins of Christianity in Palestine have written on aspects of the sociology of Palestine. See Gerd Theissen, *Sociology of Early Christian Palestine* (Philadelphia: Fortress, 1978); Richard A. Horsley and John S. Hanson, *Bandits, Prophets, and Messiahs: Popular Movements at the Time of Jesus* (Minneapolis: Winston, 1985). A study of Jewish tradition in social context during the post-exilic period is Hans G. Kippenberg, *Religion und Klassenbildung im antiken Judäa* (Studien zur Umwelt des Neuen Testaments 14; Göttingen: Vandenhoeck, 1978). On the thought world of Christianity, see John Gager, *Kingdom and Community: The Social World of Early Christianity* (Englewood: Prentice-Hall, 1975) and Howard C. Kee, *Christian Origins in Sociological Perspective* (Philadelphia: Westminster, 1980). Many other studies treat specific topics, methods or books.

chapter two will outline the sociological method followed in this book, some of the criticisms leveled against it and the precise contribution this study seeks to make to the study of first century Judaism and Christianity. Chapter three situates Palestinian society within the Roman empire, using sociological studies of agrarian empires and some social history, and describes the major social classes and roles found in such societies. Chapter four defines and classifies the types of social relations and groups which make up the fabric of society, especially those most relevant to the study of first century Judaism.

Part Two interprets the literary sources, Josephus, the New Testament and rabbinic literature, using the sociological understanding of Palestinian society derived from Part One and correcting it where necessary. In chapter five the activities of the Pharisees and Sadducees in Josephus' historical accounts are analyzed sociologically and in chapter six Josephus' descriptions of them are critically evaluated in terms of both historically known groups and the sociological models appropriate to the time. Chapters seven to nine treat the New Testament. Chapter seven covers the Pharisee, Saul of Tarsus, and chapters eight and nine the gospels. The gospels are subjected to critical evaluation in order to separate polemic from reality. Finally, in chapter ten the rabbinic sources are historically evaluated in terms of their own genres, literary contexts and the sociological and historical data derived from other sources.

In Part Three the results of the sociological and literary analyses are drawn together. In chapter eleven the scribes, who appear as an organized group only in the gospels, are set within the larger context of scribalism in the Near East and in Judaism. In chapter twelve the results concerning the Pharisees, about whom we have the most evidence, are synthetically presented and unanswered questions defined. In chapter thirteen the meager findings about the least known group, the Sadducees, are summarized and evaluated for the little they are able to tell us.

2

A Sociological Approach

Ordinarily literary analysis is used to understand the inner workings of ancient texts and historical research to set them in their proper context. This study will supplement these approaches with methods and conclusions derived from sociology and cultural anthropology. Because the literary and historical data on Pharisees, scribes and Sadducees are so sparse, numerous questions about each group remain without certain answers. Interpreters have proposed many hypotheses for understanding them, but most have been based on uncritical retrojections of modern theories of society and religion. Sociology and cultural anthropology will provide some control for the creation of hypotheses concerning the nature of these groups.

Errors in the description and understanding of the Pharisees, scribes and Sadducees have abounded. Scholars have often treated the Pharisees as a middle-class group, though there was no middle class in antiquity. They have characterized the Pharisees and Sadducees as religious groups separate from politics, even though in antiquity religion was embedded in political society and inseparable from it. The Pharisees have been seen as learned urban artisans at a time when artisans were uneducated, poor and powerless. These fundamental errors in perspective make clear that one has an assumed understanding of society whether one is aware of it or not. The first section of this study will make explicit the sociological theory and view of ancient society which will be used in the analysis of the Pharisees, scribes and Sadducees.

In order not to read modern categories and social structures into antiquity, theories of social structure must be joined to sociological studies of ancient empires and anthropological studies of pre-industrial Mediterranean civilization. Great care is needed because sociological theory is very western, based on modern philosophy and biased toward the modern view of how culture ought to be organized. Cultural anthropology is more cross-cultural and works with pre-industrial societies which are similar in some respects to ancient society.[1] However, the Mediterranean societies which anthropology has studied have all been influenced by modern industrial society and by the late medieval and modern accent on individualism. Even if one gets to what was typical in antiquity, one is left with the historical problem: was it so? If it is uncertain, how likely was it? Was there change over time in the society or group being studied? As much as possible, we must critically control both our own culture and society with its consequent interests as well as the ancient period and society with all its interests and presuppositions.

Some will object that we should not use modern sociological categories at all, but seek to determine their own social categories and understandings.[2] Though the quest for ancient categories is part of the whole enterprise, modern sociological categories are also legitimate tools of analysis. They can bring out aspects of ancient society ignored or unperceived in antiquity. Even when modern sociological categories and theories do not fit, they prove decisively how different antiquity is from the contemporary world. Finally, social science categories and theories which are part of our modern view must be acknowledged, subjected to criticism in terms of antiquity and used to evaluate critically society in antiquity.

---

[1] Bruce Malina has exploited many cultural models in order to understand aspects of the New Testament world. See *The New Testament World: Insights from Cultural Anthropology* (Atlanta: Knox, 1981) and *Christian Origins and Cultural Anthropology: Practical Models for Biblical Interpretation* (Atlanta: Knox, 1986). For Mediterranean society see J. Davis, *People of the Mediterranean: An Essay in Comparative Social Anthropology* (London: Routledge and Kegan Paul, 1977).

[2] For a concise explanation of the conflict over emic and etic categories and an argument for the complementarity of both, see Ernest Gellner and John Waterbury (eds.), *Patrons and Clients in Mediterranean Societies.* (London: Duckworth, 1977) 9-11.

The overwhelming danger in the use of the methods and especially the results of sociology and anthropology is the cookie cutter approach in which abstract categories created for organizing data and testing hypotheses are imposed on or read into texts. Such eisegesis lacks sensitivity to the texts and to the limits of scientific categories. Theories should guide and illuminate exploration of texts and be in turn corrected by what is found there. Another danger in understanding both modern and ancient categories stems from changes in society over time. The same office, group designation, or social entity may vary greatly, though the name remains the same.[3]

This study will concentrate on the social activities and roles of the Pharisees, scribes and Sadducees rather than on their thought and beliefs. There are two reasons for this. First, we have no literature directly from any of these groups and what information we have about their beliefs is not reliable because of either the biases or the dates of the sources. Along with attempts to reconstruct the thought of these groups, their activities and places in society must be determined as far as possible. Second, concentration on their beliefs has often led scholars to view them as simple theological debating societies, separate from the rest of life. To correct this imbalance stress will be placed on how these groups acted in society and what effect they had.

Once a social context is established for these groups and for first century Jewish society, the documents of the period and later documents which speak of the period can be more easily interpreted and integrated into a coherent picture. For example, the Pharisees believed in resurrection and the Sadducees did not. Many hypotheses have been created to explain this difference, but most have been loosely connected to the social situation and history of Judaism and of the Pharisees and Sadducees. Recent work on apocalyptic literature offers the hope that the social world of some documents can be recovered and perhaps even correlated with what we know of history and

---

[3]Two modern political examples may make the point. In the United States the presidency has grown enormously in power over two centuries, though the name and constitutional definition of the office has remained the same. The chairmen of political parties used to wield enormous direct power over the members, but now they are mediators and organizers among many factions.

society at the time.[4] Eventually detailed work on documents, the structure of society and the events of history may produce a more sophisticated understanding of first-century apocalyptic movements than those which see them as simply world-rejecting (Weber) or based on cognitive dissonance or relative deprivation.

THE USE OF SOCIAL SCIENCES

Social sciences have typically been used to interpret ancient texts and history in three ways:

1. heuristically, to generate questions to be used in the study of texts. This use of social sciences can produce new insights, but can also lead to inappropriate questions being asked and major aspects of the texts and period being missed.

2. descriptively, to provide categories both to describe what is in the texts and to fill gaps in our knowledge of ancient society with sociologically probable theories. The explicit acknowledgement of the outlook brought to the text by the interpreter and of the view of society used as a context for interpreting is healthy, but sociological categories often contain modern presuppositions which render them inappropriate for understanding antiquity.[5]

3. as explanation, to show how a whole social system works and how the parts affect one another. Such causal and scientific explanation is the goal of many practitioners of social science, but it is seldom reached with precision and it is challenged as a proper goal of social science by many theorists who do not have

[4]George W. E. Nickelsburg has begun the task of comparing documents from the Greco-Roman period to see which are from the same movement. See "Social Aspects of Palestinian Jewish Apocalypticism," *Apocalypticism in the Mediterranean World and the Near East*, ed. David Hellholm (Tübingen: Mohr, 1983) 641-654 and "*1 Enoch* and Qumran Origins: The State of the Question and Some Prospects for Answers," *SBL Seminar Papers 1986* (Atlanta: Scholars, 1986) 341-360. On social world see Alfred Schutz and Thomas Luckmann, *The Structures of the Life-World* (Evanston: Northwestern UP, 1973); Karl Mannheim, *Ideology and Utopia* (New York: Harcourt, 1936) and the many other works based on the sociology of knowledge.

[5]For the dangers in 1 and 2, see Stanley K. Stowers, "The Social Sciences and the Study of Early Christianity," *Approaches to Ancient Judaism, V: Studies in Judaism in Its Greco-Roman Context* (BJS 32; Atlanta: Scholars, 1985) 161-162.

an empirical model of the social sciences.

Some scholars try to use social sciences as descriptive tools and ignore theory, but the use of descriptive categories, such as class or role, carry with them an (often covert) explanatory theory concerning what aspects of human life and relationships are constitutive and causal for society.[6] Description is never self-sufficient because human understanding demands that we seek explanation. What is described depends partly on what the knower already understands. Initial description, which includes observation and insight, leads inevitably to explanation which is based on thinking and understanding and these in turn support knowledge which is based on judgment and commitment. The social sciences themselves flourish within a larger scientific and philosophical enterprise which continually seeks more inclusive insights and more comprehensive explanatory systems. The total context of social theory must be attended to.

PROBLEMS WITH SOCIAL THEORY

All modern western studies are biased in that science is assumed to be rational and right and other views wrong. Some social scientists mimic the natural sciences by restricting proof to that which can be empirically or mathematically demonstrated, but many others recognize the interplay of perception of the world and the objective experience of the world. Cultural anthropology is more sensitive to cultural patterns and views, but the dominant theories ultimately treat rites, symbols, customs and artifacts as objects to be assessed in scientific terminology rather than taking seriously a culture's stated intentions and motives.

Social studies concerned with religion face special problems because the possible truth of transcendence is systematically ignored. Such neglect is usually based on the overvaluation of the empirical and rejection of transcendent claims based on faith

---

[6]See Stowers, "Social Sciences," for problems with causality, human agency and commensurability. Wayne Meeks' seminal book on Paul, *The First Urban Christians* (New Haven: Yale, 1983) has been criticized on this score. See Stowers, 168-176; J. H. Elliott in *RSR* 11 (1985) 329-335; B. Malina in *JBL* 104 (1985) 346-349.

(which are thought to be closed to rational review). Yet by science's own principles a phenomenon which is not thoroughly explained and whose truth claims are not subjected to assessment has not been adequately studied scientifically. The prior rejection of the transcendent and of all religious truth claims is scientific bias.[7] Though many obstacles obstruct the study of religion, the task is neither impossible nor optional.

Modern social theory has been based on the modern assumption that humans are moved by self-interest and desire and that "higher" motives such as altruism, love and religious faith can be reduced to lower motives or at least subordinated to them. Though this study stresses needs and interests, not meanings and beliefs, it does not assume that human activity derives entirely from desire. Because needs and interests have often been ignored or de-emphasized by those who see the Pharisees, scribes and Sadducees as predominantly spiritual and because such interpretations cut them off from politics and society, this neglected aspect of first-century Judaism will be explored here. The faith that moved first century Jews and Christians can neither be reduced to some other phenomenon nor treated as an unassessable quirk. This study, however, concerns itself mainly with social activities and arrangements which are public and observable, to the extent that ancient texts and archaeology give us data. The social structures and relations of antiquity serve as guidelines for interpreting texts and as part of the foundation of a wholistic view of society which includes God and humans.

Functionalism

Functionalism has been the dominant sociological theory in the United States and it is the theory most used in this study.[8]

---

[7]For a sustained argument for a scientific study of religion which faces and adjudicates the truth claims of religions see Donald Wiebe, *Religion and Truth: Towards an Alternative Paradigm for the Study of Religion* (Religion and Reason 23; Hague: Mouton, 1981).

[8]Functionalism, which exists in many forms, owes much to Max Weber and Emile Durkheim. In the United States Talcott Parsons was the commanding figure in this school. It also was advanced by the work of the British anthropologists Radcliffe-Brown and Malinowski.

Functionalism assumes that all human action contributes to human living and specifically human society and seeks to understand the function (that is effect or consequence) of each action. The part that each type of action and each social group or role plays in society is analyzed and related to others in an organic way. Even negative actions have a function in society as agents for change or for dismantling structures which no longer work. Functionalism has often been challenged for its assumption that society exists and must be protected. Some have claimed that conflict theory, the study of society as a group of conflicting rather than cooperating forces, is a more true model for society. However, conflict theory is a variant of functionalism and merely brings out the positive social functions of conflict in a healthy and stable society and its role in the demise of a social structure which has outlived its usefulness.[9] Even conflicts within society serve the need of society for change, reform, modification according to circumstances and the accomodation of a wide range of needs and interests.

Many of the texts concerned with the Pharisees, scribes and Sadducees involve conflict, which is part of functioning society, not constitutive of it, in the implicit view of the sources. Josephus brings the Pharisees and Sadducees into his narrative only when they are part of crucial political events (conflicts) unfolding in Palestine.These groups appear in the gospels when they are in conflict with Jesus. In rabbinic literature the Pharisees and sages who are identified as part of the tradition often dispute over interpretations of the law and behavior. These disputes are within the fold, but fundamental disagreements between Pharisees and Sadducees and other hostile groups are seen as a threat to the community and the combatants are appropriately excoriated. All the texts treat conflict as an evil to be overcome and blame those responsible. Josephus favors a strong ruler who will keep civil order and attacks all who threaten that order. Rabbinic literature desires a well ordered community whose constitution is worked out in principled dispute, but it defends itself against those who transgress the community boundaries. The gospels promote a new understanding of God's will and

---

[9]Jonathan Turner, *The Structure of Sociological Theory* (Homewood: Dorsey Press, 1978).

thus come into conflict with the traditional Jewish community. Even here, the gospels are not revolutionary in conscious intent, but implicitly argue that they preserve true continuity in the tradition and community. Tradition and order, not change and conflict, are the virtues espoused by all parties.

The problems with functionalism are well known and often rehearsed.[10] Functionalism is heavily biased in favor of the status quo. As a theory, it assumes that society exists and is good, but it does not convincingly explain its origin or purpose. It especially seeks to know the consequences of an act, series of acts or an institution for the larger society. Because it is teleologically oriented, it does not stand the test of strict empirical causal criteria and falls victim to circularity and unverifiability.[11] Functionalism is often used descriptively as a heuristic construct to see how society fits together into a coherent structure, or how some social factors are in tension with existing structures. As such functionalism is criticized by more critical and radical theorists who object to functionalism's conservative bias in favor of the status quo and its refusal to criticize and overthrow social relations and interactions which are oppressive.[12] Finally, functionalism is criticized for ignoring the subjective motives, intentions and truth claims of social actors. A wholistic sociological method must take into account the beliefs and commitments of the people who make up society as well as the social forces and structures which act upon them.[13]

[10]A classic attack is contained in Alvin W. Gouldner, *The Coming Crisis of Western Sociology* (New York: Basic, 1970). See also Jonathan Turner and Alexandra Maryanski, *Functionalism* (Menlo Park, CA: Benjamin Cummings), 141, where the lack of explanatory power of functionalism is acknowledged. Critiques of functionalism as used in New Testament study may be found in Stowers "Social Sciences" and Richard A. Horsley, "How Functional is Functionalism for Analysis of Early Christianity," *JAAR* forthcoming.

[11]See Carl G. Hempel, "The Logic of Functional Analysis," *Aspects of Scientific Explanation and Other Essays in the Philosophy of Science* (New York: Free Press, 1965) 297-330.

[12]The Marxist critique is the best known. It sees conflict among classes as the engine of history and society in its present forms as a stage in the development of a perfect society.

[13]The ignoring of human intention in all its forms by functionalism is a central argument in Stowers, "Social Sciences." Often this approach is attributed to Max Weber, but Susan Hekman, *Weber, Ideal Type, and Contemporary Social Theory*

These limitations of functionalist method demand that it be complemented by and correlated with other studies concerned with Jewish society, Palestine in the Roman empire, the many movements and groups in Judaism, the social settings of the great variety of Jewish and other literature and the history, economics and culture of the period before a fully adequate understanding of the first century can be hoped for.

Sociology and the Sources

The first-century Jewish historian Josephus gives the most information concerning Jewish society and history in the Hellenistic and Roman empires. The events which he records, the people whom he treats and the interpretations which he offers for major events in Jewish history provide some data, but a very incomplete account of Jewish society. Since Josephus looks at society from the top with the eyes of the governing class and wishes to promote stability and continuity, he especially lends himself to functional analysis. So functionalism, which takes society as it is, will make clear the implications and limitations of Josephus' analysis of Judaism in the Roman empire. Static categories like class, status and party fit his static view of society. Before the classes in the empire are described in chapter three and used to interpret the Pharisees and Sadducees in Josephus in chapters five and six, part of this chapter will be devoted to an analysis and critique of the concept of class and the concomitant concept of power. These categories overlap but taken together they provide a very abstract and general outline of social organization and activity which can serve as a framework for understanding the more particular and unique characteristics of Jewish society. The sketchy data available concerning Palestinian society and the very abstract sociological categories of class and status will be augmented with comparative sociological studies which use historical data from similar societies. In this way hypotheses concerning Jewish society can be cautiously and fruitfully generated on the basis of cross-cultural models based

(Notre Dame: University of Notre Dame, 1983) has argued that Weber's ideal type implicitly mediates and reconciles the split between social structures and intentions.

on a coherent theory of social organization and activity. I will use two authors extensively, Gerhard Lenski and S. N. Eisenstadt.[14] Both have analyzed various types of empires in different cultures and periods of history. Lenski has developed a theoretical class system to describe the social relations within an agrarian empire, of which the Hellenistic-Roman Empire is one example. His work, supplemented by other authors and modified by their criticism, will serve as the framework of this study.

Since the Pharisees, scribes and Sadducees are small groups within the larger structures of society and since they have many relationships with others in society, more flexible models, such as networks and patron client relationships, will be introduced in order to describe many of the inner workings of society. Both the New Testament and rabbinic literature deal with the Jewish community and the emerging Christian community. For the most part they do not attend to the larger social structures of society but deal with smaller groups and small scale social relations. Thus in chapter four group formation, maintenance of boundaries, patronage, community standards of honor and shame, interest groups, social movements, schools and sects will be described as a preparation for later analysis of a variety of texts. The rest of this chapter will be devoted to a discussion and analysis of the functionalist categories which will be used to analyze the Roman empire and Jewish society (chapter three) and the activities of the Pharisees in Josephus (chapter five).

Class

Before describing Lenski's class system, some attention should be given to various concepts of class and to critiques of the use of class concepts. Weber's classic triad associated *class* with one's economic situation and possibilities, *status* with one's place

---

[14]Gerhard E. Lenski, *Power and Privilege: A Theory of Social Stratification* (New York: McGraw, 1966); S.N. Eisenstadt, *The Political Systems of Empires: The Rise and Fall of Historical Societies* (Glencoe/New York: Free Press/Collier-Macmillan, 1963) and *Social Differentiation and Stratification* (Glenview, Il: Scott Foresman, 1971). Reference also should be made to John H. Kautsky, *The Politics of Aristocratic Empires* (Chapel Hill: University of North Carolina, 1982).

in the social system according to law (estate) and one's prestige, and *party* with the political power of one's group. But these areas of life as well as others overlap considerably and many more variables conspire to give a person or a group its place, role and limitations in society. In addition, the bases for what Weber called class, status and power vary in different societies. S.N. Eisenstadt, in his study of social differentiation and stratification, notes that many scholars using Weber's three categories of class, status and party incorrectly assimilate everything to one dimension or treat the three dimensions as if they were wholly separate hierarchies involving separate people.[15] Recent studies have shown decisively that a multidimensional approach to strata formation is necessary to take into account the complexities and variations in cultures because the bases of class, status and party differ by societies.[16]

The analysis of power, with an emphasis on economic power, as a criterion for classes fits well the relationship between the upper and lower classes in hierarchical agrarian empires, such as the Roman empire. Lenski argues that class and stratification in this setting are better studied by attention to the process which produces them, the "distributive process," which may be defined as the mode of determining "Who gets what and why."[17] According to Lenski, class is not a simple concept but includes a number of determining factors, social relationships and processes. For Lenski social class includes elements of Weber's other two categories, status and party (political power). The technological stage of a society influences the economy which influences polity which in turn influences the distribution system. However, these relationships are not wholly determined because they are influenced at each stage by many factors.[18]

---

[15] *Differentiation*, 81-82.

[16] *Differentiation*, 82-83. See also, Jonathan H. Turner, *Societal Stratification: A Theoretical Analysis* (New York: Columbia, 1984), esp. chs. 4 and 8. Turner supports Eisenstadt in that the class and status system is determined by a series of complex factors and he criticizes Lenski because after distinguishing many complex factors he lumps them together as a composite and too simple phenomenon (pp. 57-58). In fact, as we shall see, Lenski emphasizes the complexity of the stratification system implicit in class and status.

[17] Lenski, *Power*, 2-3.

[18] Lenski, *Power*, 436.

The origins and processes of classes and statuses, not to speak of their desirability and morality, have been explained in several ways. The conservative functionalist tradition argues that social groups, classes and strata derive from the needs and desires of society, not of individuals. The limited number of people able to fulfill difficult and essential tasks must be motivated to act on behalf of society and they are rewarded specially and become a class. Stratification expresses the value system of the society and stresses the common advantages to society of stratification.[19] Radical conflict theory derives stratification from the conflicting needs, desires and values of individuals in sub-groups in society which are acted out in a struggle for goods in short supply. This theory stresses domination and exploitation.[20] Lenski attempts to synthesize these two traditional approaches by an empirical analysis which stresses multiple variables and their interrelations, as found in both ancient and modern societies. He works out of a fundamentally Hobbesian framework which sees society as founded on the individual and communal desire for survival, fulfillment of needs and acquisition of power.[21] According to Lenski need and power determine distribution. Basic needs come first; when they are fulfilled, power determines almost entirely the distribution of the surplus. With Weber, Lenski defines *power* as the probability of persons or groups carrying out their will even when opposed by others and it is upon power which all else depends.[22] *Privilege* is the possession or control of a portion of the surplus in society which has been produced by power. *Prestige* is one's standing or status with others and is dependent on both power and privilege.[23] It should be noted that in antiquity political power and social station led to the acquisition and retention of wealth, in contrast to modern society in which wealth often leads to power and status.[24]

[19]Lenski, *Power*, 16-17

[20]Lenski, *Power*, 16-17

[21]Lenski, *Power*, chs. 2-3.

[22]Lenski, *Power*, 44.

[23]Lenski, *Power*, 45.

[24]Kautsky, *Politics*, uses power and economic relations as the basis for his class definitions in aristocratic empires in a way similar to Lenski. The aristocracy is defined by its political and economic role in society, rather than by race, heredity or ethnic

DEFINITIONS

Lenski recognizes that class is a very complex concept which must be used in a sophisticated way with care.[25] He is especially interested in the power classes, which he defines as "an aggregation of persons in a society who stand in a similar position with respect to force or some specific form of institutionalized power," e.g., workers, the military, the wealthy.[26] A person may be a member of several power classes at once. Castes, estates, status groups and elites may be reduced to power classes in Lenski's sense. A *class is a caste* to the degree that upward mobility into or out of it is forbidden by mores. A class is an *estate* to the degree that its existence, rights and privileges are established by law.[27]

Status groups are more difficult to define, but Lenski says that some status groups are power classes and some are prestige groups. Status groups tend to be endogamous, hereditary and have a communal character. Lenski uses this term for racial, ethnic and religious groups which have social power.[28] The term *elite* refers to the highest ranking segment of any social unit, ranked by whatever criterion is chosen.

The boundaries of classes and elites are very imprecise because they are distributed continuously.[29] No one criterion for distinguishing class and group will give an adequate picture of society. In Jewish society, some hereditary priests were members of the upper classes as rulers and as retainers and others were members

---

designation. Its political role is to collect taxes and make war. From this activity the aristocracy gets prestige, wealth, privileges, freedom from taxes and control of wealth (p. 79).Thus, the aristocracy is defined by Kautsky as those who exploit and dominate the lower classes, the peasant et al. (p. 229).

[25]Lenski, *Power*, 74-82 and 443.

[26]Lenski, *Power*, 75.

[27]Lenski, *Power*, 77-78.

[28]Lenski, *Power*, 78. According to James Littlejohn, *Social Stratification* (London: Allen, 1972) 47, status can mean: a. position in social structure, irrespective of considerations of equality or inequality. This use is descriptive: an uncle is an uncle and a storekeeper a storekeeper. b. legal status in a social structure, e.g., free or slave. c. position in a hierarchical organization, e.g., manager, or position in a hierarchical scheme which embraces a total society. Social status is often used with meaning (c.) and refers to one's prestige and the way in which one is treated by others.

[29]Lenski, *Power*, 78-79.

of the lower classes as farmers and craftsmen. Landowners could be wealthy and powerful national leaders or small, local leaders or impoverished peasants just getting by. In addition, one's class and status could change over time.

A class system is the hierarchy of classes ranked in terms of some single criterion.[30] Four class systems which have an effect on the distributive system are: the political class system, the property class system, the occupational class system, the ethnic class system. Each system represents a different principle of distribution and so a struggle can go on between systems as well as between classes within a system.[31] Because the workings of a society are enormously complex and a great variety of groups, processess and arrangements are possible, a class system can aid analysis, but will never include all variations. In addition, classes looked at from the outside, which is our stance in this analysis, are large, loosely defined bodies. But for those inside the society each class contains many more fine gradations not specified by the general category.[32] Sjoberg's definition of class shows the wealth of criteria needed to define a class. A class is a "a large body of persons who occupy a position in a social hierarchy by reason of their manifesting similarity of valued objective criteria. These latter include kinship affiliation, power and authority, achievements, possessions, and personal attributes. Achievements involve a person's occupational and educational attainments; possessions refer to material evidences of wealth; moral attributes include one's religious and ethical beliefs and actions; and personal attributes involve speech, dress and personal mannerisms."[33] He also notes that pre-industrial cities, the subject of his study and part of the ancient society we are examining, display remarkable consistency in their class structures.

Class and status are part of the more comprehensive topic of stratification in society, according to J.H. Turner. Stratification is constituted by three processes: the unequal distribution of

---

[30]Lenski, *Power*, 79-80.

[31]Lenski, *Power*, 80-81.

[32]Gideon Sjoberg, *The Preindustrial City: Past and Present* (New York: Free Press, 1960) 109.

[33]Sjoberg, *City*, 109.

valued resources, the formation of homogeneous subpopulations and the ranking of these subpopulations.[34] Valued resources are threefold: 1. *material wealth* which is those material objects, or the capacity to purchase such objects with money, that people in a society value and perceive to be gratifying; 2. *power* which is the relative capacity of individuals or collective units in a society to control the actions of other individuals and collective units; and 3. *prestige* which is the respect, esteem, and honor that individuals bestow upon others in a society.[35] This is the heart of the distributive process which Lenski uses as the basis for his power classes. The degree of inequality in a society, a characteristic feature of an agrarian society, is determined by these three variables. However, their relative weight in determining inequality depends on system size, level of differentiation, productivity and other forces affecting concentration of resources. In small undifferentiated societies prestige is the most important factor. In larger ones, power and money dominate. When groups of societies are united in an empire, the role of power drops and wealth increases because the cost of exercising power effectively grows.[36] This economic pressure makes empires inherently unstable.[37]

Class, according to Turner, is defined by the intersection of the ranking and differentiation processes. More precisely, social class is used to describe "the multiplicative and interactive effects of differentiation of homogeneous subpopulations and the ranking of these subpopulations."[38] Differentiation is the "degree and extent to which subsets of members of a society reveal common behavioral tendencies and similar attitudes so that they can be distinguished from other subsets of members in a society."[39] Subpopulation formation is caused by forces which create "a sense of identity among individuals as well as a high degree of homogeneity in behaviors, attitudes, and possessions

---

[34]Turner, *Stratification*, 59.

[35]Turner, *Stratification*, 60.

[36]Note that great wealth is often needed or at least very helpful in running effectively for statewide and national office in the United States.

[37]Turner, *Stratification*, 61-63.

[38]Turner, *Stratification*, 146.

[39]Turner, *Stratification*, 147.

among subsets of a population."[40] Ranking concerns how these subsets are differentially evaluated. The process of evaluating and ranking others and categorizing them into groups goes on constantly among individuals and is the basis for the importance of ranking. Thus, Turner analytically distinguishes social processes which lead to the formation of what we call classes rather than mixing them together. Most significantly, he does not associate power in its several forms with the identification of a class, though power and the stratification it produces creates the conditions for class formation. Though this study uses the more conventional understanding of power class derived from Lenski, the distinctions and criticisms made by Turner will prove helpful in locating the place and function of the Pharisees, scribes and Sadduceees.

CLASS IN ANCIENT SOCIETY

The complexity of defining class, status and power (Weber's original triad) becomes more clear when we look at ancient society. M. Finley[41] has pointed out that Roman society was first divided by *ordo* or estate, a legally defined category which possessed clearly defined privileges and disabilities and which stood in hierarchical relationship to other orders.[42] In Weber's scheme, ordo is part of status, one's standing in society, along with prestige, social values and the honor granted by the social system.[43] But in Roman society order had its own place. Finley also points out that as order declined in significance, other groups rose to hierarchical prominence, including one called the nobility. The nobility had no legal status, but it had power and was a status group, based mostly on families who had had a

---

[40]Turner, *Stratification*, 65.

[41]Moses Finley, *The Ancient Economy* (Berkeley: Univ. of California, 1973), ch. 2.

[42]Finley, *Ancient Economy*, 45.

[43]The older meaning of status was precisely one's legally recognized place in society, that is, one's estate along with the rights and duties of that station. With the emergence of legal social equality in the modern period, the term was applied to other factors which stratified society, especially those concerned with the distribution of honor and prestige. See D.A. Sweetser, "Status," *A Dictionary of the Social Sciences*, eds. Julius Gould and William L. Kolb (New York: Free Press, 1964) 692-693.

member reach the office of consul.[44] At the same time, those who possessed Roman citizenship formed an order, that is, a legally defined group.

Legal and traditional social categories did not adequately define Roman society. Much depended on social status, which was often the road to money and political power. Social class (based on one's wealth) was much less important because one usually gained and kept wealth through political power and one achieved political power through one's status in society.[45] The economy and social class distinctions were embedded in the larger social system.[46] Status was determined by a variety of social criteria, including citizenship and family. Wealth was necessary to the upper class person, but its possession did not make one a member of the upper class. By contrast, status gained by membership in the upper class could give the opportunity for acquiring or increasing wealth. Thus, status and power were more important than wealth in ancient society.[47]

The social strata in Rome and the Empire should not be pictured as static for they were constantly in turmoil. One study shows that half of the senatorial families failed to place a member in the senate in the next generation for a variety of reasons.[48] Many new members were taken into the upper classes and orders due to the acquisition of wealth, imperial patronage and social accomplishments. These changes were even more

---

[44]Finley, *Ancient Economy*, 46-47.

[45]This is not to deny that money was very important since upper class life, which required that one not work, was impossible without it. Some of the Roman orders were limited to people with a certain wealth. However, wealth alone was not a sufficient condition to give one status or power. Ramsay Macmullen, *Roman Social Relations 50 B.C. to A.D. 284* (New Haven: Yale, 1974) 88-91. G.E.M. de Ste. Croix, *The Class Struggle in the Ancient World From the Archaic Age to the Arab Conquests* (Ithaca: Cornell, 1981) pp. 81-98 criticizes both Weber and Finley from a Marxist perspective. He reaffirms the dominance of the economy and wealth (i.e., class) over status, but his analysis is less convincing.

[46]Finley, *Ancient Economy*, 49-51.

[47]The interrelationship of these factors is well stated by Géza Alföldy, *The Social History of Rome* (Totowa: Barnes and Noble, 1985), 106: "One had to be rich, hold higher offices and thereby power, enjoy social prestige, and above all, one had to belong to a leading *ordo*, a corporately organized and privileged order which comprised men of wealth, higher offices and prestige. It was only the man who fulfilled all these conditions who really belonged in the full sense to the upper strata of society .... "

[48]Alföldy, *Social History*, 117-118.

frequent in the later Roman empire.[49]

One recent critique of these complex definitions of class must be addressed. R. Rohrbaugh in a study of the use of "class" and "status" in New Testament studies notes that class has been used in various ways by scholars writing on the social world of the New Testament. Most recently Wayne Meeks, building on Finley's work, has gone beyond large, imprecise definitions of class which lump people of different social rank to a notion of social status based on many criteria and resulting in a graded series of statuses.[50] The criteria for assigning social rank are power, occupational prestige, income or wealth, education and knowledge, religious and ritual purity, family and ethnic group position, and local community status.[51] Rohrbaugh criticizes the synthetic and gradational approach to class and social status, an approach common to most sociologists today, because its application to ancient society requires constant subjective judgments which are influenced by the author's own situation.[52]

As an alternative Rohrbaugh suggests a relational approach to defining class, one which concentrates on the social relations which define and produce social position, not on the characteristics of the social position produced by the relations.[53] The social relations offered by Rohrbaugh are the standard economic ones in terms of market or of production, for example, employer and employee, creditor and debtor, merchant and consumer, producing worker and non-productive, non-worker. The structures of ancient society follow the structures of interests but class and status were not as closely tied to occupation as they are today.[54] These relational concepts have an explanatory value for the New Testament world. For example, the relationship of debtor was relatively permanent. The landowners who had

[49] Alföldy, *Social History*, ch. 6.

[50] "Methodological Considerations in the Debate over the Social Class Status of Early Christians," *JAAR* 52 (1984) 519-546, esp. 521-527; see also Wayne Meeks, *The Urban Christians* (New Haven: Yale, 1983) Ch. 2, esp. pp. 53-55.

[51] Rohrbaugh, "Class Status," 528.

[52] Rohrbaugh, "Class Status," 530. But concrete historical data can make clear the shades of status and power of certain offices and groups as is shown in Alföldy, *Social History*.

[53] Rohrbaugh, "Class Status," 531.

[54] Rohrbaugh, "Class Status," 531-535.

enough land to make physical labor unnecessary were a relatively permanent class in society with permanent relationships with non-owners.[55]

Rohrbaugh's critique of the imprecise use of the categories class and status is accurate and the strategy he proposes, an investigation of relational terms in the ancient texts, would certainly prove fruitful. However, study of social relations is part of and not a substitute for the creation or application of general descriptive and explanatory categories which illuminate the data, allow it to be compared cross-culturally and can be related to one another within a comprehensive theory of society.

Power

Since power is so important for most definitions of class and status, a precise analysis of power in its various forms is needed. Talcott Parsons has analyzed society using action theory, his own variant of functionalism, in which "a social system is a system of the actions of individuals, the principal units of which are roles and constellations of roles."[56] He categorized social interaction in complex societies according to four generalized symbolic media of interaction, and thus specified four types of "power" available in society.[57] Symbolic media of interaction can best be explained using *money* as an example. Barter is the direct exchange of goods and does not require money or any other medium. But as society and economic interchanges become more complex, a symbolic medium is used to effect economic exchange and aid economic relationships. Money is symbolic and so has no intrinsic worth. It functions because it symbolizes physical entities which have worth and can be exchanged. As a

[55]Rohrbaugh, "Class Status," 541.

[56]T. Parsons and E. Shils, *Toward a General Theory of Action* (Cambridge: Harvard UP, 1951) 197.

[57]Talcott Parsons, *Politics and Social Structure* (New York: Free Press, 1969), esp. Ch. 15 "On the Concept of Political Power," pp. 352-404 which was originally in the *Proceedings of the American Philosophical Society* 107 (1963) 232-262 and Ch. 16 "On the Concept of Influence," pp. 405-429 which was originally in the *Public Opinion Quarterly* 27 (1963) 37-62.

symbolic medium it must exist within a system in which all parties grant to money a meaning and value. Concretely, there must be a stable, ongoing society which has enough goods available that one who exchanges goods for money is confident that he will be able to exchange the money in turn for goods.

The other symbolic media of exchange are power, influence and commitment. *Power* (now in a precise sense, not in the generalized sense which includes all these categories) is a symbolic medium of interaction within society. It is to be distinguished from a raw act of physical force, which is not in itself constitutive of social interaction in society.[58] It is best seen as political power, in that it does not require the actual exercise of physical force, though that option remains as a threat in the background and is the basis of power. Parsons defines power as "the generalized capacity to secure the performance of binding obligations by units in a system of collective organization when the obligations are legitimized with reference to their bearing on collective goals and where in the case of recalcitrance there is a presumption of enforcement by negative situational sanctions ..." Notice the reference to generalization and legitimation. Power, as a symbolic medium, is more than a physical act exercised once in a given situation; it is a capacity to be used in many situations within a society which recognizes it. Power as a symbolic medium still depends on the ultimate capacity to coerce behavior but its use in a functioning society is usually symbolic and its permanence is protected by social legitimation, e.g., by law, custom or some other type of social acceptance.[59]

The goal of power in society is effectively to mobilize resources in order to attain social goals. Power can be used to create or maintain order, to organize new social activities or institutions, or to provide better for the needs of the society. These first two

[58]Gouldner, *Crisis*, 286-297, points out correctly that Parsons undervalues the role of physical force. Parsons is interested in the workings of society and the complex interactions within a functioning society. Thus Parsons keeps violence in the background. Gouldner's critique addresses Parsons' moral claims for legitimate power and is less important for the descriptive use these categories are being used for here. Parsons' understanding of power does imply the functionalists' predisposition in favor of the major institutions which enable society to function.

[59]Parson's definition of power is a variant of Weber's, used by Lenski above. It is based on the individual's ability to carry out his/her will against opposition.

symbolic media, and the realities lying behind them, were wielded by the governing class in the Roman empire and formed the basis of the empire. The Roman ruler, and to a lesser extent the Jewish chief priests, leading elders, large property owners, and major officials, all had at their disposal power based on force and the wealth to support such a system. At the other levels of society some people had lesser amounts of power and wealth.

Commitment, the third symbolic medium, contributes to power. Generalized commitments underlie the relationships which bind the members of a society together. Commitments are symbolic of the many actual relationships a member of society has with all the other members of society. Cultural patterns and motivations shared by all are mobilized in order to get people to submit to power or to use their resources for a social purpose. One's integrity, honor and social position all depend on one's fidelity to social relationships and these relationships are symbolized by the general social and cultural commitments to which all profess adherence. In times of conflict or need, society or its members can call on others' commitment, that is, on their relationships. The goal of commitment is to maintain the cultural patterns and the integrity of the society. Both the Jewish governing class and also groups such as the Pharisees and scribes constantly appealed to their fellow Jews' commitments to Judaism. Indeed, commitment to Judaism had been the central issue of Judaism since the Maccabean war and probably played a major role in the formation of many Jewish groups. With their way of life constantly threatened by Hellenism and the Romans, Jews defended their way of life by a number of strategies, most of which required activation of the people's commitments to Jewish traditions and beliefs.

Finally, *influence* can produce action in others because it symbolizes factual knowledge and so serves to persuade others to a line of action. Influence "communicates a generalized intention on the basis of which trust in more specific intentions is requested and expected."[60] The influential person is considered to be a reliable source of information or judgment concerning the information and thus is able to influence the judgment and

---

[60]Parsons, *Social Structure*, 416.

actions of others. Influence can be exercised in the political sphere as political influence which is allied with political power; in the economic sphere as fiduciary influence which guides monetary and economic activity; and in the area of commitments as a guiding influence which enables the person to reconcile and order conflicting commitments. In all cases influence symbolizes facts, interests and rational arguments (and in the case of religion, beliefs) which persuade and motivate the person to act in a certain way. Finally, influence, which tends to integrate the other forms of social interaction into a whole, interprets the norms and laws of society which specify how commitments are to be honored, how power is to be exercised and how wealth is to be used.[61] In Josephus the Pharisees are several times said to have influence with the people and to persuade them to follow their special laws for living Judaism. The Pharisees' knowledge of Jewish law and traditions, accepted by the people, is the basis of their social standing. Presumably, the scribes and priests also had influence with some of the people. The influence of these groups of leaders varied with time and the different parts of society they were trying to influence. Jesus' struggle with the Pharisees, scribes and chief priests can be explained most easily as a struggle for influence with the people.

We may summarize and schematize Parsons' four symbolic media of social interaction thusly. Power and commitment are supported by negative sanctions. A person can be physically forced or punished if he will not act, or a person loses honor and status. Money and influence are supported by positive inducements. A person will receive something physical if he acts or he will receive the knowledge necessary to decide and act in a useful or productive way. Influence and commitment appeal to the person's mind in order to persuade or activate commitments which the person accepts. Money and power are situational in that they appeal to the circumstances surrounding a person in order to induce or force the person to act. Each of the symbolic media of interaction, according to Parsons' action theory, attempts to get other persons to act. The goals of each of the media differ. Power concerns the political system and is ordered

[61]Parsons, *Social Structure*, 420-425.

toward the coordinated attainment of social goals. Money concerns the economy and exchange of goods and it is adaptive in that it allows society to reallocate goods to achieve its goals. Commitment is related to the culture and the pattern underlying society and its goal is to maintain this pattern by keeping people firmly committed to the values and outlooks basic to society. Finally, influence, which makes a cognitive appeal to the mind, is concerned with developing laws and norms for action which are based on reliable knowledge. Influence seeks to integrate society so that all the people act in concert within a common set of guidelines.

Conclusion

The Pharisees, scribes and Sadducees must be understood as part of Palestinian Jewish society and ancient society, which differs significantly from modern society, in order to prevent an anachronistic retrojection of modern categories and concepts. Though the structural functionalist approach to sociology, with its categories of class, status and power, has been rightly criticized and modified, it is still useful for organizing the data and understanding some of the workings of Palestinian and imperial society. Great care must be taken not to impose modern concepts and rigid systems on antiquity and the methods and results of functionalism must be qualified and adjusted in response to the history and literature of the first century.

The major categories reviewed in this chapter will not suffice to understand the Pharisees, scribes and Sadducees, only to set them in their larger context in Palestinian society, a task to be undertaken in the next chapter. Further insight into the nature of these groups and their likely goals, nature and social relations will be gained by the use of other sociological and anthropological categories, models and methods which will be introduced in chapter four.

3

Social Classes in Palestinian Jewish Society and the Roman Empire

Josephus wrote his accounts of the Jews in the Greco-Roman period from the perspective of the governing classes, both Roman and Jewish. He brought persons, events and groups into his narrative only insofar as they had an impact on the highest level of national life. The relatively few passages which mention the Pharisees show their part in the political, social and religious life of Judaism. Those passages can be properly understood only in the context of the Roman Empire and Jewish society with special reference to the relationships and dynamics operative among the many groups and social forces at work in the empire. The struggles for power depicted in the gospels, and the forging of an identity for Judaism implied by rabbinic literature all took place within the larger social world of the empire. Thus an understanding of empires and their constituent parts is necessary.

Agrarian Empires

Jews in Palestine during the Hellenistic and Roman periods lived in an agrarian society which itself was part of a large agrarian, bureaucratic and partly commercialized aristocratic empire.[1] As agrarian empires, the Greek and Roman empires

[1]See Lenski, *Power*, Kautsky, *Politics*, and Eisenstadt, *Empires*, for fundamental analysis of empires and large societies. Their categories overlap and they differ on some

35

also contained agrarian societies since an empire is made up of many small societies organized into a whole.[2] Agrarian empires differ from modern industrial societies and earlier horticultural societies in many ways. In contrast to horticultural societies, agrarian societies have more efficient methods of farming, especially the plow, and consequently a greater population.[3] They produce a greater agricultural surplus, have a larger and more dominant governing class and are more highly organized and centralized.[4] In contrast to industrial societies, agrarian societies are based on agriculture, with commerce playing a very limited role in the economy. Agrarian empires are marked by a very steep hierarchy and great inequality with control and wealth in the hands of a very few.[5] Only the development of commerce beginning in the late middle ages and of industry in the modern period eroded this control and led to the transformation of society into modern industrial forms.

Agrarian societies, in contrast to modern industrial societies, are constituted by two major classes separated by a wide gulf and unmediated by a middle class. The two classes are a large peasant class which produces the food to make society run and a small, elite governing class which protects the peasants from outside aggression and lives off the agricultural surplus produced by the peasants. The surplus is not spontaneously produced, since the peasants tend to grow only what they need or can find use for. Consequently, the governing class must so organize society that the peasants are forced to produce a surplus which can be extracted from them, usually by burdensome taxes.[6] Needless to say, responsible and efficient rulers also protected the peasants so they could plant and later harvest a crop without

---

theoretical presuppositions and structural analyses, but in general their work is complementary and useful for analyzing the ancient Roman and Hellenistic empires and Judaism's place within them.

[2]Kautsky, *Politics*, 24, 120; Thomas Carney, *The Shape of the Past: Models and Antiquity* (Lawrence, KA: Coronado, 1975) 100-101.

[3]Lenski, *Power*, 117-118.

[4]Lenski, *Power*, 142-148.

[5]Lenski, *Power*, 146-176.

[6]Kautsky, *Politics*, 79-80; 229; Carney, *Shape*, 99-100; Sjoberg, *City*, 118-120; 123-133; Finley, *Ancient Economy*, 50; MacMullen, *Roman Social Relations*, 88-94.

disturbance, destruction or theft.[7] Peasants produced agricultural products and basic necessities of life such as clothes, simple tools and utensils but they seldom achieved more than subsistence and even subsistence was often threatened by the demands of the governing class and the pressure of increasing population. The activities, interests and outlooks of the governing and peasant classes totally differed from each other. The peasants, who made up the vast majority of the population, lived in a world apart from the upper classes and the townsfolk who were dependent on the governing class. The peasants lived according to the family work year whose goal was "wantlessness." In seeking this goal a peasant family had to struggle against excessive taxation (30-70% of the crop), fierce rivalries with other peasants for the limited goods available and constant political pressure limiting their freedom.[8]

The governing class did not devote itself directly to agricultural work, since one of its distinctive characteristics was freedom from the need to engage in manual labor, but rather lived off the surplus produced by the peasants. Its work was to supervise and control the agricultural work of the peasants, tend to common affairs of the empire and make provision for the security and continuation of the empire. Because the governing class usually had achieved its position by exercise of military power, most empires, including the Hellenistic and Roman empires, were conquest states founded on and often sustained by the resources made available through conquest.[9] The governing class maintained its position with the assistance of what Lenski calls retainers, whose roles in society were military, governing, administrative, judicial and priestly.[10] These retainers were mostly townspeople who served the needs of the governing class as

---

[7]Conservative and critical sociologists have divergent interpretations of the social organization of agrarian empires. Functionalists generally try to understand how the principal social structures of a society keep the society functioning and have a bias toward accepting social structures which work in an orderly way. Critical sociologists evaluate social structures for their role in promoting oppression or liberation. Neither approach is "value free."

[8]Carney, *Shape*, 99-100; Lenski, *Power*, 266-273; Kautsky, *Politics*, 79-80.

[9]Lenski, *Power*, 192-197.

[10]Kautsky, *Politics*, 161.

soldiers, educators, religious functionaries, entertainers and skilled artisans; it is here we will find the Pharisees and scribes.[11] The governing class and its retainers seldom exceeded 5 to 7% of the population.[12] In modern society the retainers' roles are fulfilled by the middle class, but in antiquity they were not a middle class because they lacked any independent power. They were a residual group dependent on the governing class and participating in its life to some extent. However, insofar as they achieved powerful posts, they could become part of the governing class, or at least enjoy much of its power and privilege.

The Economy

The development and existence of ancient agrarian societies and empires depended on economic as well as political factors. Advances in technology which allowed efficient farming (iron plows or elaborate irrigation systems) and specialized military technology (the horse, chariot, armor or fortress) were crucial in the development of centralized power.[13] The emergence of a governing class also depended on and produced a redistributative economy in which a central authority (the government or the estate) gathered agricultural produce in a central storehouse through taxation and then redistributed the goods according to status and occupational roles. As empires became very large or suffered military or economic crises, the economy tended toward a mobilization economy in which the governing class took control of the economy for major military and economic projects. Mobilization of the economy allowed empires to acquire great power and produced extensive social differentiation.

The opposite of this kind of controlled economy is a commercialized market economy, common in the modern world. It depends on the independence of the producers and on means of free exchange, including transportation, communication and either barter or money. Unlike modern economies, ancient

---

[11]Kautsky, *Politics,* 323-328; Lenski, *Power,* 243-266.

[12]Lenski, *Power,* 214-248; Kautsky, *Politics,* 229.

[13]Lenski, *Power,* 192-194.

economies were not market economies, though local markets and an international market in luxury goods did usually flourish.[14] The Roman empire from its beginning was partly commercialized which means that merchants and traders achieved some independent power apart from the aristocrats who controlled the agricultural economy. But the mass of the population, the peasants, were not free to grow and sell their produce for their own benefit, but were controlled by the governing class and impeded by difficulties in transporting and marketing food crops. Depending on circumstances, some sectors of the economy could be relatively independent but most of it was controlled.[15]

The Class System in Agrarian Empires

Lenski's analysis of agrarian empires discerns nine significant classes, five belonging to the upper classes and four to the lower. The upper classes are the ruler (a class in himself), the governing class, retainer class, merchant class, and priestly class. The lower classes are peasants, artisans, an unclean or degraded class and the expendable class.[16] These are not the only classes one could discern in ancient imperial society, but they are the most significant for the political order which held empires together and they fit the Hellenistic and Roman empires reasonably well. Lenski's categories, based on the study of several empires and historical periods, offer a general structure for understanding the places and interactions of groups such as the Pharisees, scribes and Sadducees. The class system offers a window for looking at many of the important processes at work in imperial and Palestinian society and may serve as an initial model and hypothesis.

The Pharisees fit best into the retainer class as a religious group and a political force which interacted with the governing class, often influenced society and sometimes gained power. The

[14]Carney, *Shape,* 141-142; 204-210.

[15]Kautsky, *Politics,* 18-23.

[16]Lenski, *Power,* 214-296; Eisenstadt, *Differentiation,* 88-89, makes a slightly different division of the classes.

scribes, as bureaucrats, educators and major and minor officials, also fit into the retainer class. The Sadducees were, according to Josephus, members of the governing class and the priestly class, as were some Pharisees and scribes. A quick survey of the governing classes will show how the Pharisees and scribes fit in and also why the Pharisees were not members of the common people, artisans or any other lower class, as some scholars have maintained.

1. The *ruler* of most empires and of centralized states had far reaching power and was sometimes considered to be the owner of all the land. Many rulers were functional owners if ownership is defined as the right to benefit from something. Through taxation, and occasional harsher measures such as confiscation, as well as by grants of land and political rights, the rulers were able to control all classes, especially the governing classes. The rulers were usually constrained by the need for the support and labor of the other classes and by the need to remain within the traditional framework of society.[17] The Roman emperors from Augustus on wielded great power and brought the Roman empire to the height of its wealth and power. Within Jewish society John Hyrcanus and Alexander Jannaeus to some extent and Herod certainly had this kind of power. Of course, Herod was ruler only within the limits imposed by Rome and so was simultaneously part of the governing class of the Empire.

2. The *governing class* was very small, only about 1-2% of the population. It was made up of both hereditary aristocrats and appointed bureaucrats. A strong central ruler, who had good transportation and communication, favored an appointed bureaucracy which was under his direct control and dependent on him for its power. A ruler who was militarily successful could annex foreign territories and acquire great wealth and influence which enabled him to subordinate the governing classes more effectively.[18] If the central authority of a country or empire was disorganized or weak, this favored feudalism in which the hereditary local rulers attained substantial power independent of the ruler. If the governing class was the military elite, if it kept

---

[17]Lenski, *Power,* 214-219; Eisenstadt, *Empires,* 364-365.
[18]Lenski, *Power,* 219-239.

estates large through primogeniture or if hereditary succession to the throne produced weak rulers, then the governing class was able to gain and keep power. Membership in the governing class included the right of self-aggrandizement through grants from the ruler and "honest graft" in the conduct of office. Offices were often sold and the incumbent was expected to make his fortune from his position. Land ownership, the major form of wealth, was secondary to political power because political power was used to acquire land and wealth and lack of political power could result in the loss of land and wealth through taxation and confiscation.[19] The Roman governors sent to Syria and Palestine were of this class, as were Herod and his descendants. To some extent the chief priests functioned as part of this class, but they were not as Hellenized nor as accepted in Roman society as Herod and his successors. Jewish society was ruled by the governing class (the chief priests, large landowners, notable elders and major officials) except when a strong ruler such as Herod had control.

3. The *retainer class*, perhaps 5% of the population, served the needs of the ruler and governing class. To some extent they shared in the life of the elite, but not in its direct power. Soldiers, bureaucratic government officials, various kinds of servants, religious leaders and educators were all necessary for the functioning of society and as a group they had a great impact on society and culture. However, individual retainers lacked power because any one person could be easily replaced by another. Some retainers could become very powerful and move into the governing class while others could lose their position and fall back into the peasantry. Their offices could become hereditary, but more often they were bureaucratic and so subject to the appointment of the ruler. This group gained most power when the governing class ceased to be effective rulers and left matters in their hands. When the high military officers were professionals and members of the retainer class, rather than of the governing class, then the retainers posed a serious threat to the governing class.[20]

[19]Lenski, *Power*, 210-211; 229; Richard L. Rohrbaugh, "Class Status," 542. Besides political activity, which includes military conquest, mercantile activity was the only alternate way of increasing wealth substantially.

[20]Lenski, *Power*, 243-248.

Many scribes were members of the retainer class in their capacities as bureaucrats and minor officials. Some lower ranked priests and traditional, local leaders probably fit in here too. Even despised officials, like Levi the tax collector, called by Jesus, fit into this class.[21] Since the Pharisees appear in Josephus as a recognized group which exercises religious, political and possibly educational roles, they seem to fit into the retainer class. Because they have influence with the people and strive for influence and power in Jewish government, they cannot be poor peasants or urban craftsmen who spend all their time producing enough for subsistence.[22] It is likely that the Pharisees were part of the ruling classes as retainers in some way dependent on the rich and powerful who controlled most of society's surplus. In the first century the Pharisees may have been part of the very complex leadership of Judaism, based in Jerusalem, as Josephus pictures them, or (less likely) they may have been part of or allied with the rural landowners, as the Gospel of Luke pictures them. Class analysis usually depends substantially on the economic position of a group of people, but we have no contemporary information about how the Pharisees supported themselves.[23] However, one's place in ancient society was determined much more by one's status and power than by wealth (in contrast to modern industrial society), so class analysis in Lenski's sense is not impossible.

4. The *merchant class* does not fit neatly into either the ruling or the lower classes. Merchants generally had low prestige, no direct power and were recruited from the landless. But they escaped the total control of the governing class because they stood in a market relationship to them, rather than in an

[21]Mark 2:13-17; Luke 5:27-32; Matt. 9:9-13 (where Levi is Matthew).

[22]See the next note and the sections on artisans below.

[23]Later rabbinic texts speak of rabbis who were craftsmen, rich farmers (employing others, thus gentry) and merchants. However, the rabbinic texts contain an argument about whether a rabbi should work or spend all his time studying Torah. Clearly in the third century and beyond Judaism is torn between the rabbi as full-time, supported religious functionary and the ideal of every working Jew as learned and a rabbi. See E. E. Urbach, *The Sages* (Jerusalem: Magnes, 1975) 1.599-603; 609-610. Anthony J. Saldarini, *Scholastic Rabbinism* (BJS 14; Chico: Scholars, 1982) 82-84. The dispute is contained in sayings (for example, Pirke Abot 1:9; 2:2; 3:5; 4:5) and in anecdotes about the rabbis (for example, Rav Huna in b. Megillah 105a).

authority relationship, and because the ruling class needed them for luxuries and some essentials.[24]

5. The bulk of the *priestly class* depended on the governing class, as did the retainers. The leaders of the priestly class were members of the governing class, as well as of the priestly class. Because of contributions to the religious system, such as the tithing mandated by the Bible, the priestly class often controlled great wealth. But the wealth was insecure because the priestly class was subordinate to the powers of the governing class and ruler. The priestly class tended to develop an independent power base and compete with the political governing class and ruler for power, especially because they claimed an independent, divine source of authority (see ch. 1). At certain times in Jewish history the chief priests achieved dominance, for example, under the Hasmoneans. However, they could lose power, too, as did the Hasmoneans.

6. The *peasants* made up the bulk of the population because most labor had to go into producing food. They were heavily taxed, typically at the rate of 30-70% of the crop, kept firmly under control and could gain power only when they had military importance or when there was a labor shortage. There were class differences among the peasants but they do not concern the matters covered in this study.[25]

7. The *artisan class* was similar to the peasants in lack of power. Artisans, along with the unclean class below, were only 3-7% of the population. They were not productive enough to become wealthy, for the most part, and they did not have power unless their skills were so difficult to acquire that they could command high wages and concessions.[26] Their low productivity

[24]Lenski, *Power,* 250-256. Some merchants did achieve high position and real political power, but these cases were the exception. Kautsky, *Politics,* 18-23. H. W. Pleket, "Urban Elites and Business in the Greek Part of the Roman Empire," *Trade in the Ancient Economy,* eds. Peter Garnsey et al. (Berkeley: Univ. of California, 1983), points out that in the Roman Empire many aristocrats used freedmen and slaves to conduct large and profitable businesses for them. In this case, the governing class became indirectly commercialized.

[25]Lenski, *Power,* 266-276.

[26]Lenski, *Power,* 278-280. Louis Finkelstein, *The Pharisees: The Sociological Background of Their Faith* (3 ed.; Philadelphia: Jewish Publication Society, 1966) long held that the Pharisees were part of the proletariat and made their living as urban artisans. But this is very unlikely. Urban workers and artisans were not part of the middle class, as

and dependence on the upper classes meant that they were *not* a middle class, as they are in modern society today. Some members of this group were peasants who had been forced off the land. Jesus was from this class, as was Paul and the fishermen, Peter, Andrew, James and John. Though far from indigent, they did not have power and influence in society.[27]

8. The *unclean class* usually did the noxious but necessary tasks such as tanning. Or it engaged in such difficult jobs that its health was soon destroyed, e.g., mining.[28]

9. Finally, there was the *expendable class*, about 5-10%, for whom society had no place or need. They had been forced off the land because of population pressures or they did not fit into society. They tended to be landless and itinerant with no normal family life and a high death rate. Illegal activities on the fringe of society were their best prospect for a livelihood.[29] It is likely that the bulk of the brigands, rebels and followers of messianic claimants recorded by Josephus during the Roman period were members of this class. Peasants who were forced off their land as well as peasants barely hanging on and threatened with landlessness would be attracted to movements which promised the justice not given to them by the present social system.[30]

The boundary between the upper and lower classes was fixed. Occasionally someone from the lower class moved into the upper class, but downward mobility was more common. Population pressure was the great cause of downward mobility.

they sometimes are today. Though we know almost nothing about the economic life of the Pharisees (especially if we discount the later view projected back on the first century by rabbinic literature), we do know how the artisan class lived through data from the Roman and other empires. Both the artisans and the unclean or degraded classes were similar to the peasants in lack of power.

[27]See Wilhelm Wuellner, *The Meaning of "Fishers of Men"* (Philadelphia: Westminster, 1967) who lays to rest the myth of the apostles as illiterate and indigent fishermen. On the other hand, his creation of a "middle class" is misleading (45-53). Fishermen could prosper at certain times, but they like other artisans were limited to their own labor. If they were managers, they might aspire to the upper classes but their situation was precarious like that of merchants.

[28]Lenski, *Power,* 280-281. Sjoberg, *City,* 133-137, calls this class and the expendable class "outcasts," but he emphasizes that they are part of society and perform essential menial tasks.

[29]Lenski, *Power,* 281-284.

[30]For an excellent analysis of these groups and the peasants, see Horsley, *Bandits.*

Some aristocrats became poor and dropped to the level of the peasantry. Many peasants were forced off the land and became hired labor, or members of the unclean or expendable classes. Some subordinate groups did achieve privileged status, depending on economic or political circumstances and their use to the upper classes (e.g., the Jews at certain times in the West during the Middle Ages). Ethnic or religious groups could receive privileged status through conquest.[31]

In conclusion it should be emphasized that the nine classes defined by Lenski are not watertight categories, nor are they adequate to explain completely all the complexities of Jewish society in the Roman empire. However, they provide a way of viewing first century society as a whole and seeing how different parts of the society interacted. Lenski's view of social structure, based on the study of a number of empires, fits the Hellenistic and Roman empires well enough to be useful. A detailed reading of the historical particulars of Jewish and Roman history could produce numerous modifications and additions to Lenski's system of classes, but the classes as he outlines them will provide a framework for more detailed work and guidance in understanding the relations of groups such as the Pharisees, scribes and Sadducees to the rest of society at an abstract level.

The City

The city was the home of the governing class and the classes which supported and aided them. It was also the place where political and religious struggles and change usually began. In Palestine Jerusalem was the city where power was concentrated, along with Caesarea Maritima when the Roman prefect or procurator was there and various regional centers in Galilee like Sepphoris and Tiberias. A brief survey of the ancient city will provide a context for the study of the Pharisees, scribes and Sadducees.

Cities were brought into being by the needs of the governing class who generally lived there. The function of the city was

---

[31]Lenski, *Power,* 284-296.

political, administrative, military, religious and educational and the very existence of the city and the spread of cities were caused by the need for these functions and by the people carrying them out.[32] Cities dominated the political, cultural and economic life of empires and societies. It is crucial to define city correctly, especially in contrast to huge, contemporary urban centers. A city in antiquity, as an administrative center, could be what we today would call a large village or town, but it essentially qualified as a city because the majority of the people in it did not work directly at agriculture and because the activities of the city dominated the cultural, religious, political and economic life of the empire, region or society. Cities existed to serve the needs of the governing class, including their extended families and retainers. It provided defense, communication and a forum for many other activities which enabled the governing class to dominate society.[33] Consequently, the ruling classes dominated the cities.[34] Peasants, the bulk of ancient society, were absent from the city and urban-rural tensions were common. The city included members of the artisan and unclean classes, as well as a number of the landless expendable class. All these lower classes served the upper classes and took care of the menial tasks necessary for life and luxury.

The Pharisees, scribes and Sadducees as well as other groups seem to have originated and flourished in the city. The rich and powerful lived in the city along with the classes and groups dependent on them. Most of the inhabitants of the city were bureaucrats, craftsmen, merchants, servants, religious functionaries and others directly dependent on the governing class. They did not form a middle class in the modern sense because they lacked power, like the peasants, and were almost totally dependent on the powerful for whom they worked. They were a

---

[32]Sjoberg, *City,* 67-91; Lenski, *Power,* 200-201.

[33]The phenomenon of the extended family is not common to traditional society in general, contrary to popular belief. Peasants depended on the immediate, nuclear family to provide enough labor to farm the land. Only the rich could afford the quantity and quality of means to hold together and serve an extended family. (Sjoberg, *City,* 110-133).

[34]It is notable that Josephus reports, in his account of the Jewish war against Rome, that the governing class lost control of Judaism, and thus of the government, when many outside groups, including landless peasants, took over the city and thus succeeded in revolting not only from the Romans, but from the Jewish governing class as well.

residual group between the ruling class and the peasants.[35] As a group they lacked internal coherence and were fundamentally an instrument of the powerful.[36] In dealing with bureaucrats, religious functionaries and the military, one must distinguish between the leaders who were often members of the governing class and the lower ranking members who were often peasants forced off the land by population pressure or some other event. For example, though Christian priests are in theory all members of one continuous class, the status and class of a parish priest in the middle ages was very different from that of a bishop who often came from the nobility and exercised great influence or direct control in the governing of the country.

Since the cities dominated agrarian society, change and new movements in society tended to originate in the city.[37] Much social conflict was merely the governing class in conflict within itself about who would rule. However, this conflict produced occasional new groups, movements and ideas. In general, ancient society lacked the pace of change and social mobility characteristic of modern society.

The heart of a city, if it was a center of government, was the government bureaucracy, including both high and low officials who implemented decisions, made government function and saw to the actual disposition of resources within society. A bureaucracy has its own internal organization and functions as a distinct part of society. According to Carney, the structural definition of a bureaucracy is "any group of hierarchically arranged official positions in a formal organization which persists over time, with recognized status symbols and recruitment and promotions patterns." It may have special components, such as the military or the religious.[38] The Byzantine bureaucracy which Carney studied had three major levels to the bureaucracy: high officials, the literate officials and the illiterate officials who did menial tasks. An appointive bureaucracy owes its existence originally to the ruler and is his tool. However, a bureaucracy

[35]Kautsky, *Politics,* chs. 12-13 and esp. 323-328.

[36]Kautsky, *Politics,* 333-334.

[37]Eisenstadt, *Differentiation,* 90-91 and 113-120, stresses the power of the center, that is, the ruling classes, to manipulate and change symbols in order to control society.

[38]Carney, *Shape,* 52.

tends to become self-sustaining and independent of the ruler or any other force in society. In addition, the aristocrats often strive to capture the key positions in a bureaucracy and thus regain lost power.[39]

Conclusion

The abstract sociological class categories used to describe Jewish society within the Roman empire can be seriously misleading if they are reified and imposed on the ancient world. They can be helpful if they guide the interpretation of texts and are modified by those texts to provide a descriptive and if possible explanatory theory for the events and views of antiquity. They are also a useful corrective to the unconscious application of modern social views in the ancient world.

Class is especially useful for large scale analysis of the relationships among diverse groups within society. Josephus especially looks at Judaism from the perspective of the outside world, probably because his audience was drawn from that world. The gospels are set within that world, especially in the passion narratives. The rabbinic sources ignore the non-Jewish world for the most part and we must often deduce the class and status of the Jewish community from assumptions in the text and other knowledge of the ancient world.

The Pharisees as portrayed by Josephus fit most readily into the retainer class. However, we lack one crucial piece of evidence concerning their place in society, the source of their economic support. Neither Josephus nor the gospels make clear the sources of their financial support but their power and influence are more important than their financial resources and would have been the key to their power and influence.

The limited number of categories and aspects of ancient society covered in this chapter do not do justice to the concrete social structure of the Roman empire which was very complex, involving a myriad of relationships among its peoples and classes, relationships which varied by place and over time.

[39]Carney, *Shape*, 52-53.

Before turning to the texts, it is necessary to look at the major locus of Jewish Palestinian life, the village, and at social relations on a smaller scale. Society was bound together by a web of group relationships which will be explored in the next chapter and used to explain much of the material in the gospels and rabbinic sources.

4

Social Relations and Groups in Palestine

Most gospel texts dealing with the Pharisees and some which include scribes are set in the towns and villages of Galilee. Only at the end of the synoptic gospels and periodically in John does Jesus go to Jerusalem and confront the Jewish and Roman governing class of Palestine in all its power. Thus the network of relationships which held together villages, towns and cities is crucial for understanding the Pharisees and scribes as they appear in the gospels. Sociological and anthropological categories more appropriate for small, face to face relationships and groups will be used. Since social relations and groups were many and diverse, this chapter more than others will contain a large number of definitions and may be used as a reference in conjuction with later analyses of the sources.

The Jewish and Christian groups of the first century can be linked to the class categories which have been sketched out previously. Classes are very broad categories which lump different groups together in an abstract manner. Such categories ignore many differences and important identifying characteristics of each group in the interests of a global overview. Consequently, large scale class and status categories are less fruitful for analyzing the network of relationships which bound together people in villages, such as kinship, friendship, patronage and competition for prestige, communal norms for behavior, the code of honor and the multiplicity of organizations to which they belonged. People had dozens of personal and corporate relationships which defined their place in society and their own self-concept and identity. People belonged simultaneously to a major class in society, a kinship group and a territorial group (this usually included religion), to subgroups within their class and perhaps to voluntary associations. In addition, their activities might have made them parts of coalitions and factions in the struggle for power or income. The Pharisees, scribes and Sadducees, as well as the followers of Jesus, revolutionaries, messianic and apocalyptic groups, Herodians, etc., were all groups existing within and sometimes cutting across the major classes of Jewish society.

In the Hellenistic period Jewish groups flourished and their existence has been explicitly recorded, especially by Josephus and 1-2 Maccabees. The Pharisees, Sadducees and Essenes are the most well known, but not the only ones. Christians originally were a sub-group of Judaism, as were various messianic bands and, at the time of the war with Rome, the Zealots and Sicarii. The presence of such groups in the sources bespeaks the Hellenistic milieu of Judaism and Christianity, in which private, voluntary associations for worship, socialization and other pursuits were common. The Pharisees, scribes, Essenes, Sadducees, followers of Jesus and many other groups were recognized as identifiable units within Jewish political society. They transcended the village and family and often played a role in national and local life. The lack of clear historical data about the internal organization of many first-century Jewish groups has produced many fruitless controversies. Some general hypotheses about the kinds of groups which might have existed in ancient society, how groups arose, what their social standing was and what their functions usually were will give some guidance to our subsequent detailed, historical examination of groups in the Greco-Roman Empire and in Judaism.

Village Society in Palestine

Since 90% of the people in antiquity were farmers, most village residents were farmers. The larger towns and perhaps some villages also had specialists, like skilled artisans, whose poverty and low social standing were similar to that of peasants. The leaders of a village were the elders and notable citizens who were the leaders of the prominent families. In small villages this group was usually not organized into a legally constituted body, such as a town council, though it probably was in the larger towns. Leading families were marked out by prestige derived from wealth, which meant ownership of land, by traditional leadership exercised over a long period of time and by service to the community. Representatives of the government, such as bureaucratic officials and tax collectors, were also leaders of a sort. If they were foreign or perceived as hostile to the villagers, then they were adversaries of the village leaders and competitors for power. If they were local citizens who aided the village in its relations with the national government or empire, then they were part of the leadership. In larger towns the more successful merchants and artisans as well as other specialists could attain significant wealth and exercise influence and power. Hereditary priests resident in the district and any literate and learned people who knew and interpreted the social and religious traditions of the culture were also looked to as leaders. The very limited evidence concerning the scribes in the gospels suggests that they were part of the literate leadership, though evidence for them as a coherent group is lacking. The gospels and rabbinic literature picture the Pharisees as learned leaders in the villages and towns, while Josephus restricts them to Jerusalem, a problem which will be dealt with later.

Many scholars have treated the village synagogue as a power center separate from civil leadership and under the control of the Pharisees. This reconstruction has no first-century evidence to support it. The village leadership described above probably exercised authority over the synagogue as it existed in Palestinian villages. In those villages and towns with a large plurality of Jews it is likely that the town assembly for business and celebration was coextensive with the assembly for prayer on Sabbath and feasts (the synagogue). It probably met in the town square, in the courtyard or room of a large house or in the town assembly building rather than in a building dedicated exclusively to public worship. There is little evidence for synagogue buildings in Palestine in the first century. The "synagogues" in the Jewish fortresses at Masada and Herodium were assembly halls used for many purposes, including communal prayer and the reading of scripture. It is only in the third century that buildings dedicated to worship appear regularly in Palestine.[1] It is doubtful that small poor villages had their own Torah scroll or a teacher learned in more than the basics of the law. The same prominent and (more or less) learned leaders who directed the community probably led the synagogue since political and religious society were one. This makes more understandable the opposition to Jesus, the outsider, by Jewish village leaders who saw him as a threat to their social position and disruptive of their traditional way of life.

Social Relations

Because people's multiple and complex social relationships cannot be comprehended by static class and group definitions, some sociologiest have analyzed all social relations as a network which fosters the rise of many types of groups and underlies their workings.[2] Relationships with people can be divided into at least six zones from intimate family relations to utilitarian work associations and on to mere recognition.[3] Interactions between people can be simple or multiplex (involving more than one role) and vary enormously in importance and worth. Interactions can be one-directional or mutual in varying degrees and their frequency and duration also vary. Networks as a whole can be classified according to structural features such as size, density (how many members of the network have independent interactions with each other), degree of closeness of connection among the members of the network, how the members of the

[1] For problems of identifying and dating synagogues, see Marilyn J. Chiat, "First-Century Synagogue Architecture: Methodological Problems," *Ancient Synagogues: The State of Research,* ed. Joseph Gutmann (BJS 22; Chico: Scholars, 1981) 49-60. In the diaspora and in Palestinian cities and towns which were dominated by Gentiles the Jews found it essential to organize into a formal community in order to keep their identity and carry on their communal affairs and customs.

[2] See Jeremy Boissevain, *Friends of Friends: Networks, Manipulators and Coalitions* (Oxford: Blackwell, 1974); Paul W. Hollander and Samuel Leinhardt (eds), *Perspectives in Social Network Analysis* (New York: Academic, 1979) and Samuel Leinhardt (ed.) *Social Networks: A Developing Paradigm* (New York: Academic, 1977).

[3] Boissevain, *Friends,* 45-48.

network cluster and how many intermediaries are necessary to reach a given number of people.[4]

Such an analysis of the relationships which bind society can give a detailed picture of how society works and of the causes of social activity, if the data is available. Through his analysis of networks Boissevain suggests that people are moved to act by their important personal relations as well as by their social values (Durkheim) and interests. The concept of social networks explains the patron client system (below) in which a close personal relationship underlies all the other exchanges of favors. It also explains the strong adherence to Jesus as teacher, healer and savior by his disciples and the early Christian community which turned to Jesus as its heavenly patron. It is unclear what attracted and bound the Pharisees together, but this way of looking at society will guide our investigation of that question.

Though lack of evidence impedes a detailed analysis of the Pharisees, scribes and Sadducees, the very consideration of the questions raised by network analysis will guard against a frequent fault in the treatment of these groups, which is to describe them as if they were part of a simple and static social situation.[5] In fact, social and group relations were constantly shifting, as Josephus and to a lesser extent the New Testament and rabbinic literature indicate. The isolated shards of evidence will contribute to a more ordered whole only if the interpretation is guided by a comprehensive set of questions concerning the social relations of the Pharisees, scribes and Sadducees to the rest of society.

HONOR AND SHAME

The social system of antiquity and many parts of the Mediterranean even today is best described using the ideas of honor and shame. Honor is part of one's status and was much more important in antiquity than today in industrialized society where

---

[4]Boissevain, *Friends,* 28-45.

[5]Some theorists treat groups as notional entities (used for convenience) and study instead the network of relationships which bind people together. See Ladislav Holy, "Groups," in *The Social Science Encyclopedia,* eds. Adam and Jessica Kuper (London: Routledge, 1985) 346.

one's standing in the community is controlled much more by money and position. The honor and shame are the two poles of a social evaluation based on the type of personality considered to be the social ideal in small face to face societies where standing and prestige are dependent on a person, not on an impersonal office. Thus it is typical of the Mediterranean village and town. Honor is based on relationships to others in the community and is the highest temporal ideal of a society. What is honorable may include transcendent values or be in conflict with them.[6]

Since the honor system is a mode of social ranking, it produces competition for and defense of honor. Most people in a peasant society are of the same class and lack clear criteria for assigning prestige, so they engage in constant challenge and riposte in a quest for more honor among their fellow citizens.[7] One's place in the honor system determines to some extent what material resources and what power and influence one will have in society, and these in turn reinforce or weaken one's honor and standing in society. The honor system is a clearinghouse for social conflicts and an arbiter of social standing because it embodies the concrete social norms embraced by the community.[8] Thus, the conflicts for influence and power evident in Josephus' treatment of the Pharisees, in the gospel conflicts between the Pharisees and Jesus and in the early Christian effort to gain acceptance (honor) itself in Palestine are all contests for honor in the community.

The idea of honor is a constant in Mediterranean society, but the precise idea of what constitutes honor and loss of honor changes over time. In Spain, according to one researcher, the criteria for honor have changed several times in the last three centuries. Also, honor is different for people of varied status, birth and social class.[9] The honor system alerts the twentieth-

---

[6]J. G. Peristiany, "Introduction," *Honour and Shame: The Values of Mediterranean Society* (Chicago: University of Chicago, 1966) 9-10; J. K. Campbell, "Honour and the Devil," in Peristiany, *Honour,* 152.

[7]Peristiany, "Introduction," *Honour,* 11, 14-15; J. G. Peristiany, "Honour and Shame in a Cypriot Highland Village," in *Honour,* 185-87.

[8]Julian Pitt-Rivers, *The Fate of Schechem,* (Cambridge: Cambridge Univ., 1977) 47; J. Davis, *The People of the Mediterranean: An Essay in Comparative Social Anthropology* (London: Routledge, 1977) 77, 89-90, 98.

[9]See especially Julio C. Baroja, "Honour and Shame: A Historical Account of Several Conflicts," in Peristiany (ed.), *Honour,* 81-137, esp. 122; Pitt-Rivers, *Schechem* 18-47, 77-78.

century reader to one of the major differences between antiquity and the modern period, the view of the individual. It presumes that people are community oriented and embedded in society. The type of personality produced by this kind of society is usually characterized as dyadic. A person's self-image and social standing, even in one's own eyes, is determined primarily by an external code and by public opinion and evaluation rather than by adherence to personal and internal values.[10] The modern Western emphasis on being true to oneself and actualizing one's potentialities toward fulfilment is subordinated to the needs and norms of the community in which one is embedded.

PATRON CLIENT RELATIONS

Both the Pharisees and Jesus were probably perceived as patrons by the mass of the people with whom they dealt. Josephus and the gospels show the people looking to the Pharisees as influential leaders who can help them. The same is true of Jesus in the gospels, except that his influence is not with worldly leaders, but with God. Patron client relations were common in the ancient Mediterranean world and survive there in varied forms to the present day. They help to organize social relations at the point where the large scale, corporate relationships leave off.[11] The superior and inferior in a close, familiar society are bound together by bonds of mutual obligation which are best analyzed as patron client relations. For example, the village leaders acted as protectors and intercessors for the illiterate peasants by defending the village's interests and way of life against the outside world. In contrast with the non-voluntary, impersonal, corporate relations which bind nations and empires, in patron client alliances people who know one another enter into a personal, one on one (dyadic) relationship which is not required by law, which is not perpetuated by an organization

[10]Pierre Bourdieu, "The Sentiment of Honour in Kabyle Society," in Peristiany, 211-212; Bruce Malina, *The New Testament World: Insights from Cultural Anthropology* (Atlanta: Knox, 1981) 51-68.

[11]In modern corporations rising young executives usually need patrons to support and guide them.

and which depends on a direct, personal interaction between two individuals.[12]

Patron client relationships are a very important supplement to the class categories developed by Lenski. Class structure stresses the vertical differences among people in a society, based on power and wealth. However, the metaphors of class, stratum, etc. do not totally comprehend reality. Ancient society, more than modern, industrial society, has a very strong horizontal dimension based on interpersonal loyalty, commitment and influence, both within and across class boundaries. Thus attention to patron client relations fills out the picture of how society works and especially shows how all four dimensions of power analyzed by Parsons operate to keep society together and aid different groups in their social conflicts. They explain the Pharisees' relations with both the governing class and the people and partly explain Jesus' relation to his disciples and the early Christian community's relation to Jesus as savior.

A patron client relationship is often between two unequal persons, long lasting and diffuse; by this relationship the patron and client each commit themselves to exchange favors and come to each other's aid in a time of need.[13] The favors and aid rendered may be different in each case, but they are valuable to the recipients. If the client receives much more from the patron than he gives, for example, physical protection from harm, a permanent alliance is formed since the client is permanently indebted to the patron by a debt which cannot be repaid. Often these relationships are characterized by personal loyalty, as

[12]Carl H. Lande, "Introduction: The Dyadic Basis of Clientelism," in *Friends, Followers, and Factions,* (eds.) Steffen W. Schmidt et al. (Berkeley: University of California, 1977) xiii. For additional data, analysis and bibliography, see S. N. Eisenstadt and Louis Roniger, "Patron-Client Relations as a Model of Structuring Social Exchange," *Comparative Studies in Society and History* 22 (1980) 42-77; *Patrons, Clients, Friends: Interpersonal Relations and the Structure of Trust in Society* (Cambridge: Cambridge UP, 1984); *Patrons and Clients in Mediterranean Societies,* (eds) Ernest Gellner and John Waterbury (London: Duckworth, 1977). For patronage at the level of empire, see Richard Saller, *Personal Patronage under the Early Empire* (Cambridge: Cambridge UP, 1982).

[13]Lande, "Clientelism," xiv; "A patron-client relationship is a vertical dyadic alliance, i.e., an alliance between two persons of unequal status, power or resources each of whom finds it useful to have as an ally someone superior or inferior to himself." xx.

well.[14] Within society dyadic relationships such as patron-client relations are non-corporate and based on implicit contracts which supplement the explicit contracts which are part of formal, corporate society and government. A society needs structure in addition to what is legislated and dyadic relationships give that structure to society. When the central institutions of a society are weak, dyadic alliances proliferate and fill a more basic need for social structure.[15] Yet, patron client relations are always appended to and presume a corporate body, that is, society at large.

Healthy patron client relationships demand that the patron treat the client fairly, but the power and wealth of the client can foster oppression and exploitation rather than concern for the welfare of the client. Both the strengths and weaknesses of this kind of relationship can be seen in the relationships of tenant farmers to the owner or serfs to their lord. The client can ameliorate an oppressive situation only by seeking greater favor with the patron or by two other alternatives unusual in antiquity, revolt or withdrawal from the relationship. The Gospel of Luke charges that the Pharisees, as patrons of the people, are failing in their duties and it claims that Jesus, acting as an intermediary with God, fulfills the role of patron in a new and more effective way. The patron-client relationship depends greatly on the person of the patron, in contrast to the corporate relationship which has a built-in structure which tends to sustain it independently of any particular person.

Since villages and towns existed within a larger society and empire, the mass of uneducated villagers needed wise and influential patrons to intercede for them with the bureaucracy. Such patrons are usually called *brokers,* that is, intermediaries between more powerful patrons or officials and the less powerful who depend on them. It is likely that the Pharisees and scribes, as leaders and perhaps low level officials, were perceived as brokers by the people in their dealings with the world at large. The group gathered around a patron is called a clientele. *Clienteles* are composed of a patron and all of his clients. The group does not have a corporate structure but is bound together by loyalty

---

[14]Lande, "Clientelism," xv-xvi.

[15]Lande, "Clientelism," xvii-xviii; xxi-xxii.

to the patron and can be mobilized only by him. A clientele offered the patron support in his dealings with other, often higher officials or patrons, and thus increased his prestige and indirectly advanced the clientele's interests. For a wealthy person a clientele would consist of dependent farmers, servants and other community members dependent on them or owing them a favor. The dependent officials and servants of Herod the Great, the high priest, and the "Herodians" (Mk 3:6) associated with Herod Antipas should probably be conceived of as a clientele.

The Origin of Social Groups

Between the overarching common structures which bind a society together and the personal relations of patron and client lies a profusion of corporate and non-corporate groups. Normal social relations, changes in society and the give and take of patron client relations produce a number of voluntary, mostly non-corporate groups which further bind society together and are the basis for cooperation and conflict within society. Jesus led such a group and the Jewish leaders formed such groups as they made alliances to oppose Jesus. The Pharisees, Sadducees and early Christians were voluntary groups which were probably non-corporate, at least for part of their history.

The emergence of the Pharisees, Sadducees, Essenes and other groups in the Hasmonean period can be effectively explained by the sociological process of group formation. Judaism struggled for four or five centuries to adjust to Greco-Roman culture, from the conquest by Alexander the Great in 332 B.C.E. to the formation of the Mishnah about 200 C.E. In its battle to retain its Jewish identity, with emphasis on monotheism, the Bible, circumcision, sabbath observance and a host of other practices, Judaism assimilated many characteristics of the Greco-Roman way of life and thought.[16] It is very likely that the emergence of identifiable, voluntary associations, which struggled for control of Jewish society, disagreed over how Judaism was to be lived, and reacted to the activities of foreign rulers differ-

---

[16]See E. Bickerman, *From Ezra to the Last of the Maccabees* (New York: Schocken, 1962) and M. Hengel, *Judaism and Hellenism* (Philadelphia: Fortress, 1974).

ently, is itself a Hellenistic phenomenon used by some Jews to combat Hellenism.

The emergence of a diversity of groups in Jewish society fits the pattern of agrarian empires when they become large and complex. Society became differentiated and stratified and that led to the development of social groups in addition to basic kinship and political groups. An empire tends to develop a political bureaucracy which includes religious, cultural and economic leadership along with the military and administrative. It also develops a variety of groups beyond the kinship and political structure, each group with a different composition and goals. Some groups mimic kinship groups and are thus called fictive kinship groups. For example, the Christians often refer to each other as brothers and sisters and to God as their father, thus turning themselves into a "family." But the groups are voluntary and membership is achieved by commitment and proper behavior, rather than heredity. This process of differentiation is pervasive and even leads to limited differentiation on the village level.[17] These new groups competed with traditional ethnic, territorial and ascriptive groups for social resources such as power, status, and wealth.[18]

In antiquity voluntary groups were based both on social function and on solidarity. Social groups based on function gathered people of the same role or status in society or with the same interests. Examples of groups based on function are associations of artisans or merchants, religious associations and cult groups; those based on social solidarity included people with similar social needs, desires and outlooks such as aliens in a given place, people of many statuses dissatisfied with the prevailing world view, etc.[19] Early Christianity provided solidarity for those searching for a different view of the divine and for salvation. When a society, such as the Roman empire, included a large number of these groups, the groups tended to recognize each other's similarities and common interests and so they evolved more general cultural symbols and developed the non-

---

[17]Eisenstadt, *Empires,* 79 and 92.

[18]Eisenstadt, *Empires,* 91.

[19]Eisenstadt, *Empires,* 79-80. M. Finley, *Ancient Economy,* 138 notes that these groups were especially popular among the urban poor, and even the rural poor.

ascriptive, voluntary parts of society to the detriment of the traditional, ascriptive elements of society. In addition these associations often established a broad influence over all parts of the lives of their members so that they performed integrative functions of wider scope than those inherent in their purely specialized explicit objectives.[20] As these groups became stronger and the attraction or hold of the empire or political structure became weaker, people might identify more strongly with a non-ascriptive, voluntary group than with kinship or political units. The gospel saying about leaving one's father and mother[21] and Augustine's defense of Christians as good citizens of the Roman empire in the *City of God* bespeak this tension and competition.

Eisenstadt warns that the rise of ancient associations should not be seen as identical to processes in modern society:

> "These developments in the associational structure of the historical bureaucratic societies cannot be equated with the growth of associational activity and national consciousness in modern societies. Though varying from society to society, participation in most of the historical associations was still limited to relatively select urban or aristocratic groups, and by many traditional orientations and patterns of organization. Moreover, the extents to which such associations became oriented toward central values and symbols were greatly different; and many of them were limited to small localities. The same applies to their participation in the common cultural life and their identification with common collective and cultural symbols. Nevertheless, each of these associations, whatever the scope of its membership or orientation, brought a distinct element of differentiation to its society."[22]

With this warning in mind, these conditions and consequences of the rise of associations help to explain the variety of movements and positions which developed in the intellectual, religious

---

[20]Eisenstadt, *Empires,* 81-82.

[21]Mt. 10:37; Luke 14:26.

[22]Eisenstadt, *Empires,* 82.

and political life of the Hellenistic and Roman Empires. It is in this context that the rise of the Pharisees, Sadducees and other Jewish groups is to be sought.

Social Groups

Moderns usually picture the aristocratic and monarchic societies of antiquity as fixed and unchanging and thus fail to understand the role of groups like the Pharisees and other Jewish groups. Though the status system of ancient empires looked very rigid, it was often fairly flexible. Wealth, power and prestige as determinants of social position became separate from one another and competing hierarchies arose within society.[23] Thus various leadership and power groups competed with traditional groups in the workings of society:

> "Another extremely significant manifestation of the existence of different status hierarchies is the development of special elite positions and activities. In most of the societies studied here, there developed special categories, of groups or of people, whose members engaged in leadership and communication in various institutional spheres, while these categories were not rooted in any ascriptive status groups, roles, or positions. In the religious and cultural organizations, there arose several such positions, whose incumbents were recruited from many, though not necessarily all, status groups, and whose activities cut across these groups.[24]

Though the presence and power of the new elite reached even to some of the small villages and weakened the powers of the traditional and legally recognized groups in society,[25] fundamentally the free urban groups and associations had power because they were in the city, the center of power. They provided some upward mobility for their members, though few actually reached

[23]Eisenstadt, *Empires,* 82-83.

[24]Eisenstadt, *Empires,* 83.

[25]Eisenstadt, *Empires,* 84-86.

the top of the governing class.[26] Those who did achieve higher status tried to retain it by the usual ascriptive means, heredity and permanent social status. Such a development of new elites can be found in the emergence of Jewish groups such as the Pharisees, scribes and other groups.

Space does not allow a treatment of the myriad of groups which emerged in Palestine and the Roman Empire. As an aid to understanding ancient groups, a useful set of distinctions drawn from the sociological analysis of groups will be presented; then the data concerning Greek voluntary associations will be reviewed. Finally, because the Pharisees and Sadducees are often called sects, recent work on sects will be addressed. Josephus' designation of the Pharisees as a *hairesis,* a choice (often translated as sect or school of thought) will be treated in ch. 6 along with Greco-Roman data on schools of philosophy.

In its most simple sense a *social group* is any collectivity of humans. From a social psychological point of view a social group is "a number of individuals who have internalized the same social category membership as a component of their self-concept."[27] Such a cognitive and internal definition of a group is not very useful in our discussion at this point, but it indicates how flexible and complex group definition may be and how little we say when we designate a collectivity as a group.

A *formal social group* is what we usually mean by a group and it commonly refers to "a plurality of individuals bounded by some principle of recruitment and by a set of membership rights and obligations."[28] It is an organization and implies "the existence of procedures for mobilizing and coordinating the efforts of various, usually specialized, subgroups in the pursuit of joint objectives."[29] Social organizations, in turn, are usually divided into involuntary, voluntary, corporate and non-corporate. Familiar *involuntary groups* are family, political communities, social classes, castes, and other collectivities into which we are

---

[26]Eisenstadt, *Empires,* 86-87.

[27]John C. Turner, "Social Group," in Henri Taifel (ed.), *Social Identity and Intergroup Relations* (European Studies in Social Psychology; Cambridge/Paris: Cambridge University/Maison des sciences de l'Homme, 1982) 36.

[28]Holy, "Groups," 346.

[29]Peter Blau, "Organizations," *IESS,* 298.

born or which impose themselves upon us. They are usually *corporate* groups which have explicit goals and make concrete demands on their members.[30] In antiquity one usually was born into a kinship group (extended family) and into a political group which might be an independent ethnic group or nation or subordinate to an empire. The Jews in Israel were a subordinate nation and ethnic group in the Greek and Roman empires. Such social relationships were usually *ascriptive,* meaning that one is assigned a certain group membership and a social status, role, or place within that group by birth or an outside force, such as a political entity or a culture. By contrast, *achieved* membership or status is based on the activities of the person and the effects produced on social relationships by those activities. Achieved status or membership is usually voluntary because it is based on one's own efforts.

Voluntary groups are much more varied than involuntary groups because they are organized for a great variety of purposes, some comprehensive and some very restricted.[31] Voluntary organizations usually exist within the larger, more basic framework of involuntary, corporate society and seek to fulfill more restricted goals or needs of parts of the society. *Corporate voluntary groups* have fixed goals, modes of action, and relations among the members.[32] Hellenistic associations, political parties, interest groups and institutionalized coalitions belong to this type. *Non-corporate, voluntary groups,* such as movements, coalitions, factions, etc., usually lack fixed structure, are held together by temporary and narrow common interests, cannot by right claim the resources of the members and have an identity which is less clear than stable, corporate groups. Any of these groups may become corporate if it remains in existence long enough and takes steps to ensure its permanent existence.

Since many of the social conflicts in Josephus and the gospels can be understood in terms of political interest groups, coalitions, factions and movements, brief definitions of these voluntary groups will be helpful. A *political interest group* is a voluntary

---

[30]Lande, "Cleintism," xix.

[31]Michael Banton, "Voluntary Associations: Anthropological Aspects," *IESS,* 357.

[32]Boissevain, *Friends,* 171.

association which seeks to convert its interest into public law or gain control over social behavior.[33] Such groups, which compete for power, usually seek to label their opponents deviant. The give and take of political, social and religious life and the struggles for power among groups can be explained as the attempts of dominant and deviant groups to have society follow their rules. Many of the conflicts among the Jewish leadership and the early Christian community can be explained in these terms.

Compared to corporate groups which are permanent and organized and have a set identity, coalitions and factions are much more temporary and limited. It should be noted, though, that coalitions and factions which remain in existence for a long time may acquire corporate characteristics. A *coalition* is "a temporary alliance of distinct parties for a limited purpose" and so *political coalitions* make joint use of resources to affect political decisions. A coalition differs from a corporate group in that the resources used by the coalition remain linked to the original members of the coalition and the wider goals of each member may vary considerably.[34] The coalition is thus temporary and not the primary identity of the members. The parties united against Jesus such as the Pharisees and Herodians in Mark 3:6 are typical of a coalition as is the Pharisees' alliance with Pheroras' wife against Herod (see ch. 5).

A *faction* is a coalition which is "recruited personally according to structurally diverse principles by or on behalf of another person."[35] Factions tend to be "characterized by unstable membership, uncertain duration, personalistic leadership, a lack of formal organization, and by a greater concern for power and spoils than with ideology or policy."[36] When two clients with their clientele compete in society, the rivalry is usually factional because the two groups are formed by their adherence to a leader. In the period before the great war with Rome, as depicted

---

[33]E. Pfuhl, *The Deviance Factor* (New York: Van Nostrand, 1980), 122. Modern political interest groups are political parties, pressure groups, special interest groups and lobbies.

[34]Boissevain, *Friends,* 171-173.

[35]Boissevain, *Friends,* 171-173, 192 and 195.

[36]Lande, "Clientism," xxxii.

in Josephus, Jerusalem was rife with coalitions and factions. Paul seems to be trying to break up factions in the Corinthian church by reorienting them to their primary patron, Jesus (1 Cor 1-4).[37]

When social activity is very diffuse and lacking in organization, it is often referred to as a movement. The term covers a variety of groups. For example, early Christianity is increasingly called the Jesus movement by New Testament scholars. A *social movement* defined very abstractly and psychologically is "an effort by a large number of people to solve collectively a problem that they feel they have in common."[38] More concretely, a social movement is aimed at promoting or resisting change in society at large. Such social movements can range from popular sentiment which might result in social activity to complex reformist or revolutionary groups. They often begin as voluntary, non-corporate groups but can become corporate social movement organizations, which may be coalitions, political interest groups or other kinds of organizations.[39] It is certainly possible that the Pharisees, with their program for reviving or reforming Judaism and the Jesus movement, with its new interpretation of Jewish life and revelation, functioned as social movements or as social movement organizations at some periods in their existence.

Corporate and non-corporate voluntary associations, such as coalitions, and factions, along with non-voluntary corporate groups such as the family and the state itself serve many of the same economic and social needs in that they organize production and protection. Coalitions are as basic a form of social organization as the family and serve many of the same functions, including economic production and physical protection. Factions tend to predominate in societies which are weak and in which the state cannot provide security.[40] Palestinian society in

[37]L. L. Welborn, "On the Discord in Corinth: 1 Corinthians 1-4 and Ancient Politics," *JBL* 106 (1987) 85-111 shows that the groups in Corinth were political factions competing for power in the community and not based on theological disagreements.

[38]Hans Toch, *The Social Psychology of Social Movements* (Indianapolis: Bobbs, 1965) 5.

[39]John D. McCarthy and Mayer N. Zald, "Resource Mobilization and Social Movements: A Partial Theory," *American Journal of Sociology* 82 (1977) 1212-1241, esp. 1217-1219.

[40]Boissevain, *Friends*, 203.

the Hellenistic and Roman periods was rife with the types of groups described here. Concretely and historically, of course, the actual groups covered by these general definitions had diverse and particular characteristics which are very important for understanding society and their place in it. However, the significant common characteristics highlighted by the general categories sketched above will illuminate some of the important workings of Palestinian society and enable us to understand the Pharisees, scribes, Sadducees and other groups more accurately.

Greek Associations

Since the Pharisees especially and other Jewish groups as well have often been compared to various groups in the Greco-Roman world, some discussion of the possibilities is needed. Greco-Roman associations, which existed in great variety, and sects will be treated here. Philosophical schools of thought and the meaning of Josephus' designation of the Pharisees and other groups as *hairesis* will be treated at the end of chapter six.

Private voluntary associations were numerous and varied in the Hellenistic and Roman periods. They existed in both the city and country and among the upper and lower classes and they are extremely difficult to categorize.[41] The terms used for associations and the members of the associations are many: *orgeones, thiasos, schola, eranistai, synodos, collegium, synagōgē, koinon, hairesis.* Each word has many meanings and no one has a consistent technical meaning.[42] Collegia could be burial societies or religious societies or both; *thiasos, secta,* and *synodos* are sometimes used for collegia and schools.[43] *Thiasos,* which most

[41]Marcus N. Tod, *Sidelights on Greek History* (Oxford: Blackwell, 1932) 77; MacMullen, *Social Relations,* 18-20; 73-80; Finley, *Ancient Economy,* 138. The most useful compendium of material for the Hellenistic world, now incomplete because of continuing discoveries, is Franz Poland, *Geschichte des Griechischen Vereinswesens* (Fürstlich Jablonowskischen Gesellschaft zu Leipzig 38; Leipzig: Teubner, 1909).

[42]Poland, *Geschichte,* 152-168. Trade guilds or associations often had religious titles and met in worship of a deity, but were not really religious associations, much less sects or cults. Tod, *Sidelights,* 76-77.

[43]Robert Wilken, "Collegia, Philosophical Schools, and Theology," in *The Catacombs and the Colliseum,* (eds.) Stephen Benko and J. J. O'Rourke, (Valley Forge: Judson, 1971) 279.

often means a religious association, is also used of trade associations.[44] In addition, associations often had multiple purposes. A craft guild might engage in the protection of the craft, but it might be a social group. Burial societies met regularly and had rules for their banquets. A street or neighborhood might have a society for the regular worship of a deity or the organization of a festival. Collegia were common among the lower classes, but they usually had no economic function. They were both social and religious and were used to gain honor and status in society. Many titles and honors were distributed in these groups, mimicking the state.[45]

The Hellenistic institution of voluntary associations very probably prompted the formation of the voluntary Jewish groups, the Pharisees, Sadducees and Essenes.[46] However, Greek and Roman associations were so varied that the analogy of association has only the most general meaning and is not useful for precise definition. Hundreds of associations existed, many of which had only 10-25 members.[47] No generalizations about Greek associations can be used confidently to describe or define a group.

We know so little about the internal organization of the Pharisees and even less about the scribes and Sadducees that it is difficult to connect them to Hellenistic associations, except in a very general and a priori way. That an influence from Hellenistic associations is possible can easily be granted. Proof for such hypotheses and concrete description of how such associational behavior was adapted to Jewish life is very difficult to come by. Twenty years ago Hugo Mantel suggested that the

---

[44]Abraham Malherbe, *Social Aspects of Early Christianity* (Baton Rouge: Louisiana State Univ., 1977) 86-91.

[45] MacMullen, *Roman Social Relations,* 73-80; Finley, *Ancient Economy, 138, Poland, Geschichte,* 337-338; 423-445.

[46]Henry Fischel, "Story and History: Observations on Greco-Roman and Pharisaism" in *American Oriental Society Middle West Branch Semi-Centennial Volume,* ed. D. Sinor (Bloomington, IN: Indiana Univ., 1969) 82; Morton Smith, "Palestinian Judaism in the First Century," *Israel: Its Role in Civilization,* ed. Moshe Davis (New York: Harper, 1956) 67-81; Ellis Rivkin, *A Hidden Revolution: The Pharisees' Search for the Kingdom Within* (Nashville: Abingdon, 1978) 242-243 on the Pharisees; Martin Hengel, *Judaism and Hellenism* 1:230-247 on the Qumran community.

[47]Poland, *Geschichte,* 282-283.

Great Assembly of Jewish leaders, alleged to have ruled Judaism in the Hellenistic period, bore many structural and terminological characteristics of Hellenistic associations.[48] Mantel has used later rabbinic sources as accurate representations of history centuries earlier and has accepted the existence of the Great Assembly as historical. Both of these conclusions are inaccurate.[49] His study does show how the later rabbinic sources understood earlier history and that these sources were influenced by Hellenistic ways of thought in their own reconstructions of the past, but not how the Pharisees of the second Temple period were organized. Others have tried to connect the community of the Dead Sea Scrolls (*yaḥad*) to Greek associations characterized as *koinon*.[50] The concrete complexities of local organization and the bewildering variety of associations over time in diverse places render such comparisons of very limited explanatory or descriptive value.

Surely the Pharisees, about whose organization we know very little, may have been similar to these Greek associations in some respects and stimulated in their organization by models from the larger culture in which Judaism existed. The evidence indicates that they played an active role in society and this suggests that they engaged in common activities and had meetings and meals in order to foster their identity and aid their activities.[51] They probably had an organized leadership; they certainly had rules, common patterns of worship, and some kind of training; they were a relatively small group which knew each other personally, socialized with one another and received the protection and patronage of wealthy sponsors, whether members or friends of the organization. These things we can indirectly surmise, but neither the direct evidence on the

---

[48] H. Mantel, "The Nature of the Great Synagogue," *HTR* 60 (1967) 69-91.

[49] On the non-historicity of the Great Assembly as an institution, see Ira J. Schiffer, "The Men of the Great Assembly," *Persons and Institutions in Early Rabbinic Judaism,* ed. William S. Green (BJS 3; Missoula: Scholars, 1977) 237-276.

[50] Bruno W. Dombrowski, "*Ha-Yahad* in IQS and *tó koinón:* An Instance of Early Greek and Jewish Synthesis," *HTR* 59 (1966) 293-307.

[51] Jacob Neusner has interpreted them as a table fellowship society with religious purpose. This topic will be taken up in detail in ch. 10.

Pharisees nor the patterns common in Greco-Roman associations can tell us certainly what they were like.[52]

Sects

Since the Pharisees and Sadducees, as well as the early Christians and other Jewish groups, have often been described as sects and since the category, sect, is so popular and so unclear, a more extended treatment of sect is needed. Sect formation must be understood as a form of deviance. Since society includes many systems of belief or many interpretations of the prevailing system of belief, much social activity involves conflicting social groups which often label one another deviant.[53] Minority groups labeled deviant are out of power, dissatisfied with society and often interested in changing it. When such groups compete for power like political interest groups, they try to label the dominant group as deviant. At other times they accept their deviant status and form voluntary organizations to promote their way of life apart from society.[54]

The popular usage of sect is far less sophisticated and usually connotes a group with peculiar, minority beliefs and practices; sects are conceived of as withdrawn from society and politics and as critical of society. Sects are often identified by a loose congeries of characteristics without internal coherence. In Troelsch's classic typology, especially as popularly used, sect is contrasted with church on theological and behavioral grounds and within a Christian context.[55] However, the term has come

[52]For an application of this category to the Pauline community, see Wayne Meeks, *The First Urban Christians* (New Haven: Yale, 1983) 77-80.

[53]E. Pfuhl, *Deviance* 122.

[54]Pfuhl, *Deviance,* 263-266. Pfuhl categorizes deviant groups by two pairs of factors, whether they are directed to inner concerns or to attempts to change society and whether their attitude toward society is alienated or conformist.

[55]For difficulties and imprecisions endemic to the church sect distinction, along with that of denomination or free church, see B. Johnson, "On Church and Sect," *American Sociological Review* 28 (1963) 539-549; Alan W. Eister, "Toward a Radical Critique of Church-Sect Typologizing: Comment on 'Some Critical Observations on the Church-Sect Dimension,'" *Journal for the Scientific Study of Religion* 6 (1967) 85-90. For the argument that Troelsch uses this term as proper to Christianity and as an historical

to have a wider meaning and to embrace groups reacting against any society on a variety of grounds. In modern sociology the word sect is increasingly applied to religiously based groups which are politically active in their society. In view of these developments, if the Pharisees are to be characterized as a sect, such a categorization does not entail their separation from politics or their ceasing to work as a political interest group in Jewish society.

Bryan Wilson has created a working typology of seven kinds of sects, based on the group's relationship with its host society. His emphasis on the sect's relationship with society and its activities fits the approach taken in this study. A quick review of his typology will aid in understanding the groups contained in ancient texts.[56] Wilson defines the seven types of sect based on response to the world and he rejects explicitly the more usual criteria of doctrinal deviance or lack of formal organization.[57] Sects are defined by deviance from what is dominant in society, as might be expected: "Concern with transcendence over evil and the search for salvation and consequent rejection of prevailing cultural values, goals, and norms, and whatever facilities are culturally provided for man's salvation, defines religious deviance." The seven types of sect respond to the world differently, partly because they have different ideas of salvation based on different definitions of evil and how it is to be over-

---

explanation of the development of Christianity, see Theodore M. Steeman, "Church, Sect, Mysticism, Denomination: Periodiological Aspects of Troeltsch's Typology," *Sociological Analysis* 36 (1975) 181-204.

[56]See *Magic and the Millennium: A Sociological Study of Religious Movements of Protest Among Tribal and Third-World Peoples* (London: Heinemann, 1973) 16-26. His earlier typology had only four types and was based on different principles. See *Patterns of Sectarianism: Organization and Ideology in Social and Religious Movements* (London: Heinemann, 1967) edited by Wilson, esp. the introduction, pp. 1-21; "An Analysis of Sect Development" pp. 22-45. This latter work contains a list of characteristics of sects which is often used as a shopping list of things to look for in groups. The presence of a number of characteristics does not make a group a sect unless these characteristics can be related to one another in some systematic way in a theoretical context.

[57]Wilson, *Magic,* pp. 16-17; 19. Wilson is generally sympathetic in his analysis of sects, but like most modern Western social scientists, he assumes a "higher absolute value for Western political organization and rationality." Cf. Hillel Schwartz, "The End of the Beginning; Millenarian Studies, 1969-1975," *RSR* 2 (3, 1976) 7.

thrown.[58] 1. The *conversionist* seeks emotional transformation now, with salvation presumed to follow in the future after evil has been endured. Because of alienation from society a new community is formed. Early Christians fit this type. 2. The *revolutionist* awaits the destruction of the social order by divine forces. Apocalyptic groups fit this type. 3. The *introversionist* withdraws from the world into a purified community. The Essenes fit this type. 4. The *manipulationist* seeks happiness by a transformed subjective orientation which will control evil. The gnostics fit this type. 5. The *thaumaturgical response* seeks relief from specific ills by special, not general dispensation. Magicians and healers with their followers fit this type. 6. The *reformist* seeks gradual, divinely revealed alterations in society. The Pharisees and Jesus with his disciples probably fit this type.[59] 7. The *utopian* seeks to reconstruct the world according to divine principles without revolution.[60]

The seven types of sects can be sorted according to three larger categories: a. the objectivist, seeking change in the world: revolutionist, introversionist, reformist, utopian; b. the subjectivist, seeking change in the person: conversionist; c. the relationist, seeking to adjust relations with the world: manipulationist, thaumaturgical. The seven types are not totally separate from one another, nor are they rigid. A group can have more than one response to the world at one time, though usually one is dominant. Though these kinds of sects seek some change or good effect, they are more than interest groups because of their vigorous life. Most operate as self-selected and intermittently operative communities.[61] In addition, sectarian responses change over time and eventually sects can mutate into other kinds of groups, e. g., the development of denominations from sects in the second generation.[62]

Wilson's seven types of sect allow us to sort groups which have a religious base and a strong positive or negative relation to

[58]Wilson, *Magic,* 21.

[59]See ch. 12 for a discussion of the Pharisees as a sect.

[60]Wilson, *Magic,* 23-26. See also 38-49.

[61]Wilson, *Magic,* 32.

[62]Wilson, *Magic,* 49, 38, 35.

society. The types focus on the goals of the groups so they allow us to understand their choices and activities. Thus sects are not simply groups with certain doctrinal views, but active units of society which cause reactions among other groups and sometimes directly effect changes in society.

This review of some historical and sociological work on groups and social relations demonstrates the complexity of society and the inadequacy of descriptions of the first century which imagine the Pharisees, Sadducees, Essenes and Jesus as isolated religious groups debating matters of belief. Political and religious life were one and each person belonged to several socially operative units at once, including family, nation, social class, social roles, etc. Any claim concerning Jewish teaching or behavior had major ramifications in all quarters of life and society and any political, social or religious initiative had the potential to affect the whole people, including the governing class and the empire itself. In the next section attention will be paid mainly to the social relations and activities of the Pharisees, scribes and Sadducees in order to understand their place in society and the relationship of their teaching, way of life, social position and political goals.

Summary

The inner web of society was composed of networks of relationships which held together the villages where most of the people lived as well as the upper reaches of society. The most fundamental community relationships were involuntary and based on kinship and political society. Religion, economics, education, culture, ethical norms and all other aspects of society were imbedded in the familial and political relationships which held society together. In such a closely knit society people defined themselves by their standing in the community according to common social norms for honorable behavior.

In a village the elders and leaders of prominent, landed families tended to lead the community in both its internal and external relations. They were representatives to the government, patrons of those in need, intercessors (brokers) for the weak with the powerful, judges in disputes and leaders in religious affairs. They governed their actions by accepted community norms and, true to peasants in most cultures, resisted change and the attempts of outsiders to impose new ways or interfere in the closed life of the village. However, since most villages in Galilee and Judea were proximate to major trade routes and often drawn into intense political disputes involving foreign powers, Jewish villages must not be pictured as isolated or unaffected by happenings in the world at large.

The relationship which governed those of unequal status at all levels of society can best be described as that of patron and client. The relationship was personal between individuals and often involved the exchange of many favors over a long period. Such relationships were non-corporate and based on implicitly accepted understandings, rather than the formal contracts of corporate organizations, especially political society. Wise and influential patrons often interceded as brokers for their weak, uneducated or needy clients who were threatened by larger and impersonal government taxes and regulations.

Voluntary associations were the pre-eminent mode of social organization in the Hellenistic eastern Mediterranean both before and after the coming of Rome. Both long lasting corporate and more spontaneous non-corporate groups gathered to achieve specific social purposes affecting their members. The upper and lower classes organized into corporate societies which could be as simple as social clubs or as complex as movements to reform society. Prominent among these groups were political interest groups which tried to control or influence the direction and leadership of society. The Pharisees seem to have been such a group, varying in effectiveness according to political circumstances. Changing political events also produced shorter-lived, more fragile, non-corporate associations, such as coalitions of different powerful groups and individuals and factions centered on a forceful leader as well as popular movements for reform, revolt or special interests of the movement.

Jewish voluntary groups such as the Pharisees and Sadducees have often been called sects. If sect is limited to a withdrawn protest group, the term is inappropriate. If sect is used in its more adequate and varied contemporary sense, which includes political protest and action and the exercise of power and influence and makes allowance for several responses to social and cultural pressure, then it may be used. Still, probably these groups are best understood as schools of thought (see the discussion of *hairesis* in Ch. 6) and their roles in society defined by a more precise, descriptive typology of groups such as that proposed in this chapter.

Part II

THE LITERARY SOURCES

5

The Pharisees and Sadducees as Political Interest Groups in Josephus

After a brief introduction to Josephus' social viewpoint, the activities of the Pharisees and Sadducees in Josephus' works will be treated in this chapter and the descriptions of them in the following chapter. At the end of chapter six the results of both chapters will be summarized and synthetically analyzed.

Because the Pharisees are prominent among Jewish groups mentioned in the New Testament, Biblical scholars tend to inflate their importance. From the viewpoint of the whole culture, and especially that of the ruling classes, the Pharisees were of minor importance. Josephus reflects this larger perspective by mentioning the Pharisees on less than twenty occasions in his many volumes. Like the Pharisees the Sadducees are mentioned seldom (six times) and always in contrast to the Pharisees, except on one occasion. The scribes never appear as a separate group, the way they do in the Gospels. Thus, Josephus' scattered references to scribes will not be treated here, but in the chapter eleven where evidence from many sources will be marshalled to elucidate the scribes' place in society.

In the *War* the Pharisees are mentioned four times. Their great influence on Queen Alexandra and consequent political power in the early first century, B.C.E. are recounted disapprovingly. Later in that century Herod accused his brother Pheroras' wife of subsidizing the Pharisees against him. After the long, laudatory description of the Essenes the Pharisees are described briefly with the Sadducees as one of the three traditional Jewish philosophies. Finally, at the beginning of the Great War the most notable Pharisees along with other Jewish leaders tried to prevent the cessation of the sacrifices offered for Rome.

Pharisees as a group or as individuals are mentioned nine times in the *Antiquities,* three of which are parallel to passages in the *War.* Josephus gives a brief description of the Pharisees in Book 13, as he treats the Hasmonean period, and a longer one at the beginning of Book 18 (beginning of the first century, C.E.), parallel to the description in the *War.* He recounts their conflict with John Hyrcanus which led to loss of influence, their later regaining of influence on Alexandra, and their loss of it again at her death. During the Herodian period, Samias and Pollion, who are Pharisees, appear in several incidents. Samias (or Pollion) defended Herod (in a manner of speaking) at his trial before the Sanhedrin. Herod showed favor to Samias and Pollion when he took Jerusalem and later exempted them from taking an oath of loyalty to him.[1] Near the end of Herod's life the Pharisees formed an alliance with Pheroras' wife and her faction against Herod, an association which led to the execution of a number of Pharisees.

In the *Life* Josephus says that he tried the Pharisaic way of life along with the Essenes, Sadducees and an ascetic named Bannus; finally he chose the Pharisees. On the eve of the revolt, the leading Pharisees along with the chief priests and Josephus, appeared as a leadership group. Simeon ben Gamaliel, a Pharisee, is the prime mover in Jerusalem to have Josephus removed from command in Galilee and finally the delegation sent to remove Josephus from command had a priest Pharisee and two lay Pharisees along with a young chief priest.

The Sadducees are mentioned along with the Pharisees in the three descriptions of the three Jewish "sects" and as successful rivals of the Pharisees for John Hyrcanus' affections (in both the *War* and *Antiquities*). One individual Sadducee appears, a first century high priest named Ananus who was rigorous in legal judgment.[2]

---

[1] There may have been two occasions on which Pharisees refused to take a loyalty oath. See below.

[2] *Ant.* 20.9.1 (199). The text and translation of the Loeb Classical Library edition will be used, with modification where problems arise. This is published in nine volumes, eds.

Josephus

Because Josephus is such an important source for knowledge of Judaism and because his outlook and interpretation of Judaism is integral to his narrative, a brief review of his life, work and viewpoint will provide a foundation for interpreting his account of the Pharisees and other Jewish leaders. The rich body of scholarship on Josephus will be used but no adequate discussion can be given of the many scholarly problems which underlie this brief review.[3]

Josephus was born in 37-38 C.E. of a priestly family. He was well educated and well connected with the chief priests and other leaders of Judaism in Jerusalem. He says that he studied or tried all the major philosophies and finally chose the Pharisees, though no Pharisaic tendency can be found in his interpretation of Judaism (see the section on the *Life* below). When he was twenty-six, he was part of an embassy to Rome (63-64) and he was firmly sympathetic with the ruling classes' unsuccessful attempts to retain control of Jewish society and suppress the popular movement which led to revolt against Rome. He was an active military leader in Galilee during the first part of the war. Josephus' military activities in Galilee, his purposes in developing support for himself and the war in Galilee and his disputes with the Jerusalem and other Galilean leaders are complex and have not been definitively worked out.[4] After defeat, Josephus surrendered to Rome and joined the entourage of Vespasian and his son Titus, the Roman generals who eventually became emperors, and after the war, Josephus went to Rome as a client of the Flavians and wrote his *War*. Later, sponsored by others, he wrote his *Antiquities* and *Life*.

Soon after the war Josephus wrote an account of the events

H. St. J. Thackeray, R. Markus, A. Wikgren and L.H. Feldman (Cambridge, MA: Harvard University, 1926-1965).

[3]The best brief review of Josephus scholarship is by Harry Attridge, "Josephus and His Works," *Jewish Writings of the Second Temple Period*. Ed. M. Stone (*Compendia*, 2:2; Assen/Philadelphia: Van Gorcum/Fortress, 1984), pp. 185-232. A complete, annotated, topical bibliography is also available in Feldman, *Josephus and Modern Scholarship*.

[4]Attridge, "Josephus," 188-192, has a review of the problems.

in Aramaic for the Jews in Mesopotamia.[5] It has also been suggested with some probability that Josephus wrote a memoir of the war which he used in his account of his own activities in the *War* and his later *Life*.[6] The first book of Josephus which we possess is the *War*, the first six books of which were probably published during the reign of Titus (79-81). In the *War* Josephus manifests several tendencies and biases. He presents the best possible picture of himself, absolves the Romans from blame for the loss of Jerusalem and praises the Flavians, especially Titus. He blames the revolt on revolutionaries whom he calls brigands and distinguishes from them the majority of Jews whom they misled. He also attributes the destruction of the Temple and attendant events, as well as all history, to God's will and in his accounts of Jewish losses arouses sympathy for their fate and suffering.

In the *Antiquities*, which was published with its appendix, the *Life*, in 93-94 after Agrippa's death (he did not die in 100 as some have held), Josephus presents Jewish history as a record of the workings of divine providence and the divine laws. He uses history to give moral and religious instruction by pointing out how ignoring the laws of God (as Herod did, for example) leads to disaster. He provides information to his Greek readers concerning Judaism and defends Jewish rights in the Greco-Roman world and the worth of Jewish laws in comparison with Greek and Roman laws. Josephus has been accused of being a deceptive, untrustworthy sycophant of the Romans and defended as a worthy historian in the Greek tradition.[7] Read with care his

---

[5] *War*, Preface, 1 (3, 6).

[6] The differences in the accounts in the *War* and the *Life* make it unlikely that the latter is based on the former directly. Thus, the hypothesis of a common source, rewritten in two different ways. Cf. R. Laqueur, *Der jüdisch Historiker Flavius Josephus: Ein biographischer Versuch auf neuer quellenkritischer Grundlage* (Giessen: München, 1920) who first proposed the theory. It has been ably defended recently by Shaye J.D. Cohen, *Josephus in Galilee and Rome: His Vita and Development as a Historian* (Columbia Studies in the Classical Tradition 8; Leiden: Brill, 1979), pp. 24-83.

[7] Cohen, *Josephus*, is very negative on Josephus' trustworthiness. Horst Moehring, "Joseph ben Matthia and Flavius Josephus," *Aufstieg und Niedergang der Römischen Welt* II.21.2, ed. H. Temporini (Berlin/New York, deGruyter, 1984), pp. 864-944, shows convincingly that Josephus follows the conventions of good Greek historiography and tries to balance his Jewish loyalties with his relationship with his patrons and his appreciation of Roman power.

works can yield solid historical information as well as an intelligent first century interpretation of Jewish affairs. Critical control of Josephus' claims is possible in many cases because Josephus' biases and viewpoint are so clear and obvious.

In both the *War* and the *Antiquities* Josephus uses the Jewish history of Nicolaus of Damascus; in the *Antiquities* he uses many other sources, including the Bible and certain non-Biblical books which we possess. The identification of Josephus' sources and the evaluation of how Josephus used them or rewrote them is a most complex discussion for which decisive evidence is lacking in many cases.[8] Josephus explicitly refers to Nicolaus in a number of places and may have used him in many others.[9] Nicolaus was a chief counselor to Herod for a time and wrote a history of eastern monarchies, including a detailed and sympathetic account of Herod's reign. Josephus used Nicolaus as a major source for the treatment of Herod's reign in the *War* and also in the *Antiquities,* Books 12-17 where Nicolaus' pro-Herodian bias is balanced by an anti-Herodian source. Josephus' inconsistencies of tone and evaluation are often attributed to his use of inadequately edited sources.[10] Though some passages concerning the Pharisees fall within parts of Josephus dependent on Nicolaus, Josephus' attitude toward the Pharisees is fundamentally consistent whether he is using Nicolaus or not. Several scholars have claimed that in the *Antiquities* Josephus is more pro-Pharisee than in the *War* and that this shift reflects the Pharisaic ascendancy in Palestinian Judaism after the war with Rome and Josephus' desire to promote their power in the interests of peace and order. Our analysis of the texts from Josephus, will show that this thesis does not stand.

---

[8]The best recent discussion of how Josephus uses his sources is in Cohen, *Josephus*. See also Daniel R. Schwartz, "Josephus and Nicolaus on the Pharisees," *JSJ* 14 (1983) 157-171.

[9]Fifteen passages which are explicitly attributed to Nicolaus, eleven of them from Josephus, are collected with an introduction and notes in Menahem Stern, *Greek and Latin Authors on Jews and Judaism*, Vol. 1 (Jerusalem: Israel Academy of Sciences and Humanities, 1974) 227-260. Scholars attribute many other passages in Josephus to Nicolaus.

[10]Cohen, *Josephus*, is especially critical of Josephus for his inconsistency and sloppiness.

Josephus' View of Society

The bulk of the *War* and of the *Antiquities* from the Hasmonean period on describes the fortunes of the Hasmonean and the Herodian rulers and the other ruling groups and families of Judaism. Only when individuals or groups gained ruling power or became important for the rulers does Josephus give them extensive treatment. He does not give a full description of the aristocracy, much less of the people, nor does he talk about bureaucrats, scribes, priests (other than chief priests) or local leaders as separate classes or groups. From the viewpoint of the governing class, which is the viewpoint Josephus takes,[11] the Pharisees and many other Jewish groups and classes are unimportant, minor forces on the social scene and so they are neglected, except when they have major political effect. He narrates the power and fervor of Jewish religious beliefs and customs only when they affect politics, for example in the dispute over Roman images in Jerusalem and the furor after one of Cumanus' soldiers destroyed a Torah scroll.[12] His chief interest in the latter half of the *Antiquities* and the *War* is the politics of the governing class and the relationship of the nation to the empires surrounding it.

In all his writings Josephus favored a strong, stable ruling force. Thus, he presented both the Hasmoneans and Herod the Great favorably. Though Josephus acknowledged Herod's personal failings with his family (he executed many of them) and as a pious Jew (he built pagan temples), he appreciated Herod's ability to work with the Romans and keep order. Thus, in times of order he focused on the leaders who controlled society, but in times of political change and upheaval (for example in the late Hasmonean period and again after the death of Herod, when Jewish leadership broke down) he gave an account of all the major leaders and groups competing for power and recognition. It is during these times that the Pharisees and other groups

---

[11]Tessa Rajak, *Josephus: The Historian and His Society* (Philadelphia: Fortress, 1984) 154. Rajak has a helpful presentation of Jewish society as seen by Josephus, especially at the time of the war with Rome. The scope of the study is different from this one and she is more eclectic in her method and speculative in some hypotheses.

[12] *War* 2.9.2 (169-174); 2.12.2 (228-231).

became important for the nation's politics and were noticed by Josephus. Josephus approved such leaders and groups when they promoted stability and disparaged them when they threatened it.

The Hasmonean Period

The relationships between the Pharisees and Hasmonean rulers were often troubled. The Pharisees sought influence with the Hasmoneans by serving as retainers to them and by recruiting them as patrons. At the same time they pursued their own ends like any other political interest group. Once, under Alexandra, they achieved direct political power, but for much of the period, they were in conflict with John Hyrcanus and Alexander, lacked power and influence and consequently are mentioned by Josephus only during crises and conflicts.

JOHN HYRCANUS

The Pharisees first appear on stage in Josephus during a conflict with John Hyrcanus (134-104). Josephus strongly approved of Hyrcanus and pictured him as a successful ruler who engaged in a number of conquests in the principalities surrounding Israel, renewed the treaty with Rome, destroyed the Samaritan temple on Mount Gerazim and thus established his sovereignty over Samaria.[13] As a sign of his approval Josephus concludes with an extraordinary story *(paradoxon)* that Hyrcanus the high priest was alone in the temple burning incense when he heard a voice saying that his sons had been victorious in battle. Josephus, who attributes the gift of revelation and prophecy to favored leaders of the nation and to holy men,[14] approved of John Hyrcanus as a strong and successful ruler who was favored by fortune, or in Biblical language, was chosen and favored by God. As proof of this he attributed to

---

[13] *Ant.* 13.9.1-10.3 (254-283).

[14] J. Blenkinsopp, "Prophecy and Priesthood in Josephus," *JJS* 25 (1974) 239-262, esp. 250, 256.

Hyrcanus a successful reign and the gift of prophecy as well as the God-given offices of high priest and ruler.[15]

Josephus explains that Hyrcanus had problems because "the envy of the Jews was aroused against him by his own successes and those of his sons; particularly hostile to him were the Pharisees who are one of the Jewish schools *(haireseis)*, as we have related above."[16] According to the story, the Pharisees originally had great influence on Hyrcanus who was a disciple of theirs and greatly loved by them. The story of their conflict begins at a banquet given for them by Hyrcanus.[17] At the banquet Hyrcanus said that he wished to be righteous and please God in everything, and thus he wanted to please them because they pursue knowledge *(philosophousin)*.[18] Hyrcanus then asked the Pharisees to correct him if he was doing anything

---

[15] *Ant.* 13.10.7 (299-300). Specifically, Hyrcanus foretold that his two elder sons would not remain masters of the state.

[16] Ant. 13.10.5 (288).

[17] *Ant.* 13.10.5-6 (288-298). This story is told also in rabbinic literature (b. Qidd. 66a) but the king is Jannai, that is, Alexander Jannaeus. The relationship between the two stories and their historical reliability have been often discussed with most scholars favoring Josephus' account. In rabbinic literature John Hyrcanus (Johanan the high priest) is presented positively most of the time and Yannai negatively. Some have tried to solve the conflict by reference to the history of their reigns. Recently M.J. Geller, "Alexander Jannaeus and the Pharisee Rift," *JJS* 30 (1979) 202-211 has favored the talmudic account on the basis of the talmudic approval of John Hyrcanus and the evidence of other turbulence in Alexander's reign. Schwartz, "Josephus," 158-159 argues that the story of the banquet is inserted into the framework of Nicolaus of Damascus' history and so is not originally about John Hyrcanus. He notes that it is not present in the equivalent place in the *War* 1.2.8 (67-68). See also Lee I. Levine, "The Political Conflict Between Pharisees and Sadducees in the Hasmonean Period," [in Hebrew] in *Jerusalem in the Second Temple Period: Abraham Schalit Memorial Volume*, (eds.) A. Oppenheimer et al. (Jerusalem: Ministry of Defence, 1980) 70-72. The Talmud itself discusses the confusion of these two Hasmonean rulers in b. Ber 29a.

It is likely that the conflict with John Hyrcanus was historical. Since the Talmud generally approves of Johanan the High Priest, it transferred the banquet story to Jannai because he was the one the Pharisees were supposed to have had conflict with. For a convincing analysis which suggests that the rabbis used Josephus in some cases and that the rabbinic retelling of these stories often changes people, times and places, see Shaye J.D. Cohen, "Parallel Historical Traditions in Josephus and Rabbinic Literature," *Proceedings of the Ninth World Congress of Jewish Studies* (Div. B, Vol. 1; Jerusalem: World Union of Jewish Studies/ Magnes, 1986) 7-15.

[18] The Loeb translates this phrase as "for the Pharisees profess such beliefs." The idea is that the Pharisees know and love God's laws and so anyone who pleases them must be pleasing God as well.

wrong. But the Pharisees testified that he was virtuous and he was delighted with their praise.

This opening scene reveals much about the Pharisees' place in society. Hyrcanus is the Pharisees' political ruler and patron; the Pharisees are clients dependent on him and act accordingly by not criticizing him.[19] The Pharisees are pictured as part of Hyrcanus' circle of retainers and as a group they have achieved considerable influence, especially over how a proper Jewish ruler ought to carry out the ancestral laws and customs. The story also implies that they are an intellectual force in society with a particular way of interpreting the tradition. Though the Pharisees have access to Hyrcanus, any power they have is based on influence with Hyrcanus and not held directly in their hands.[20] This political patron-client relationship explains why Hyrcanus held a banquet for his valuable and influential clients and why the Pharisees tactfully praised their powerful patron when he asked whether they had any criticism of him.

The Pharisees' unity was broken by a Pharisee named Eleazar, "who had an evil nature and took pleasure in dissension," and suggested that Hyrcanus give up the high priesthood because of a story that his mother had been a captive.[21] Hyrcanus was furious as were the Pharisees because the story was false and more importantly, because Hyrcanus' position as ruler was tied to his high priesthood.[22] Not only Hyrcanus but also the Pharisees, who were dependent upon the good will of Hyrcanus, were angry at the attack on Hyrcanus by one of their number.

---

[19]Hyrcanus is spoken of as subordinate to the Pharisees spiritually and religiously and the philosophical language of disciple (and teachers) is used and acted out at the banquet, but this is not the primary relationship which emerges.

[20]Note that the Pharisees have influence as a group. No individuals or leaders are mentioned, nor are requirements for membership or internal organization detailed. It seems that Hyrcanus is interested in them because of their corporate influence as a political group.

[21]The people bring up this story later in *Ant.* 13.13.5 (372). If a woman had been a captive, she may have been sexually violated. This put the heredity of a priest in doubt. Priests were forbidden to marry captives for this reason (Lev. 21:14).

[22]*Ant.* 13.11.1 (301) and *War* 1.3.1 (70) say that Aristobolus (104-103) assumed the title king, but coins do not confirm this. Strabo 16.2.40 (762) says that Alexander Jannaeus was the first to assume the title and coins confirm his use of the title king. See E. Schürer, G. Vermes and F. Millar, *The History of the Jewish People in the Age of Jesus Christ (175 B.C.-A.D. 135)* Vol. 1 (Edinburgh: Clark, 1973) 217, 227.

Though the break with Hyrcanus might seem to be caused by a misunderstanding, a serious political attack is implicit and must reflect some Pharisaic opposition to Hyrcanus. Sensing disloyalty in his allies, Hyrcanus demanded that the Pharisees recognize this and make amends.

The Pharisees' political position as influential retainers is further clarified by their rivalry with another group of retainers, the Sadducees. Jonathan, a close friend of Hyrcanus and a Sadducee, slandered the Pharisees with the charge that Eleazar had acted with the approval of the Pharisees and suggested a test to see if they really disapproved of what Eleazar said and wished to see him severely punished. When the Pharisees did not recommend death for Eleazar, because of the leniency of their teaching concerning punishment, Hyrcanus was further angered and Jonathan the Sadducee inflamed that anger until Hyrcanus rejected the Pharisees as clients and allies and accepted the Sadducees in their place. Thus Sadducean practices and policies replaced the Pharisaic in the governance of the nation.

Hyrcanus' shift of favor from the Pharisees to the Sadducees is typical of the relations between a ruler and the retainer class.[23] Many groups and individuals compete for royal favor and the consequent power and wealth. Josephus acknowledges that the Pharisees were rejected through misunderstanding and intrigue, but he does not bemoan their rejection. Groups coming into favor and falling out of favor with their political patron are normal and not to be especially regretted. The consequences of this dispute were dire for the Pharisees. Hyrcanus abrogated the regulations peculiar to the Pharisees and punished those who observed them. As a consequence the people, who followed the Pharisees, came to hate Hyrcanus and his sons. This is part of Josephus' explanation for the unrest under Alexander Jannaeus and ultimately for the failure of the Hasmonean house and the intervention of the Romans in 63 B. C. E. Unfortunately, Josephus did not specify the customs and regulations of the

---

[23]Lee Levine, "Political Conflict," 74-75, argues that Hyrcanus initiated the break in order to shift his allegiance to the Sadducees, who were the rising military party in the emerging Hasmonean kingdom. The evidence for this position is slim, though Levine is correct to suspect the influence of some political issue not brought out by the text. His study agrees with this one in seeing all the groups of the time as political forces in society.

Pharisees and then Sadducees which John Hyrcanus adopted. Clearly they pertained to public and significant behavior and were not minor sectarian practices or beliefs.

ALEXANDER JANNAEUS AND ALEXANDRA

During the reigns of Alexander Jannaeus (103-76) and his wife Alexandra, who succeeded him (76-67), the Pharisees continued to seek influence and power and to act as a political interest group which sought out the ruler as patron or forged alliances with other dissident groups against the ruler. This period was rife with factional strife and shifting coalitions competing for control of Jewish society. Josephus disapproved of the disorder and leveled blame against Alexander, Alexandra, the Pharisees and all others who disrupted Jewish society.

At the death of John Hyrcanus a dynastic struggle ensued. His sons, Aristobolus and Antigonus, competed for power but eventually another son, Alexander Jannaeus (103-76) gained control.[24] Josephus recounts at length the wars of Alexander Jannaeus, his success at taking advantage of Seleucid dynastic struggles and weakness, his territorial gains, his conflicts with the people and other groups and his oppressive cruelty.[25] Josephus disapproved of Alexander because his untactful policies aroused the people to disturbance and revolt and filled his reign with conflict.[26]

On his death bed Alexander bequeathed his kingdom to his queen, Alexandra, and quieted her fears about the hostility of the people with the advice that she win the Pharisees over to her side so that they would control the people.[27] The *Antiquities* has no account of Alexander's disputes with the Pharisees, but Alexander, in his final speech to his wife, admits that his conflict with the people was partly caused by his mistreatment of the

---

[24] *Ant.* 13.12.1 (320) ff.

[25] Alexander killed 6000 when he was pelted with citrons at the festival of Tabernacles and he later crucified 800 opponents and slaughtered their families. *Ant.* 13.13.5 (372-373); 13.14.2 (379-383).

[26] *War* 1.2.8 (67-69) and 1.4.1-8 (85-106).

[27] *Ant.* 13.15.5-16.3 (399-417).

Pharisees. Alexander stresses to his wife the ability of the Pharisees to harm or help people by influencing public opinion, despite the fact that they sometimes act out of envy. He also reveals the Pharisees' political agenda, that is, their desire for power over the laws governing domestic Jewish life. Alexandra is to render them benevolent by conceding to them a certain amount of power. Later on he tells her to "Promise them also that you will not take any action, while you are on the throne, without their consent."[28]

Alexandra followed this advice and also let the Pharisees have control over Alexander's corpse and burial, as he advised. The Pharisees, in turn, forgot their anger and gave speeches praising Alexander as a great and just king and they moved the people to give him a splendid burial. Josephus neither praises nor blames the Pharisees for their actions. He sees them as one of the political interest groups competing for power and influence and he sees their influence and power over the ruling class as dependent on their status and influence among the people. He seems to approve of Alexander's advice to his wife to win over the people and end the civil disorder which marked the end of his reign. The Pharisees are seen here as a force for order and thus win Josephus' approval. Josephus shows no interest in the details of the Pharisaic program, nor their motives. He takes for granted their self-interested quest for power and cynical posthumous praise of Alexander, but quickly criticizes them for causing disorder.[29]

Josephus begins the account of Alexandra's reign by noting that the people loved her because they thought that she had disapproved of Alexander's cruel crimes. Josephus himself expresses admiration for her in the *War* because she was not cruel like Alexander, was more in tune with the people and conducted herself in such a manner as to gain popular support.

---

[28]*Ant.* 13.15.5 (404).

[29]Though the *Antiquities'* account of the Pharisees' influence on the people is more extensive than that in the *War*, Josephus' viewpoint has not become more positive. Longer and more detailed accounts are common in the *Antiquities*, but the Pharisees' influence in society is presumed in both accounts and the Pharisees' ultimate influence on Alexandra is seen as negative in both. In fact, Alexandra herself is presented more negatively in the *Antiquities* than in the *War* for having succumbed to the Pharisees.

She kept the peace, ruled effectively and was pious. She studied the ancient customs of her country and expelled from government men who offended against the holy laws. Lest she be pictured as an overly pious holy hermit, Josephus notes that Alexandra built up the army, conducted military campaigns and engaged effectively in foreign negotiations.

Josephus accuses Alexandra of weakness in letting the Pharisees rule and the Jewish people of weakness in letting a woman rule them. Alexandra carried out her promise to give the Pharisees power by permitting the Pharisees to do as they liked in all matters and commanding the people to obey them. She also restored the Pharisaic regulations which had been abrogated by John Hyrcanus.[30] Josephus comments: "There grew up beside her into her power Pharisees, a certain body *(syntagma)* of Jews with the reputation of being more pious than others and expounding the laws more accurately." Alexandra listened to them with too great deference because she was pious and they gradually took advantage of her simplicity (or sincerity[31]) "and became administrators *(dioikētai)* of everything, to banish and recall whom they wished, to loose and to bind. In short, the advantages of royalty were theirs; the expenses and burdens were Alexandra's."[32] In the *Antiquities* Josephus summarizes the Pharisees' power with an exaggeration: "While she had the title of queen, the Pharisees had the power," and then adds that they in no way differed from absolute rulers.[33] The Pharisees had substantial direct bureaucratic power in domestic affairs, recalled exiles and freed prisoners, but did not have unlimited power because they could not punish on their own authority Alexander's old advisors and allies who had crucified the eight hundred.

The Pharisees' powerful but limited role in society can be seen most clearly in their attempt to take vengeance on those who had been responsible for the eight hundred rebels crucified by Alexander Jannaeus.[34] They assassinated several of Alexander's

[30]*Ant.* 13.16.2 (408).

[31]*haplotēta.*

[32]*War* 1.5.1-3 (107-114).

[33]*Ant.* 13.16.2 (409).

[34]*War* 1.4.6 (96-98); *Ant.* 13.16.2 (410-415). The anti-Pharisaic passage in the *War* is

old supporters and urged the queen to execute others. Alexander's retainers appealed to Queen Alexandra against her new powerful retainers and clients, the Pharisees, using her son Aristobolus as spokesman. Stressing their loyalty to the Hasmonean house and their reluctance to become mercenaries or advisors for another king in the area, they asked to be allowed to guard her fortresses and be safe in exile from the Pharisees. Josephus does not approve of any of the participants in this conflict because all parties contributed to instability. The partisans of Alexander had been responsible for unrest and had allowed Alexandra to take over; Alexandra had allowed the Pharisees to get too much control; the Pharisees were disrupting society.[35]

Alexandra's solution to the conflict between her old and new retainers and clients recognized the old guard's claim on her and kept them in reserve. "The queen, not knowing what to do consistent with her dignity, entrusted to them the guarding of the fortresses with the exception of Hyrcania, Alexandreion and Machaerus."[36] Alexandra clearly trusted these out of favor retainers and felt an obligation to care for them, so she minimally satisfied the requirements of a patron to treat her clients fairly.[37] She also kept the Pharisees from gaining total control over their enemies and her government. But this compromise caused her trouble near the end of her reign when the old guard threatened her rule and fought on the side of Aristobolus in his attempt to seize the throne by force.[38] Josephus' ultimate judgment is that the Pharisees had promoted conflict within society and Alexandra had not resolved the conflicts or ruled with the long

---

commonly said to have come from Josephus's source, Nicolaus of Damascus, who was a member of Herod's court and wrote a history of his reign. But that Josephus would include this assessment of the Pharisees and otherwise pay little attention to them is consistent with his interest in the ruler and the top of the governing class and with his support of civil order. See Rajak, *Josephus*, 34. For an assessment of Josephus' use of Nicolaus, as well as the text of some passages explicitly attributed to him, see Stern, *Greek and Latin Authors*, Vol. 1, 227-260, esp. 229-230.

[35] In *Ant.* 13.16.3 (417). See also 13.16.6 (430-432) for a more extensive negative evaluation of Alexandria.

[36] *Ant.* 13.16.5 3 (417).

[37] Lande, "Clientism,' xxiii.

[38] *Ant.* 13.16.5 (423-429).

term interests of her dynasty in mind because "she expressed the same opinions as did those who were hostile to her family."[39]

SUMMARY

During the reigns of John Hyrcanus, Alexander Jannaeus and Alexandra, Josephus portrays a struggle for power within the governing and retainer classes. The Pharisees appeared during the reign of Hyrcanus competing for power with other political interest groups. They had their own program for Jewish society, contained in a set of traditions and rules which Josephus does not describe. They gained and lost great influence and were still in existence during the reign of Alexander. Though they are not mentioned among the groups opposing Alexander, they are strongly in sympathy with those executed by him.[40] Josephus sees the Pharisees as an organized group, which he calls a *syntagma,* something which is ordered, such as a military unit, a political constitution or a civil group recognized by a constitution. Josephus (or his source Nicolaus before him) keeps the Pharisees at arms length and does not embrace them as authentic leaders or exemplars of Jewish life by saying that they were *reputed* to be more pious and accurate in interpreting the laws than others.

During the time of unrest at the end of Alexander's reign the outgoing king himself proposed to his wife and successor, Alexandra, that she gather around herself a new group of supporters and retainers, the Pharisees. Both Alexander and Alexandra realized that their position as rulers was in jeopardy and they took steps to consolidate their power by making a coalition with the most influential group among the people, the Pharisees. The Pharisees entered into the coalition and stabilized

---

[39]*Ant.* 13.16.6 (431). Josephus is probably alluding to the Pharisees, since he has previously shown that they were hostile to the Hasmoneans.

[40]Many commentators identify the 800 opponents of Alexander who were executed as Pharisees, but Josephus does not. Since Jewish society contained numerous political and social groups, alliances and coalitions with complex relationships, scholars should hesitate to identify one group with another. Levine, "Political Conflict," 69, argues that Josephus does not identify the 800 as Pharisees in order not to show them as rebels. But, as will be seen at the end of ch. 6, their political involvement and resistance is clearly presented in *Ant.*

the transition from Alexander to Alexandra by quieting the people. Alexandra gave the Pharisees what they wanted, legal support for their particular interpretation of Judaism and some direct power to run domestic affairs. The Pharisees used their power to attack their rivals, the old governing class. The soldiers, advisors and high bureaucrats under Alexander, now out of power, appealed to Alexandra for justice on the basis of their loyalty to her and Alexander and she met their demands.

In the confusion which followed the death of Alexandra the Pharisees are not mentioned and it is likely that they lost influence and popularity with the people because of the way they had exercised power over them and thus lost political power to rival interest groups, coalitions and factions. Though both of Alexandra's sons, Aristobolus and Hyrcanus, had followings among the governing class, the retainer class and possibly the lower classes, neither is said to have turned to the Pharisees for support. The rise and fall of the Pharisees fits the pattern found in many other countries and empires outlined in chapters two and three. In bureaucratic empires and states, such as the Jewish state, religious functionaries and groups tend to emerge as partially independent political power centers. Especially in times of turmoil and change such as the period after Alexander's death, they, as well as many individuals and groups, can be expected to compete for power. Sociologically, the Pharisees are part of Lenski's retainer class, in the service of the ruling class as bureaucrats, educators and officials. In a readjustment of ruling power they could gain power in the bureaucracy and become part of the ruling class temporarily, as they did under Alexandra.

In their relationship with Alexandra the Pharisees can best be seen as a religio-political interest group, a corporate, voluntary association "organized for the pursuit of one interest or of several interests in common." It probably recruited people along recognized principles and had common interests and rules governing the members' behavior.[41] Alexandra and the Pharisees found it mutually beneficial to become allies and form a coalition. The alliance was not a permanent change in class and

[41]Boissevain, *Friends of Friends,* 171.

status, but a temporary position attained in society and based on the patronage of the ruler and the Pharisees' prestige attained through religious practice and knowledge. Thus, the Pharisees' position in society was part of a complex network of relationships and depended heavily on circumstances.

Josephus tells us little directly about the Pharisees' organization, stated goals, size or leadershp. He sees them as a vital social force which has its base in knowledge and observance of the ancestral laws of Judaism. They probably functioned as a social movement organization seeking to change society.[42] Because of the Hellenization of the Hasmoneans and the governing class which had followed non-traditional laws in controlling society the Pharisees probably sought a new, communal commitment to a strict Jewish way of life based on adherence to the covenant. They probably capitalized on popular sentiment for rededication to or reform of Judaism and created a formal or informal social movement. In such a time of change, with some of the governing class probably unobservant, groups such as the Pharisees could exert great influence with the support of the people.

The Herodian Period

The Pharisees remained influential actors at the highest levels of society, both in Herod's court and in the Sanhedrin. Early in Herod's reign the Pharisees were favored by Herod as supporters and clients, but later they joined a faction opposed to Herod and suffered his wrath. The Pharisees, like all the upper classes, were controlled by Herod and failed to attain any real power while he lived, yet they did not withdraw, but remained active participants in political life. Reasons for their support of Herod are given by Josephus, but difficult to separate from Josephus' own views. Some Pharisees seem to have espoused a view of Israel's destiny

---

[42]A social movement organization is "a complex, or formal, organization which identifies its goals with the preferences of a social movement or a counter movement and attempts to implement those goals." See Henri Taifel, *Differentiation between Social Groups: Studies in the Social Psychology of Intergroups Relations* (London/New York: Academic, 1978) 28-46 and McCarthy and Zald, "Resource Mobilization", 1212-1219, esp. 1217-1219.

which could include Herod as leader, at least early in his reign.

SAMAIAS AND POLLION

About twenty years after Alexandra's death, in 47-46 B. C. E., the political situation was confused, with Antipater and his sons, Herod and Phasael, governing, much to the consternation of the traditional Jerusalem leaders. In an attempt to rein in this new power, they summoned Herod to trial before the Sanhedrin on the charge that he acted illegally in executing some brigands without the verdict of the Sanhedrin in Jerusalem.[43] The Sanhedrin's claim to power was opposed by the high priest Hyrcanus, who had been Herod's ally, the Roman governor in Syria who ordered Hyrcanus to acquit Herod and finally by Samaias, a prominent member of the Sanhedrin and a disciple of a Pharisee named Pollion.[44] When Herod appeared with a strong bodyguard, he so awed the Sanhedrin that no one arose to accuse him. Samaias rebuked the members of the Sanhedrin for their cowardice in allowing Herod to dominate them and predicted that they would regret releasing Herod because he would one day punish all of them. Later when Herod and the Roman general Sossius besieged and captured Jerusalem from the partisans of Antigonus, Samaias advised the people of Jerusalem to allow Herod into Jerusalem because their sins made his victory inescapable. Samaias' prediction came true when Herod punished those who had opposed him and showed special favor to his supporters, among whom were Pollion the Pharisee and Samaias his disciple who had advised the people to admit him.[45]

---

[43]On the social context of banditry and its connection with peasant revolt, see R. Horsley, "Josephus and the Bandits," *JSJ* 10 (1979) 37-63.

[44]*Ant.* 14.9.3-5 (163-184); Samaias is identified as a disciple of Pollion in *Ant.* 15.1.1 (3) and there Pollion is said to have been the one to have rebuked the Sanhedrin, contrary to *Ant.* 14.9.4 (172). On attempts to link these figures with the rabbinic figures Shamaiah and Abtalyon, see bibliography in the Loeb edition, vol. 14, Appendix K. Also A. Guttmann, *Rabbinic Judaism in the Making* (Detroit: Wayne State, 1970) p. 53; S. Zeitlin in *The Rise and Fall of the Jewish State* (Philadelphia: Jewish Publication Society, 1964-   ). Vol. 2, p. 104 and L. Feldman, "The Identity of Pollio, the Pharisee, in Josephus," *JQR* 49 (1958) 53-62.

[45]*Ant.* end of Book 14 and beginning of Book 15.

Since Samaias' rebuke of the Sanhedrin agrees with Josephus' own thought very closely, it is likely that his speech does not represent Pharisaic teaching directly. Josephus did not like Herod, but liked even less Jewish leaders who were weak and allowed disorder in the state and its institutions. Thus in practice, Josephus favored Herod because he was the best leader available. In Josephus' view weakness always leads to disaster and in this case weakness ended any vestige of Hasmonean rule and led to Herod's ascendancy. As a spokesman for Josephus' views, Samaias is presented very positively. He is said to be an upright man *(dikaios)* who was superior to fear and able to make a true prediction of the future (a sure sign of God's favor in Josephus' eyes).[46] Josephus through Samaias interprets the rise of Herod to mean that God was punishing the Hasmoneans and those in Jerusalem who supported them.

Samaias, as a member of the Sanhedrin, was a member of the governing class and perhaps his teacher Pollion was also. It is not surprising that a Pharisee or perhaps a number of Pharisees should be counted among the group of elders and leaders who make up the Sanhedrin.[47] Pharisees had been both influential and powerful in the government and some continued to participate in political activity. But, Samaias and Pollion were in a weak position because Samaias' rebuke to the Sanhedrin in 47-46 and their advice to admit Herod into Jerusalem in 37 were ignored. They still attempted to influence the people, as they did in the days of John Hyrcanus and Alexander Jannaeus, but they lacked noteworthy success. However, by supporting Herod at crucial points in his quest for power, they attained favor as clients of Herod.

---

[46]Josephus did the same with Vespasian (*War* 3, 8, 6 [387-408]).

[47]The Sanhedrin in Jerusalem was the supreme council, included the most powerful and influential citizens at any given time and thus probably had a shifting membership which reflected the power struggles and social currents of history. In order to reconcile seemingly conflicting statements in Josephus and rabbinic literature some scholars have espoused a theory of two Sanhedrins, one political and one religious. The inextricable union of political society and religion make this impossible. For a convenient summary of theories, see Hugo Mantel, "Sanhedrin," *IDBS*, 784-786.

THE PHARISEES UNDER HEROD

Herod's continuing support for the Pharisees and his perception of them as his allies, or at least as not a threat, is clear later in the middle of his reign. About 20 B.C.E., he undertook a series of actions to suppress dissatisfaction with his rule.[48] As part of this program he required the people to take an oath of allegiance to him and any who refused were gotten rid of with the exception of the Pharisees and Essenes. Herod tried to persuade Pollion the Pharisee, Samaias and their disciples[49] to take the oath but they refused. Herod, however, did not punish them, but showed them respect because of Pollion.

Josephus does not say why these groups refused to take an oath. The Essenes are consistently presented as an ascetic and atypical group and they might be expected to have special scruples. The Pharisees had their own interpretations of Jewish law but nothing explicit is said in Josephus about restrictions on taking oaths. The Pharisees' active role in Jewish political and legal life would suggest that they had no problem with oaths. Josephus' account of Pollion and Samaias' prediction concerning Herod, their acquiescence to his rule, and their theological explanation for Herod's ascendency suggest that they did not oppose him, perhaps because he was the best alternative available in Palestinian society at the time. The Pharisees seem to be uneasy allies of Herod; they may have kept their distance from Herod either because they feared his autocratic power or disagreed too fundamentally with his policies. The Pharisees remained an active political force which Herod recognized, sought to keep benevolent and treated with great seriousness when they were a threat, as will be seen in the next incident involving the Pharisees.

CONFLICT WITH HEROD

Domestic conflicts and palace intrigues over succession dominated the final part of Herod's reign, according to Josephus. The Pharisees participated in one factional intrigue as a minor

---

[48]*Ant.* 15.10.4 (368-372).

[49]*sundiatribontōn autois,* literally, those spending time with them.

political force, with catastrophic results for themselves. Herod's brother Pheroras, the tetrarch of Perea, along with Pheroras' wife, mother and sister and Antipater's mother conspired to have Antipater, Herod's son, succeed him. Herod's sister, Salome, reported on their plots to her brother, but Herod, who was still influenced by the conspirators, took a long time to act against them.[50] During this time of scheming Josephus recounts disapprovingly the Pharisees' long relationship with Pheroras' wife and their role in the plots. "There was also a group of Jews priding itself on its adherence to ancestral custom and claiming to observe the laws of which the Diety approves, and by these men, called Pharisees, the women (of the court) were ruled."[51] The Pharisees are here pictured as influencing prominent women just as they had Alexandra in the previous generation. Josephus keeps his distance from the Pharisees by reporting but not affirming their reputation for observance and their claim to know the laws, just as he did earlier. For Josephus, they are just one more group of retainers surrounding Herod and scheming for power. "These men were able to help the king greatly because of their foresight [prediction], yet they were obviously intent upon combating and injuring him."[52] As an instance of the Pharisees' ill will toward Herod, Josephus cites the refusal of six thousand to take an oath of loyalty to Caesar and the king's government.[53] Such an act weakened the government and

---

[50]*War* 1.29.2 (567-571); *Ant.* 17.2.4-3.3 (32-60).

[51]*Ant* 17.2.4 (41). The Greek word translated here as "group" is *morion* which means literally a "part" and is used idiomatically of groups. It is used of the Pharisees here only.

[52]*Ant.* 17.2.4 (41). A.I. Baumgarten, "The Name of the Pharisees," *JBL* 102 (1983) 414-416, citing the common view, holds that this hostile passage derives from Nicolaus of Damascus who was pro-Herodian. He and others fail to note that Josephus is completely consistent in all his works in condemning troublemakers.

[53]It is likely that this refusal to take an oath is not the same as the refusal by Pollion, Samaias and their students recorded in *Ant.* 15.10.4 (368-371). 1. In Book 15 Herod excused Pollion and his students because he considered him an ally and did not impose a fine. 2. In book 15 the group is Pollion and his disciples. Here it is six thousand Pharisees, who seem to be an organized group. 3. In book 15 only an oath to Herod is mentioned. Here it is an oath to Caesar and Herod. 4. Here Herod protests that Pheroras' wife has opposed him by a series of acts including the paying of the Pharisees' fine. The context is not the first refusal to take an oath about 20 B.C.E. but the intrigues near the end of Herod's life in 7-4 B.C.E. See G. Alon, "The Attitude of the Pharisees to the Roman Government and the House of Herod," *Scripta Hierosolymitana* 7 (1961) 53-78 and E. Schürer, G. Vermes and F. Millar, *History*, Vol. 1, 314, n. 94. D. Schwartz,

promoted disorder, a result which Josephus constantly deplores.[54] If the number of members of the Pharisees, six thousand, is accurate, it suggests that the Pharisees were an organized group or movement with clear enough boundaries to be identified.

The Pharisees' refusal of the loyalty oath and their coalition with Pheroras' camp are linked because Herod punished the Pharisees with a fine which was paid by Pheroras' wife.[55] She acted as their patron and they in return shifted their allegiance from Herod and served as her clients: "In return for her friendliness they foretold—for they were believed to have foreknowledge of things through God's appearances to them—that by God's decree Herod's throne would be taken from him, both from himself and his descendants, and the royal power would fall to her and Pheroras and to any children that they might have."[56] Josephus records the Pharisees' reputation for prediction, a gift which would indicate divine favor, but the way he speaks of it, the cynical motive they have for making the prediction and the fact that the prediction did not come true all show that in Josephus' view the Pharisees are political opportunists manipulating their patron. Josephus also reports that the Pharisees predicted that another powerful court official, Bagoas, a eunuch would come to power and even have children.[57] The Pharisees are in the thick of the political battles and they have considerable influence on the opponents of Herod, an influence which Josephus considers harmful.

Herod responded to this hostile coalition by executing Bagoas, Karos, those of Herod's household who approved of what the

"Josephus," 160 defends a single conflict over oath taking told in divergent accounts by Nicolaus of Damascus and Josephus.

[54] Josephus does not say why the Pharisees refused to take the oath. An oath to Caesar might be religiously repulsive to them, though not necessarily. Politically they are portrayed as opponents of Herod and so most probably of the Roman empire which created him as king. Refusal to take the oath certainly functioned as and probably was meant as a political protest and attack.

[55] *Ant.* 17.2.4 (42-45).

[56] *Ant.* 17.2.4 (43).

[57] Richard A. Horsley, "Popular Messianic Movements Around the Time of Jesus," *CBQ* 46 (1984) 483, notes that the acceptance of the Pharisees' predictions suggests an eagerness for an anointed king in response to Herodian repression.

Pharisees said and those Pharisees most responsible for corrupting his people (that is, turning them against him). Then, he put Pheroras' wife on trial for her plotting and made a number of accusations against her, for example, that she helped the Pharisees evade the fine imposed on them by paying it for them. The result of his charges was to decrease the power of Pheroras' faction and consequently of the Pharisees.[58]

The First Century

The Pharisees are mentioned several times in Josephus' account of the first century. The final reference to the notables of the Pharisees in the *War* occurs in the dispute over whether to cease offering the daily sacrifices sent by the Emperor to be offered for his welfare and that of the nation.[59] Eleazar, son of the high priest Ananias and captain of the Temple, convinced the Temple priests not to accept sacrifices from foreigners. The chief priests and notables (*gnorimoi*) tried to keep the priests from rejecting the Emperor's sacrifices because this was an act of war. Then the principal citizens (*dunatoi*) assembled with the chief priests and the notables of the Pharisees to deliberate concerning the problem. This group decided to address the people in order to change the minds of the revolutionaries, a tactic which failed. In the course of the assembly the leaders produced priestly experts on the traditions who testified that all their ancestors had accepted sacrifices from aliens. Because the leaders had lost authority and influence in the chaos of the civil

---

[58]One further event during Herod's life deserves mention, the tearing down of the golden eagle over the Temple gate by the disciples of Judas and Matthias (*Ant.* 17.6.1-4 [148-167]; *War* 1.33.2-4 (648-655). Many commentators treat these teachers and disciples as Pharisees. However, they are not identified as such. It is true that Pollion the Pharisee has disciples and John Hyrcanus was said to be a disciple of the Pharisees. But teachers with circles of disciples seem to have been common and there is no reason to treat this group as Pharisees. The two teachers exhort their students to zealous action and to martyrdom for the law. The Pharisees in this part of the *Antiquities* are presented more as political operators entering into sophisticated coalitions to gain power rather than nationalistic and religious zealots inciting revolution.

[59]*War* 2.17.2-4 (409-417). Philo, *Leg. ad Gaium*, 157, 317, also gives information on these sacrifices.

war, their attempt to persuade the people failed and war with Rome ensued.

Josephus includes in the governing class the chief priests, the principal citizens and the notables of the Pharisees and he makes a clear distinction between these legitimate leaders and the people, of whom some were revolutionaries. The notables among the Pharisees were consulted but the basis for their status is not clear. They may have come from hereditary families which had aristocratic position in the city or they may have been powerful by virtue of their leadership of the Pharisees. In addition, we do not know whether the Pharisees *as a group* had a position in the dispute over whether to revolt against Rome. Earlier they were united in their opposition to Alexander and Herod, but in this they were at one with much of Palestinian society. Here most of the people of Jerusalem seem to have been for revolt but it is probable that the Pharisees, through their leaders, were allied with the governing class.

The Pharisees in the "Life"

Josephus mentions the Pharisees on the eve of the revolt against Rome.[60] Upon his return from an embassy to Rome he had sought asylum in the Temple from the brigands controlling Jerusalem. After their leader Menahem was killed, Josephus says that he again "consorted with the chief priests and the leading Pharisees."[61] According to Josephus he and these leaders feared the people and so pretended to agree with their revolutionary ideas, all the while trying to stall them and hoping for the arrival of Roman troops. Josephus is himself a priest with links to the high priestly family and the Hasmoneans, [62] so his presence among the leaders is reasonable. Since he has claimed to be a Pharisee as well as a priest, he may be presenting himself as linked with the leaders of his two groups. Nevertheless, here as in the *War* the leading Pharisees are part of the governing

---

[60] *Life* 20-23 (5).

[61] The notables of the Pharisees are mentioned along with the chief priests in the *War* also (2.17.2-4 [409-417]).

[62] *Life* 1-6 (1).

class and their membership in the Pharisees is noteworthy. Thus the Pharisees must have been a social and political group which was important, influential and powerful enough to be heard through its leaders.

Later in the *Life*, during Josephus' tenure as commander in Galilee, he is opposed by Simon ben Gamaliel. John of Gischala (in upper Galilee), who was a rival of Josephus, sought to have Josephus removed and himself appointed instead.[63] He sent his brothers to Jerusalem to ask his old and intimate friend, Simon ben Gamaliel, to convince the assembly to make this change. "This Simon was a native of Jerusalem, of a very illustrious family, and of the school of the Pharisees, who have the reputation of being unrivalled experts in their country's laws (*nomima*). A man highly gifted with intelligence and judgment, he could by sheer genius retrieve an unfortunate situation in affairs of state." Simon urged "the high priest, Ananus and Jesus, son of Gamalas, and some others of their party" to remove Josephus. Ananus reminded them of the good reputation Josephus had with many of the chief priests and leaders of the people and advised against trumping up charges. Simon then instructed John's brother to bribe Ananus and in this way succeeded in getting Ananus and his party to agree to remove Josephus without the knowledge of others in the city.

The governing class in Jerusalem was composed of many groups, with the high priests and their party at the center. Simon has more power and influence than John of Gischala or Josephus because of several factors, including his family, his ability and most probably his connection with the Pharisees. Simon is presented as a political operative within the governing class who helps an ally achieve his purpose against substantial opposition. Josephus belongs to the same circles and has his own supporters, but, absent in Galilee, he lost the battle for continued support and was slated for removal.

The delegation sent to remove Josephus reveals more of the political class structure in Jerusalem and the status of the Pharisees.[64] The delegation was made up of four equally edu-

[63] *Life* 189-198 (38-39)
[64] *Life* 196-198 (39).

cated men from different classes of society. Two Pharisees were from the lower rank of society,[65] another Pharisee was a priest and a third person, the youngest, was from the high priestly family. The instructions which the delegation received on setting out for Galilee are instructive. If the people of Galilee resist their removing of Josephus, they are to ascertain the basis for Josephus' hold over the people and refute it.[66] Three possible warrants for Josephus' authority are given: being a native of Jerusalem, knowledge of ancestral laws and priesthood and obviously the delegation is Josephus' equal on all points. The three Pharisees in the group are from Jerusalem and knowledgable in the laws; one of them is a priest. The three bases for one's acceptance as a leader are consistent with what Josephus had shown of Jewish history. In the absence of a king, the priests and especially the chief priest and high priestly families held the center of power. A prerequisite for rule and an entreé into the ruling classes is knowledge of the ancestral laws and customs of Judaism. Especially since the Maccabean wars, when the Jewish way of life had been threatened, fidelity to the laws had been a distinguishing mark of Jewish society. Those who were known for their knowledge and observance of the laws, such as the Pharisees, achieved influence and often power among the people. By contrast, those who did not observe the Jewish way of life, like Herod, were despised and if possible rejected. Finally, being a native of Jerusalem implies that the people recognized Jerusalem as their center and as the center of Jewish government; those who lived in Jerusalem and who were educated were considered to be the ruling class, even by Galileans who lived in another region and were directly controlled by different Jewish authorities. In this case, however, they failed. It may be that the Galileans perceived Josephus and the work he had done in

---

[65] Josephus calls the two Pharisees *demotikoi,* that is, commoners, the people, citizens without rank.

[66] The authorities in Jerusalem did not have direct control over Galilee. As usual the local leaders were the "notables," that is, the prominent and wealthy citizens. For the notables of Galilee, see *War* 2.12.3 (233) and for the leading (*dunatoi*) Samaritans, see *War* 2.12.5 (239). For a convenient summary of the regional difference within Galilee and between Galilee and other parts of Palestine, see Eric M. Myers and James F. Strange, *Archaeology, the Rabbis and Early Christianity* (Nashville: Abingdon, 1981), ch. 2.

Galilee as closer to their interests than the delegation and its policy sent from Jerusalem.[67]

The Sadducees in the "Antiquities" and "Life"

Jonathan the Sadducee, who brought the Sadducees to power under John Hyrcanus, has already been treated. The next Sadducee appears in Josephus during the war against Rome when Ananus the high priest is identified as a Sadducee and like the Sadducees under John Hyrcanus, is singled out for his rigor in rendering legal judgment.[68] Ananus was appointed by King Agrippa during the interim between the death of the procurator Festus and the arrival of his replacement, Albinus. Because he had James the brother of Jesus and some others executed, some who thought that he had acted illegally or unfairly protested and he was removed after three months.[69] Josephus, as usual, does not approve of anyone who causes unrest, including the Sadducee Ananus in this case. Later in the *War* Ananus as senior of the chief priests is praised for resisting the Zealots and putting the public welfare above is own.[70] Later still, in the *Life* Josephus claims he was bribed to give his support to those opposing Josephus.[71] Josephus is neither for nor against the Sadducees, Ananus, James or the early Christians. He supports order and praises anyone who resists the revolutionaries.

[67]On the whole problem of the *Life* and of this episode, see Cohen, *Josephus*, esp 223-227.

[68]*Ant.* 20.9.1 (199-203)

[69]Ananus' opponents are described as those "who were considered the most fair-minded and who were strict in observance of the law." Some commentators identify the opponents with the Pharisees and say that Josephus was shielding them from apparent disloyalty. See G. Baumbach, "Das Sadduzäerverständnis bei Josephus Flavius und im Neuen Testament," *Kairos* 13 (1971) 22 and Baumgarten "*Name,*" 413-414. However, all groups in Jewish society need not be reduced to the Pharisees and Sadducees. Josephus, who disapproves of anyone who causes disorder, disapproves of Ananus here and supports the more level headed leaders who would have avoided conflict. See J. LeMoyne, *Les Sadducéens* (Paris: Etudes Bibliques, 1972) 240.

[70]*War* 4.3.7 (151) to 4.5.2 (325).

[71] *Life* 195-196 (39).

The Sadducees appear much less often in Josephus because they have an impact on national leadership less often than the Pharisees. Two Sadducees are named but the group to which they belonged remains in the background and unknown. The named Sadducees, Jonathan and Ananus, belonged to the governing class since the one is a friend of Hyrcanus and the other is high priest. This does not necessarily imply that all Sadducees were of the governing class and certainly not that all the governing class were Sadducees.

Summary

Both Pharisees and Sadducees were small groups within the complex social fabric of Judaism in Judea. The Pharisees are certainly a political interest group who wished to influence the way Jewish life was lived religiously, socially and politically. The Sadducees were probably such a group too. The Pharisees were for the most part retainers, that is, a group whose members do not have independent wealth and power, but who are dependent on the governing class. Some Pharisees were part of the governing class and of the Sanhedrin and the Pharisees had at times a partly independent power base through their influence on the people. The few Sadducees who appear in Josephus are from the governing class, but their nature, numbers, program and influence on the governing class are unclear. Though Josephus has written to further his own interpretation of Jewish society, his picture of the Pharisees and Sadducees is consistent with what we know of agrarian empires and thus sociologically probable in its general outlines. A full evaluation of the Pharisees and Sadducees in Josephus must await a consideration of Josephus' descriptions of these two groups.

6

Josephus' Descriptions of the Pharisees and Sadducees

Josephus provides comparative descriptions of the Pharisees, Sadducees and Essenes once in the *War* and twice in the *Antiquities*. Additional descriptions of the Pharisees and Sadducees are contained in the account of John Hyrcanus' break with the Pharisees in the *Antiquities* and in Josephus' description of his own involvment with the three groups at the beginning of his *Life*. Each was written for a particular purpose and must be interpreted in its context. The descriptions are especially helpful for analyzing the nature of these groups and their inner workings, insofar as this is possible. They must be compared to one another to detect shifts in Josephus' views or purposes and then all the descriptions compared with his accounts of the Pharisees' activities in the previous chapter.

The Pharisees and Sadducees are best known from the parallel descriptions of them and the Essenes in the *War* and *Antiquities*.[1] The context of this major description is identical in both works and crucial for its interpretation. After Herod's death and before Archelaus, his son and heir, could gain control there were many revolts and disorders stemming mostly from the people[2] and led

---

[1]The description is contained in the *War* 2.8.2-14 (119-166), with the Pharisees and Sadducees treated in 2.8.14 (162-166). The parallel in the *Antiquities* is in 18.1.2-6 (11-25), with the Pharisees and Sadducees in 18.1.3-4 (12-17).

[2] *War* 2.1.1. (1) ff.

by various Jewish political and messianic figures. Archelaus governed with great brutality for nine years until both the Jews and Samaritans asked Augustus to remove him.[3] From 6 C.E. until the Great War in 66 (except for three years) Judea and Samaria were governed by Roman prefects and procurators, the first of whom was Coponius.

At this critical juncture in Josephus' narrative, when Herodian control of Jewish affairs ended and the road to revolt began, Josephus recounts that under Coponius a Galilean named Judas led a revolt in which he encouraged his countrymen to refuse to pay tribute to Rome and to acknowledge only God as their ruler (*despotēs*).[4] This rebel was different because he was "a teacher (*sophistēs*) of his own school (*hairesis*)," the founder of the fourth philosophy.[5] With the aid of Saddok a Pharisee, according to the *Antiquities*, Judas inflamed the people to rebellion and began a process which culminated sixty years later in the war which destroyed Jerusalem.

Josephus takes this occasion to warn that innovation and reform are very dangerous and that the fourth philosophy intruded into and ultimately destroyed the Jewish body politic.[6] Josephus hastens to add that this fourth school of thought which encouraged rebellion had nothing in common with the other three kinds (*eidē*) of Jewish philosophy, the Pharisees, Sadducees and Essenes.[7] Josephus seems to imply that from here on the three previous schools of thought, presumably traditional, ancient and legitimate, were joined by a fourth kind

---

[3] *War* 2.7.3 (111-113).

[4] *Ant.* 18.1.6 (23). Judas' origin is confused. The *War* says that he is from Galilee (2.8.1 [118]) but the *Antiquities* 18.1.1 (3) that he is from Gamala in Gaulanitis, east of the Sea of Galilee.

[5] *War* 2.8.1. (118). *Hairesis* is often translated as sect. It is a choice of a way of life, which can be a sectarian choice in the modern sense or a choice of a school of philosophy or thought which one was expected to live up to in antiquity. The presence of the terms teacher and philosophy in this context make "school" (of thought) an apt translation here.

[6] He also details the poor policies of some of the procurators, which contributed to Jewish revolutionary feelings.

[7] In the *Antiquities* Josephus acknowledges that the fourth pilosophy is the same as the Pharisaic philosophy, except for its passion for liberty, its acceptance of God only as ruler and its revolutionary aims, but because of the disorder and suffering it caused, Josephus brands this philosophy novel and intrusive (*Ant.* 18.1.6 [23] and 18.1.1[9]).

which led to rebellion. Josephus presents the three traditional philosophies for his gentile readers as a respectable and permanent part of Judaism, but he discredits the fourth philosophy, which led to the war, here and all through his book.

The *War*

Though Josephus may have gotten his descriptions of the three traditional philosophies from an independent ethnographic source,[8] his choice and positioning of the source furthered his goals. In his treatment of the three philosophies in the *War* Josephus lists them in the order Pharisees, Sadducees and Essenes and immediately moves into a long and laudatory description of the Essenes' ascetic and eremitic way of life.[9] Clearly this group is the one he wishes the Romans to notice, probably because their withdrawn way of life presented no political threat. In addition, their unusual community life would appeal to the Roman interest in eastern philosophies and religions during the first century.[10] A brief, comparative description of the Pharisees and Sadducees follows the long description of the Essenes. Their beliefs about three philosophical and theological issues are contrasted: first, fate (or divine providence), second, free will and human responsibility, and third, immortality with reward and punishment. Then their communal relations among themselves and with others are contrasted. A detailed comparison of the Pharisees and Sadducees is contained in the following chart.

---

[8]George F. Moore, "Fate and Free Will in the Jewish Philosophies According to Josephus," *HTR* 22 (1929) 374; 383-384; Morton Smith, "The Description of the Essenes in Josephus and the Philosophumena," *JQR* 49 (1958) 292-300; H. Attridge, *The Interpretation of Biblical History in the Antiquitates Judaicae of Flavius Josephus* (HDR 7; Missoula: Scholars, 1976), 178-179, n.4.

[9] Josephus *lists* the three groups in the order Pharisees, Sadducees and Essenes in *Ant.* 13, the *War* and the *Life*. In the *Antiquities* 18 he lists them in the order Essenes, Sadducees, Pharisees. He *treats* them in the order Essenes, Pharisees, Sadducees in the *War;* Pharisees, Essenes, Sadducees in *Ant.* 13; and Pharisees, Sadducees, Essenes in *Ant.* 18.

[10]Smith, "Palestinian Judaism," 75 and H. Attridge, "Josephus," 186.

Pharisees	Sadducees
Way of Life	*Way of Life*
They are affectionate with one another.	Boorish with each other.
Cultivate harmonious relations with the community.	As rude to their peers as to aliens.
Thought	*Thought*
Attribute everything to fate and to God.	Deny fate. God beyond both the commission and the very sight of evil.
To act rightly or wrongly rests mostly with humans but fate cooperates in each action	Humans totally in control of the choice of good and evil.
Every soul is imperishable	No endurance of the soul.
Only the soul of the good passes into another body.	No rewards or punishments.
The souls of the wicked suffer eternal punishment.	
Influence	*Influence*
Considered the most accurate interpreters of the laws.	*(no information)*
Hold the position of the first/leading school.	

The Pharisees and Sadducees, both of whom are treated as established and well known groups in Judaism, are neither praised nor blamed by Josephus in the *War*. After his long and enthusiastic treatment of the Essenes, he turns to the first two groups named, taking up the Pharisees first and the Sadducees, "the second order (*tagma*)," after. He introduces the Pharisees by saying that they *are considered* the most accurate interpreters of the laws and hold the position of[11] the leading[12] school. Josephus keeps his distance from the Pharisees' reputation as the most accurate interpreters of the laws by the use of the Greek verb *dokeō*, just as he did when speaking of their activities during Alexandra's reign. Though Josephus says in his *Life* that he was a Pharisee, he certainly does not write as if he were one. The Pharisees are one of the schools of thought in Judaism but not the one in which Josephus is most interested, though he does note their prominent reputation.[13]

Josephus briefly describes the Pharisees' and then the Sadducees' distinct philosophical and theological outlooks on fate/providence, human responsibility and freedom, and life after death. Josephus does not make evaluative comments nor does he comment on the origins of or reasons for these positions.

After the review of the stances of the Pharisees and Sadducees on the philosophical issues, Josephus explicitly compares the social relations of the two groups in a way which favors the Pharisees and explains their prominence. The Pharisees foster warm internal social relations, and harmonious relations with the public while the Sadducees are boorish among themselves and with their peers. No explanation is given for the Sadducees' behavior nor does Josephus connect the Pharisees' and Sadducees' behavior with their beliefs.

---

[11]"Hold the position of" is Thackeray's translation of *apagontes*. The Whiston translation has "introduce" which makes no sense. The form means "take for oneself."

[12]"Leading" is the Greek word for "first" which could also have the sense first to come into existence or most ancient. The verbal form suggests that Josephus means that the Pharisees have achieved prominence.

[13]Josephus did not radically change his views because he refers back to this description of the three schools of thought twice in his *Antiquities* and once in the *Life*. See *Ant.* 13.5.9 (173); 18.1.2 (11); *Life* 10, which is a general reference to all the descriptions.

THE *ANTIQUITIES,* BOOK 18

In the parallel description in the *Antiquities* Josephus gives his most detailed presentation of the belief and behavior of the Pharisees as a group and a philosophy. He lists the three philosophies in the order Essenes, Sadducees and Pharisees and then treats them in the reverse order with the fourth philosophy added to the list by way of contrast. The Pharisees and Essenes receive equally detailed treatment, with the Sadducees and fourth philosophy getting briefer treatment. Josephus gives a cross reference to his treatment of these groups in the *War* but by contrast, in the *War* the Essenes received a longer treatment and the Pharisees a briefer treatment than in the *Antiquities.*

The descriptions contain many points of comparison and contrast among the groups. The characteristics which Josephus assigns to the Pharisaic and Sadducean way of life, thought and influence are contrasted on the following chart:

Pharisees	Sadducees
Way of Life	*Way of Life*
They simplify their standard of living, making no concession to luxury.	
They show respect and deference to their elders and they do not rashly contradict their proposals.	They dispute with the teachers of the path of wisdom which they follow.
Thought	*Thought*
They follow the guidance of what *logos* says is good.[14]	They accept no observance apart from the laws.

---

[14]*logos* here probably means their beliefs or doctrines, not Greek or Stoic "reason."

Human activity is explained by a combination of fate and human will.	
The soul survives death.	The soul perishes along with the body.
There are rewards and punishments under the earth.	
Influence Influential among the townsfolk (*demois*) because of their views.	*Influence* Few know this *logos*, but they are those of the highest standing.
Worship conducted according to their views.	They accomplish little in office because the masses force them to follow Pharisaic teaching.
The citizenry (*hai poleis*) witness to the excellence of the Pharisees by practicing the highest ideals in their way of living and discourse.	

Josephus' list of characteristics does not have any inherent unity or intelligibility. He has previously compared the teaching on free will and life after death of the Pharisees, Sadducees and Essenes and he repeats that here. He alludes somewhat obscurely to the *logos* of the Pharisees and Sadducees, to the commandments the Pharisaic *logos* gives them to guide their lives and to the laws which the Sadducees follow to the exclusion of any other observance. Josephus does not say explicitly that the Pharisees follow oral law, nor does he say that the Sadducees only follow the laws written in the Bible, contrary to the claims made in many descriptions of these groups. This passage says that their traditions differed, but not how.

The Sadducees are said to make a virtue of disputing with their teachers. This suggests that the Sadducees had their own traditions and interpretations which were a matter of dispute. The Pharisees are said to show respect for their elders and not contradict their proposals rashly. Perhaps their mode of interaction hints at a respect for a certain body of traditions which they passed on and lived by. This respect for their elders and tradition also gives the impression that they are humane and pleasant in their social relations and lends support for Josephus' contention that they are influential among the people. The people's inclination toward the Pharisees' traditions may also have derived from the content of those traditions, a content unknown to us. If the Sadducees were drawn from the governing class, they may have used an interpretation of the law which was politically and economically disadvantageous for the lower classes. The Pharisees may have developed or adopted a set of customs and legal interpretations which favored the needs of the lower classes. In the end, though, the meager description given by Josephus in the *Antiquities* tells us little about the Pharisees and Sadducees.

Josephus treats the Pharisees and Sadducees as known, organized groups with influence. The Sadducees are drawn from the leading citizens (note that not all chief priests or leading citizens are said to be Sadducees) and often hold power through high office. The Pharisees are influential on the townsfolk or citizenry which indicates that they are most probably a specialized sub-class, based in cities and towns, politically and socially active, and powerful or influential in restricted areas. These descriptions fit the Pharisees and Sadducees as they appear in Josephus' narrative. The Pharisees are not the governing class, but a part of the retainer class, subordinate to the governing class. Josephus mentions them in times of turmoil and weakness among the governing class, when retainers like the Pharisees could be expected to gain political power.

Josephus does not praise either the Sadducees or the Pharisees for their activities, but merely notes their power and influence. They along with other forces are important parts of society. Though Josephus presents an unflattering portrait of the Sadducees, compared to the Pharisees, he remains faithful to his dominant aim, to show that the traditional Jewish ways of thought are as respectable as Greek philosophy and not revolutionary. Many say that Josephus has exaggerated the Pharisees' influence here in order to establish the post-70 heirs of the Pharisees as legitimate Jewish leaders in the eyes of the Romans. An evaluation of this claim will be made at the end of the chapter. If Josephus has exaggerated, he has not contradicted his own consistent position that a group is to be praised if it promotes order.

THE ANTIQUITIES, BOOK 13

The Pharisees are first mentioned in the *Antiquities* in Book 13 where Josephus briefly introduces the Pharisees, Sadducees and Essenes in order to establish Judaism's respectability in the Greek world.[15] After Jonathan, the brother of Judas Maccabee, attained military victory over the Seleucid king Demetrius II in 143 B.C.E. he sent diplomatic missions to Rome and Sparta in order to gain recognition and support in the larger Mediterranean world against the Seleucids. Within this context Josephus informs his readers that Judaism had three schools of thought (*haireseis*) concerning human affairs and he identifies each according to its view of fate and free will, a question which divided several schools of Greek philosophy such as the Stoics, Epicureans and Cynics. Like other respectable Hellenistic states, the Jewish state too has its philosophies and Josephus distinguishes them in a way that his Greek-speaking readers would understand. Josephus acknowledges that his description is brief and refers the reader to his more lengthy account in the *War*, Book 2. The description of the three schools of thought also prepares the reader to meet both the Pharisees and Judas the Essene later in the book.[16]

Josephus lists the three groups in the order Pharisees, Sadducees and Essenes, but treats them in the order Pharisees,

---

[15]*Ant.* 13.5.9 (171-173).

[16]Schwartz, "Josephus," 161-162 conjectures that the description comes from Nicolaus of Damascus and originally included an attack on the legitimacy of the Hasmoneans, based on the Essene and Sadducee (Zadokite) rejection of their high priesthood. This proposal is overly speculative and lacks evidence.

Essenes, Sadducees. Each group is treated equally and Josephus gives no evaluations. The Pharisees believed in both fate (divine providence, in theological language) and human responsibility, the Essenes attributed everything to fate and the Sadducees denied fate and placed all responsibility on human action. The Essenes are called a *genos*, which is best translated by the neutral term group.[17] No description has yet been given in the *Antiquities* of the roles of these groups in society or of their historical importance, nor do we learn of their origin or internal constitution. This brief description merely informs the readers that Judaism has philosophies and prepares for the mention of them in succeeding passages.

PHARISEES AND SADDUCEES UNDER HYRCANUS

After Josephus has recounted the contest between the Pharisees and Sadducees for the favor of John Hyrcanus (treated in the previous chapter), he explains that the conflict over regulations was based on the Pharisees' affirmation of *nomima* (laws/customs/practices) handed down by former generations (*paterōn*), but not written down in the laws of Moses.[18] The Sadducees accepted only written *nomima* and were not obligated by those handed on by former generations. The Pharisees and Sadducees consequently had controversies and great disagreements and each group competed to have its characteristic teachings concerning the political and religious laws of Judaism and its distinctive way of living Judaism accepted. These controversies were not just academic or matters of personal preference

[17]The Essenes are called a *genos* several times in Josephus: *War* 1.3.5 (78); 2.7.3 (113); *Ant.* 13.11.12 (311); 15.10.4 (371); 17.13.3 (346). The Sadducees are called this once in *Ant.* 13.10.6 (297). The Greek word has a wide range of meaning, such as "race, family; class, genus, kind, sort of." In the Loeb translation Marcus translates *genos* as "sect" here and in Book 17 but as "group" in reference to the Sadducees and also in reference to the Essenes in #311 and in Book 15. In the *War* Thackeray translates the first use of *genos* as "of Essene extraction" and the second as "sect" with a footnote that the Greek word means race. Whether Josephus was trying to hint at a more physical unity among the Essenes or mark off their group as a special kind of genus is unclear from his usage. In *Ant.* 18, #119 Josephus uses *genos* of the Essenes, but both the context and the grammar show that the word means that the Essenes were Jewish by birth, not that their group was a *genos*.

[18]*Ant.* 13.10.6 (297-298).

because the views of these groups affected the running of the Jewish state.[19]

Josephus notes that the Sadducees had the confidence of the rich, but he does not say that all the Sadducees were rich; much less does he say that all the rich, the rulers and the chief priests were Sadducees, a position often assumed by scholars. Both the Pharisees and Sadducees were political interest groups with a special expertise and interest in the laws (and so religion) of the nation.[20] Unfortunately, Josephus does not tell us any of the regulations specifically in question nor does he tell us why the rich favored one group and the people another. We may speculate why the Sadducees were favored by the rich and powerful. They favored harsher punishments for crimes, something which would appeal to those keeping order in society. More importantly, they limited authority to written (Biblical and other?) regulations and not to other traditions accepted by the Pharisees, perhaps because the governing class preferred to be as unconstrained by custom as possible. The Scriptural rules, uninterpreted by detailed traditions, were more often than not vague or inapplicable as written. Thus the governing class would be free to decide what they meant. It is certain that the governing class had their own traditions and that the people in various places had customs and traditional rules to guide their behavior.

The Life

In his *Life*, which was a reply to attacks on his person and was written as an appendix to the *Antiquities*, Josephus speaks of his training with several groups and his choice of the Pharisees. According to his own account, he made initial contact with these groups when he was sixteen and "determined to gain

[19]This is a classic effect of influence in Parson's sense (see ch. 2). The special knowledge of a group gives it standing in the community and the ability to guide others' actions without the use of direct political power. The influence may also affect those with political power and cause them to make certain teachings sanctioned policy.

[20]In this passage Josephus refers to the Sadducees as a *moira* and as a *genos*. *Genos* has already been treated above. *Moira* is another word with a wide range of meaning. It can mean a division, section or even a political party. Josephus uses it of the Sadducees only here and never of the other groups. It is unlikely that he uses the word in other than a general sense.

personal experience of the several *haireseis* [schools of thought] into which our nation is divided.... So I submitted to hard training and laborious exercises and passed through the three courses (of the Pharisees, Sadducees and Essenes)."[21] In addition Josephus spent three years with and became a devoted disciple of Bannus, a man who resided in the wilderness, lived off the land and purified himself frequently in cold water. Finally, at age nineteen he decided to govern his life "according to the *hairesis* of the Pharisees, [a *hairesis*] having points of resemblance to that which the Greeks call the Stoic [*hairesis*]."

Each of the four groups was a way of life which required a change in one's personal life and some specialized knowledge. Josephus had already received his basic education and he claims that he had such a reputation for love of letters that at age fourteen "the chief priests and the leading men used constantly to come to me for precise information on some particular in our ordinances (*nomima*)."[22] Josephus does not tell us what kind of training he received with Bannus, though living in the wilderness presumably involved asceticism. Nor does he say where he was trained by the Pharisees, Sadducees and Essenes, nor how long he spent with each, except that he covered all three in a year.[23]

Doubt has frequently been cast on Josephus' account of his training.[24] If he spent only a short time with the three sects, what could he have learned and what effect could they have had on him? Though he says he was three years in the wilderness and was a devoted disciple of Bannus, he returned and chose the Pharisees. Even if this is so, Josephus' writings, actions and interpretations of Scripture do not manifest any connection with what we know of the Pharisees. Cohen notes that Josephus' identification of himself as a Pharisee and as one respectful of Jewish traditions in the *Life* fits his overall apologetic purpose and may not be reliable.[25] Josephus habitually identifies himself

---

[21] *Life* 9-12 (2).

[22] Note the similar claim made for the twelve year old Jesus in Luke 2:41-51.

[23] Rajak. *Josephus*, 34-36, suggests that Josephus spent about three months each with the Pharisees, Sadducees and Essenes to learn the basics of their way of life and refers to this practice as a common Greek practice.

[24] Attridge, "Josephus," 188.

[25] Cohen, *Josephus*, 144-151. Cohen's negative evaluation of Josephus is standard, though better worked out than previously. For example, Rasp follows Laqueuer in

as a priest and community leader but not as a Pharisee. In speaking of his choice of the Pharisees, he does not say that he joined the Pharisees as a group, but that he began to govern his life by the rules of the Pharisees. Perhaps he was guided by some aspects of their teaching and practice without becoming a social and political ally and active in their organization. If this is so, most probably their program for remaining Jewish while living within and accommodating the Roman empire was what attracted Josephus.[26] Rajak speculates that Bannus, living in the wilderness, may have led a politically radical group, similar to others mentioned in Josephus. If so, Josephus' choice of the Pharisees would have been a rejection of revolution and acceptance of accommodation to the empire.

Summary: The Pharisees and Sadducees in Josephus

The minor role played by the Pharisees and Sadducees in Josephus is explained by his concentration on the governing class and its political and military fortunes which were so crucial for Jewish society as a whole. Neither the priesthood, the aristocrats nor the peasants are treated except when they have an impact on the fortunes of the nation as a whole. The Pharisees and Sadducees are mentioned at times of change, crisis or transition in government because when power shifted they and many other social and political forces in Jewish society became active in the competition for power and influence. When John Hyrcanus shifted his allegiance from the Pharisees to the Sadducees, when Alexandra struggled to maintain control after her husband's death, at the beginning and end of Herod's reign, at the transition from Herodian rule to Roman procurators and in the complex events at the beginning of the war against Rome, the Pharisees and Sadducees are treated by Josephus as part of the political and social competition for power and influence.

evaluating Josephus as an opportunist in his self-presentation ("Flavius Josephus," p. 46).

[26]See Rajak, *Josephus*, 34-39 and 224. She accepts Josephus' statement that he was a Pharisee. Attridge, *Interpretation*, 176-179 says that the first half of the *Ant.* gives no evidence that Josephus was a Pharisee.

The Pharisees functioned as a political interest group which had its own goals for society and constantly engaged in political activity to achieve them, even though they did not always succeed. They were not themselves the leaders of the Jewish community, though prominent leaders of the Pharisees, either by their station in the Pharisaic group or because of family status, were part of the governing class. The Pharisees as a group did not have direct power (except to a limited degree under their royal patron, Alexandra) and were not as a whole members of the governing class. They were a literate, organized group which constantly sought influence with governing class. As such they fit into Lenski's retainer class, a group of people above the peasants and other lower classes but dependent on the governing class and ruler for their place in society. The members of the retainer class usually fulfilled administrative, bureaucratic and military functions in society. Josephus does not make clear what functions the Pharisees fulfilled in society, but in each era of Jewish history from the Hasmonean period until the destruction of the Temple they were present and struggling to gain access to power.

The Pharisees' precise goals for society and the laws by which they wished society to live are not described by Josephus, but the traditions which they promoted were popular with the people, especially in the Hasmonean period, according to Josephus.[27] Both their activities in the Hasmonean period and the description of them at the end of Archelaus' reign imply that they were allied with traditional, non-revolutionary Judaism. Whatever influence they achieved, they usually achieved with the help of a powerful patron and they entered into coalitions with other groups among the upper classes in order to gain influence and move those who had power.

---

[27]Richard Horsley, "'Like One of the Prophets of Old': Two Types of Popular Prophets at the Time of Jesus," *CBQ* 47 (1985) 444-445, points out that the lower class did not always look to the literate class, which formed a tiny middle stratum, for leadership. These literate groups had their own interests to pursue and if they differed from those of the common people, the people were quite capable of producing their own leaders, such as prophets. This seems to be what happened at the time of the war against Rome. He notes elsewhere that the people would not have looked to the landed gentry for leadership because they were implicated with Herod and other "alien leaders" ("Messianic Movements," 484-485).

Josephus tells us little about the Sadducees. Though the members of the Sadducees are mostly from the governing class Josephus does not say that all or most of the priests and aristocrats were Sadducees, contrary to the assumptions of many scholars. It is probable that the Biblical traditions and interpretations which the Sadducees promoted favored the status quo and the political and financial interests of the governing class. This would explain their constituency and their unpopularity with the people and conversely the popularity of the Pharisees' views.

Josephus' *descriptions* of the Pharisees and Sadducees are generally consistent with his accounts of them in action. However, the descriptions are far from complete and do not present a coherent picture of the groups' thought and organization. The Pharisees were noted for their practice of the law and their ability to interpret the law in their own way. This implies that they had particular views about how to live Jewish life and probably followed communal customs within an organizational structure. However, Josephus does not give us any information about the inner workings of the Pharisees or their presumably learned leadership. The Pharisees' acceptance of life after death and resurrection as well as reward and punishment is contrasted with the Sadducees' rejection of these teachings. These characteristic teachings are witnessed most often in Josephus and also in the New Testament. Likewise, their positions on fate (meaning divine providence) and on free will and human responsibility are contrasted. Their positions on life after death and on divine providence are consistent with one another and probably derive from their eschatology and apocalyptic expectations. The Sadducees picture humans as independent and distant form God both in life and after it; the Phariseees picture God and humans as in a close relationship both in this life and the next. (The Essenes attribution of everything to fate probably reflects their strong apocalyptic orientation, reflected in the Dead Sea Scrolls, with its concomitant rejection of Jewish society.)[28]

The Pharisees are said, both in the *War* and in the *Antiquities*, to be the leading and most influential school of thought. The Sadducees are said to come from the governing class in the

[28]Blenkinsopp, "Prophecy," 249.

Antiquities, but the social class of the Pharisees is not specified, except that one can infer that most of them were of a lower social station than the Sadducees. This fits the conclusions drawn from the events recounted by Josephus above. The description of social relations among the members of these groups and with outsiders may fit their place in society, also. The Sadducees are pictured as competitive, argumentative and hard to get along with. The Pharisees cultivated harmonious relations with all, had great respect for their traditions and elders and consequently, had a large following for their attractive way of life.

Though the descriptions which Josephus gives are very incomplete, some cautious speculation about these groups will be helpful. The attitudes and behavior of the Sadducees fit the governing class which has hereditary access to high office and power. They competed for power with one another and aroused the enmity or envy of those around them. The Pharisees, most of whom did not have hereditary ties to positions of power, struggled to influence society as a group by winning influence. Consequently, they stressed social relations to build up their own group and win it favor and influence with others. That their struggle for power and influence was a group struggle is shown by the absence of names of Pharisaic leaders in most cases. Only Eleazar who attacked John Hyrcanus, Samaias and Pollion who struck up a peculiar and ambivalent relationship with Herod, Simon ben Gamaliel and the three Pharisees who were part of the delegation sent to Josephus in Galilee (Jonathan, Ananias and Jozar) are named.

We learn little about the Pharisees' and Sadducees' internal organization from Josephus' descriptions.[29] The Pharisees seem to have been a more cohesive group than the Sadducces and it is probable that they had a leadership structure, education for their members and clear criteria for membership. The beliefs which they espoused in afterlife, divine activity in history and human freedom, were most probably different enough from the traditional Jewish teachings and attitudes to require some

---

[29]This casts doubt on Josephus' claim in his *Life* that he was a Pharisee. He shows no special interest in the Pharisees and manifests no intimate knowledge of their position, practices, or organization.

positive commitment. By contrast, the Sadducees maintained the older, more traditional view of Judaism, that there is no afterlife, and probably also they followed post-exilic tradition in seeing God as more transcendent than immanent and less directly involved in the events of history. Consequently, the Sadducees could be an identifiable school of thought without having a highly articulated communal structure and without attracting many to their views.

HAIRESIS: SECT OR SCHOOL?

Josephus provides so little information on the internal organization and leadership of the Pharisees and Sadducees that the nature of these groups is controversial and unclear. His indiscriminate and non-technical use of several Greek words to designate these groups suggests that they were not exactly like anything in the Greco-Roman world.[30] As was argued in chapter four, to designate them as Greek voluntary associations does little to clarify their nature due to the variety of those organizations. The closest Josephus comes to a precise naming of these groups is when he calls them *haireseis*. *Hairesis*, a Greek word most familiar in its pejorative Christian sense, heresy had a neutral or even positive meaning in non-Christian Greek usage. Because of Josephus' use of this *hairesis*, scholars have often identified the Pharisees and Sadducees as philosophical schools of thought or religious sects. Each of these possibilities will be examined in turn.

A *hairesis* was a coherent and principled choice of a way of life, that is, of a particular school of thought.[31] In the view of the ancients and most importantly Josephus, once a few basic principles of a tradition were accepted one could then expect some diversity, that is, some choice of particular ways of life and

[30]For a chart of the words Josephus uses, such as *genos, moira, tagma*, see LeMoyne, *Sadducéens, 19*. There seems to be no consistent, significant pattern to Josephus' usage.

[31]Marcel Simon, "From Greek Hairesis to Christian Heresy," in *Early Christian Literature and the Classical Intellectual Tradition* (in honorem Robert M. Grant), eds. William R. Schoedel and Robert L. Wilken (Théologie Historique 53; Paris: Beauchesne, 1979) 101-116, esp. 110 and 104. Henri I. Marrou, *A History of Education in Antiquity* (New York: Mentor, 1964) 157 and 504 notes that *hairesis* can also mean a year's class of ephebes in Egyptian usage.

thought. Greek philosophical schools were usually ways of life based on a certain understanding of the universe and of moral law. Thus, Josephus uses *hairesis* to describe the great currents of thought and practice in Judaism, the Pharisees, Sadducees, Essenes and "Fourth Philosophy" revolutionaries, in such a way as to bring respectibility to Judaism and attest to the antiquity and value of its traditions.[32] *Hairesis* only received its pejorative meaning of heresy in the middle of the second century with Justin Martyr; even then its neutral sense persisted into the third century in Christian literature.

Translations of *hairesis* in Josephus usually alternate between *sect* and *school* (of thought), but neither may be completely accurate. *Sect* in the popular usage usually refers to a religious group which is in reaction to the main religious tradition and which sees itself as the true religion and an exclusive replacement for the dominant tradition.[33] Such a stance is not characteristic of the Sadducees, if Josephus is correct that they came from the leaders of society. They would be a sub-group of the governing class seeking to solidify its traditional position and interpretation of how society should run. In the more precise typology developed by Bryan Wilson (in ch. 4) the Pharisees with their expectations for Jewish life and their political involvement might be a reformist sect, but too little is known of them at this point to be certain. We are especially uncertain how much community life and organization the Pharisees had and so we lack knowledge of a prime determinant of sects. The Essenes, especially the Qumran group, are closest to the modern idea of sect because they withdrew from society in protest and had active conflict with the religious authorities of the society. They fit Wilson's introversionist type, those who withdraw into a purified community. The Essenes who lived within Palestinian towns, if they were apocalyptically oriented, as the Dead Sea Scrolls suggest, would be Wilson's revolutionist type, awaiting divine intervention to destroy the evil social order.

School of thought, as a translation of *hairesis*, may be closer to what Josephus meant, though not necessarily to what the Pharisees were. Josephus is certainly comparing the Pharisees,

[32]Simon, "Hairesis," 104-105.

[33]See the summary of sectarian analysis in chapter 4.

Sadducees and Essenes to the Greek schools of philosophy in order to show that Jews are a respectable, civilized people with all one would expect in thought and practice.[34] But are these groups really schools which trained their members and lived some sort of communal life or at least had strong social bonds? Did they think of themselves as schools in the Greek mode? This is possible because Judaism had been thoroughly influenced by Hellenistic civilization which put a high premium on both philosophical schools and voluntary associations. Morton Smith urges us to take seriously Josephus' designations of the Jewish groups as schools of thought because to the ancient world a philosophy was the most accurate term for groups practicing a certain kind of wisdom.[35] It is very difficult to prove that these Jewish groups were philosophical schools, however, or to know what education was like in Jewish circles.

The Greek schools of philosophy did not just engage in the academic study of a group of doctrines, but urged on their members and students a way of life. Students often sampled several schools of philosophy, but to devote oneself to one of the schools involved a lengthy period of study, life according to a moral code, communal activities with other members of the school and often a distinctive dress.[36] Whether the Pharisees, Sadducees or Essenes are this type of group must be determined from the evidence of the sources. Neither Josephus nor the New Testament describe the complete inner organization of the Pharisees, but some hints and bits of information will allow cautious hypotheses. That the Pharisees actually were similar to

---

[34]Josephus uses "philosophy" and "philosophize" of the schools of thought in the descriptions in *War*, Book 2 and *Antiquities*, Book 18 and also in the John Hyrcanus story in *Ant.* 13.10.5 (289). In *Ant.* 18 he designates the revolutionaries as the "fourth philosophy" (18.1.1.[9]).

[35]Smith, "Palestinian Judaism," 79. He also suggests that the Pharisees were self-consciously philosophical schools and seen as such by the people (79-81). In drawing this conclusion, however, he uses later rabbinic sources uncritically.

[36]See R. Alan Culpepper, *The Johannine School: An Evaluation of the Johannine-School Hypothesis Based on an Investigation of the Nature of Ancient Schools* (SBLDS 26; Chico: Scholars, 1975) 258-259 for a convenient list of characteristics of ancient schools. This list, however, is a composite and does not distinguish different types of schools with precision. See Stanley Stowers, "Social Status, Public Speaking and Private Teaching: The Circumstances of Paul's Preaching Activity," *NovTest* 26 (1984) 59-82 for the distinction of some types.

a philosophical school or other Hellenistic association is likely because the formation of voluntary social groups was a characteristic of Hellenistic society. Even the rabbinic evidence, though of a later date, shows the impact of Hellenistic categories on its understanding of its own institutions and those of the earlier Pharisees, though the evaluation of the historical validity of this understanding of the Pharisees must await a later chapter.[37]

In speaking of schools we must distinguish different types. The rough equivalent of modern primary and secondary schools were often organized in cities for the children of the upper classes; such institutions included a building, formal classes, etc. Higher education, including philosophy, was most often informally arranged. The Academy, Stoa and Lyceum in Athens and the schools in Alexandria were exceptions to the general rule. More often a single philosophical teacher gathered a group of students under the patronage of and within the house of a wealthy sponsor.[38] The members lived a full or partial community life, were expected to adhere to a code of behavior which could also include dress and food, studied and argued in a lively fashion and devoted their lives, partially or entirely, to the goals proposed by the way of life and school of thought they were pursuing. But his generalized picture must not be applied rigorously. The philosophical schools differed among themselves about how schooling ought to be accomplished[39] and each culture and locale adapted the Greek model to local circumstances.

We know little concerning higher education in Palestine in the Hellenistic period. Presumably the chief priests and leaders of the prominent families were trained in Jewish traditions and also in Greek so that they could communicate with the imperial government. The concluding hymn to Ben Sira mentions a school (51:23) though the literary form makes it unclear whether

[37]See Mantel, "Great Synagogues," 69-91 for a concise, though often uncritical, review of the evidence.

[38]For this model as it applies to the Pauline Christian communities Stowers, "Teaching," 59-82. Meeks, Urban, 81-84, also compares the Pauline community to philosophical schools and notes that such schools were sometimes modified households or Greek associations.

[39]Stowers, "Teaching," 76-77.

a metaphorical or literal school is being referred to. In either case the idea is present. Payment for instruction is also mentioned (51:28). The proliferation of Jewish literature from the Hellenistic period and preservation and study of earlier Biblical traditions all argue for a lively intellectual, literary tradition which included education on all levels.

We do not know how educated the Pharisees were as a group. Josephus presents them as reputedly accurate interpreters of the Jewish tradition, a claim which implies that all learned their own traditions and some were highly educated.[40] In the gospels they are informed and subtle adversaries of Jesus, a role which implies familiarity with tradition and custom. It is perhaps more probable to imagine the Pharisees in general as learned leaders of the people. The scribes, too, were literate as a condition of their job and the higher their function in society, the more learned they must have been. Presumably, the Sadducees, who were upper class according to Josephus, were educated, but whether they formed a definable school is unknown.

Whether the Pharisees and other groups can be profitably treated as philosophical schools or schools of thought in the Hellenistic mode is uncertain. We do not have sufficient evidence of their organization, self-concept and public role to be sure of their similarity to Greek schools, beyond some broad similarities. The Pharisees as depicted by Josephus acted as a political interest group and thus went beyond the activities of many Greek schools. On the other hand, they had a program of reform for Jewish life, a particular interpretation of Jewish tradition and a definable and sometimes controversial outlook on fundamental matters crucial to Judaism. Josephus' use of *hairesis* for the Pharisees is best translated as school (of thought) as long as this expression is understood to mean an interpretation and a way of life which is not exclusively academic and theoretical. Even with this characterization, the problem of the exact nature of the Pharisees, Sadducees and also Essenes as historical groups is more complex than indicated by Josephus' characterization of them.

---

[40]See Baumgarten, "The Name," 411-428 on the accuracy in interpretation attributed to the Pharisees in the sources.

Excursus
Pro-Pharisaic Bias in the Antiquities?

Many have held that Josephus exaggerated the role and influence of the Pharisees by retrojecting into the pre-war period the role the rabbis were playing in the later first century. R. Laqueur, Hans Rasp, Morton Smith and Jacob Neusner have all claimed that Josephus is much more positive toward the Pharisees in the *Antiquities*, that he favors them because they have become the leaders of Palestinian Jewry and that he consequently provides a more important role for the Pharisees than is historically justified.[41] Neusner has argued on the basis of the Mishnah and the gospels that the Pharisees were a sect-like group in the first century C.E. and not politically active.

The claim that Josephus was pro-Pharisee is weakened by several difficulties. In the *Antiquities* Josephus treats them the same way he treats other groups and is anti-Pharisaic in many places, does not treat them at great enough length to make a case for them and reveals their revolutionary activity more fully than in the *War*. Finally, the rabbinic heirs to the Pharisees were probably not yet prominent enough to be promoted as Jewish leaders.

Though Josephus has often been characterized as pro-Pharisee, especially in the *Antiquities*, it is more probable that Josephus' larger view of society and government determined his attitude toward the Pharisees, Sadducees and all other Jewish groups and figures. Josephus valued, above all, a strong, orderly government which would guarantee peace. The disorder and disaster of the Jewish war against Rome led him to criticize any groups which caused instability and revolution in Jewish society in the Greco-Roman period. Consequently, he disapproved of the Pharisees when they avenged themselves against their enemies under Alexandra because they caused social strife. He approved of Pollion and Samaias for supporting Herod at the beginning of his reign because Herod was a strong ruler who

---

[41]Laqueur, *Josephus;* H. Rasp, "Flavius Josephus und die Jüdischen Religionsparteien," *ZNW* 23 (1924) 27-34; M. Smith, "Palestinian Judaism," 75-77; J. Neusner, *From Politics,* 65-66.

would bring stability in contrast to the chaos of the final years of Hasmoneans. He disapproved of the Pharisees' coalition with Pheroras' family against Herod at the end of his reign because it was part of the factional strife which led to the disorders of the first century. He approved of the Pharisees who joined other Jerusalem leaders in an attempt to quiet the people at the beginning of the war with Rome. He approved of both the Pharisees and Sadducees as ancient Jewish schools of thought which lent Judaism stability and respectability, especially in contrast to the new and revolutionary fourth philosophy. He gave a critical picture of the Sadducees' relations with the rest of society which deprived them of useful and stabilizing influence with the people. He was critical of the Sadducee Ananus because his stern Sadducean approach in favor of capital punishment provoked social unrest and led to his loss of power. Later he approved of the same man's heroic resistance to the revolutionary zealots in Jerusalem because he was properly fulfilling his leadership role. He was indifferent to the transfer of John Hyrcanus' favor from the Pharisees to the Sadducees because it did not promote social instability or a crisis of leadership.

In many places where Josephus is clearly anti-Pharisaic in tone and judgment, many claim that he is not giving his own view, but quoting Nicolaus of Damascus, Herod's court historian who was staunchly pro-Herodian and consequently anti-Pharisaic. This argument is not cogent. Though Josephus is sometimes inconsistent in his use of sources, his accounts of Pharisees, as well as other Jewish groups, form a coherent whole. He approves of the Pharisees when they are a force for stability and he disapproves of them when they challenge the dominant, traditional and stable government and way of life of Judaism. Josephus used both Nicolaus and other sources, especially in *Antiquities*, Books 14-17, but his main themes and interpretations of events come through his (sometimes careless) use of sources and communicate his view of many aspects of Jewish history.

Some have claimed that because the *Antiquities* treat the Pharisees at greater length than the *War*, it is pro-Pharisee and reflects Josephus' support for the rabbis who had emerged as the reliable, non-revolutionary leaders of Judaism about 90 C.E. But the *Antiquities* have more about the Pharisees because the account there is more lengthy and detailed. In fact, neither the *War* nor the *Antiquities* has very much coverage of the Pharisees and thus it us unlikely that one of Josephus' major purposes was to promote the Pharisees in the eyes of the Romans.[42] Josephus does stress Jewish laws, customs and high moral character as worthy of the respect of Greeks and Romans. Thus, the Pharisees, as interpreters of Jewish custom, are to be praised,[43] but nowhere does he say that they should be rulers of society.

D. Schwartz has argued convincingly that far from giving a uniformly positive and pacific picture of the Pharisees in the *Antiquities*, Josephus is more frank about their involvement in the war than he was in his earlier work which was closer to the events.[44] He shows that there is no clear evidence that the Pharisees left politics under Herod or immediately after, a conclusion which was reached in a different way in this study.[45] In the *Antiquities* Josephus admits that the Pharisees are very close to the fourth philosophy in everything except revolutionary zeal, that they engaged in political plots under Hyrcanus and Herod (he uses Nicolaus of Damascus for his source here) and (in the *Life*) that Simon ben Gamaliel and three Pharisaic delegates were involved in the early revolutionary leadership.[46] Schwartz suggests that in the *War*, soon after the end of the revolt against Rome, Josephus was careful to separate the Pharisees and others from politics, but two decades later in the

---

[42]Attridge, *Interpretation*, p. 14 notes that there is some change in Josephus' treatment of the schools of thought from the *War* to the *Antiquities*, but that Josephus' connection with and attitudes toward the sects is not significant in his overall work.

[43]Attridge, "Josephus," 224-227. See *Ant.* 3.9.1-3.12.3 (224-286) and 4.8.4-43 (196-301) for extensive apologetic summaries of Jewish law. Also, *Apion* 2. 145-220 and 291-296.

[44]Schwartz, "Josephus," distinguishes Josephus from Nicolas of Damascus and then shows the evolution of his treatment of the Pharisees.

[45]"Josephus," 166. Schwartz agrees with the position that Josephus is pro-Pharisee in the *Antiquities*, but not in such a way as to obscure or misrepresent their political involvement. Cohen, *Josephus*, 236-37, notes that the *Antiquities* acknowledges that the responsibility for the war against Rome was more widespread than admitted in the *War*. In addition, the Pharisees are explicitly connected with the revolt in the *Antiquities*, though no school of thought had been connected with it in the *War* (pp. 154-157). Despite this, according to Cohen the *Antiquities* are more pro-Pharisaic than the *War* (pp. 237-238).

[46]Schwartz, "Josephus," 169; Rast, "Flavius Josephus," p. 33 notes that the Pharisees are more political in the *Antiquities* than in the *War*.

Antiquities he was less cautious in some cases, though he still favors the Pharisees and keeps them mostly out of politics.[47]

Since Josephus' accounts of Pharisaic disruptive and revolutionary political involvement in the *Antiquities* do not derive from or especially serve his political purposes, these accounts are to be trusted as representative of Pharisaic political involvement. My position is that Josephus is not discernibly pro- or anti-Pharisaic in his overall attitude toward them, but that his evaluation of the Pharisees and all other groups is guided by larger political principles, especially the desire for orderly government and keeping the peace.

The theory that Josephus was promoting the Pharisees as leaders in Judaism is also weakened by uncertainty about their role in Palestine about 90 C.E. Though most treatments of the Pharisees based on Talmudic sources see the rabbinic "prince" (*nāśī*) or patriarch as firmly in charge of Judaism, it is far from clear that the Pharisees had taken over Judaism by 90 C.E. The rabbinic leadership which gradually took shape over the decades following the destruction of the Temple was composed of priests and scribes, as well as pre-war Pharisees.[48] It is likely that many of the rabbinic leaders came from Pharisaic groups, but there is no evidence that the Pharisees as a coherent group survived the destruction of the Temple.[49] The emerging rabbis did not immediately take over Judaism and receive recognition from the people and the Romans. Evidence that Gamaliel II was recognized as the leader of Judaism by the Romans is slim and highly ambiguous, rendering this often repeated claim historically uncertain.[50] Though the Romans characteristically recruited local

[47]Schwartz, "Josephus," 169-170.

[48]See Jacob Neusner, *Judaism: The Evidence of the Mishnah* (Chicago; Chicago UP, 1981), pp. 230-256 and other essays as well for the contributions of the priests, scribes and householders.

[49]See a fresh analysis of the arguments for the connection between the Pharisees and rabbis in Shaye Cohen, "The Significance of Yavneh: Pharisees, Rabbis, and the End of Jewish Sectarianism," *HUCA* 55 (1984) 36-38. Cohen argues, probably correctly, that no one argument is convincing, but that the cumulative effect of several arguments makes the connection probable. What must be borne in mind is that we know very little about the emergence of the new Jewish leaders after the destruction of the Temple and that the usual harmonious picture constructed from the Talmud is not historically proven.

[50]Schwartz, "Josephus," 167-168. See further discussion in ch. 10.

leaders as their proxies, there is no conclusive evidence that they did so after the war. Even if they did recognize Gamaliel as the representative of the Jewish community, he and his associates (rabbis) would have had only limited control over how Jewish life was lived at first. Control was not complete even by the time of the Mishnah (200 C.E.). The Mishnah presents itself as an ideal view of Judaism and shows little sign of being a practiced law code with effective enforcement and penalties. Stories and conflicts in the Palestinian Talmud of the third and fourth centuries indicate that the rabbis were only then succeeding in their struggle to gain control over how the people lived Jewish life.

PHARISAIC POLITICAL INFLUENCE

Jacob Neusner has claimed that the Pharisees ceased to be a politically active group, left the political arena during the time of Herod and the Romans and took on more sectarian characteristics.[51] However, such a separation of the political and religious is too sharp. It seems that the Pharisees were a politically and religiously based group in a complex society and that they were always interested in political power and always a factor in society at large. But they were a minor factor, or better, one of a large number of forces which made up Jewish society. It may be that at the time of the revolt the Pharisaic notables were not acting for the organization, but were just prominent individuals. But the fact that Josephus identifies them as Pharisees argues that membership in the Pharisees had a social and political value. They had been competing for power at the end of Herod's reign and the confusion and breakdown of traditional leadership during the first century was a perfect opportunity for the Pharisees and many other groups to gain power. In the *Life* Josephus recounts that a delegation sent to control his activities in Galilee had three Pharisees as members (see below). The Pharisees were probably less visible and

---

[51]See *From Politics to Piety*, 65-66; "Josephus' Pharisees: A Complete Repetoire," *Formative Judaism: Religious, Historical and Literary Studies. Third Series: Torah, Pharisees, and Rabbis* (BJS 46; Chico: Scholars, 1983), 61-82 for a convenient summary. In this he follows Smith, "Palestinian Judaism."

influential and so less reported by Josephus during the first century, C.E. because they had no royal patron like Alexandra and there was no central Jewish authority, like Herod, with whom to come into conflict. That the Pharisees did survive after the reign of Herod as a political force is attested to by the presence of Pharisees among the Jerusalem leaders at the beginning of the war with Rome and on the delegation sent from Jerusalem to Josephus in Galilee. Their presence in Markan traditions which derive from the middle of the first century also suggests that they were still struggling for influence with the people, in this case in competition with Jesus.

7

Paul the Pharisee

Paul is the only person besides Josephus whose claim to be a Pharisee is preserved (Phil. 3:5) and he is the only diaspora Jew identified as a Pharisee. This single passage in Paul's letters where the word Pharisee is used can show something of Paul's understanding of the Pharisees only when it is interpreted in the context of Paul's biographical statements and social world. The information from Paul's own letters will be separated from the interpretation of Paul presented in Acts because Luke's view of Paul from the late first century is heavily influenced by his interpretation of Christianity and does not fully accord with Paul's letters. It is noteworthy that Acts does not identify Paul as a Pharisee, though he is portrayed as a zealous and active Jew who eventually came to believe in Jesus.

Though Paul's letters are generally more reliable than Acts, they must be read critically because Paul always wrote to make a point with his listeners and never presented a complete account of himself in a relatively objective manner. The major questions to be put to the pauline texts concern what Paul understood a Pharisee to be and what social value he associated with Pharisaism. We will also inquire about the kind of commitment required to become a Pharisee and what effect or influence Pharisaism had in the diaspora.

The only text to mention Pharisees, Phil 3:2-4:1, attacks Paul's opponents who stress circumcision. Scholars who think that Philippians is a composite of several pre-existing literary units identify this section as one of those units.[1] Paul contrasts

[1]Helmut Koester, *Introduction to the New Testament* (Philadelphia: Fortress, 1982)

those who "mutilate the flesh" (Phil 3:3) with the Christians who are the "true circumcision" and who "put no confidence in the flesh" (3:4). Paul argues that, though he has every reason to have confidence in the flesh, that is, in his Jewish birth and heritage (3:4-6), he counts all that as loss in comparison with Jesus (3:7-11). It is in this section on his Jewish heritage that Paul mentions his connection with Pharisaism.

Paul recites his Jewish genealogy and accomplishments in Phil 3:4-6 (presented here in a very literal translation which will reflect the concise style of the Greek).

> If anyone seems to put confidence in flesh, I more;
> with respect to circumcision an eighth day one;[2]
> from the people/nation[3] Israel, of the tribe Benjamin;
> in relation to law, a Pharisee,
> in relation to zeal, a persecutor of the church,
> in relation to righteousness in law, being blameless.

Paul interprets his former life as worthless in comparison with his present life in Jesus. His physical descent is treated as loss; his past way of life as a Pharisee, a persecutor of Christians and a blameless adherent of the law has been replaced by a desire to be found having the righteousness based on faith from God (3:8-9).

Paul's single allusion to his having been a Pharisee is related to law, that is, the Jewish way of life as an interpretation of the Torah. Paul's concise claim, "in relation to (*kata*) law, a Pharisee," most naturally means living Jewish life according to the Pharisaic interpretation of the law. The two characteristics of his Jewish way of life which follow his claim to be a Pharisee

---

2.132-134 sees this section as the third letter against Judaizing and gnosticizing missionaries, written in the form of a testament and using biographical history, ethical admonition, eschatological instruction, blessings and curses. See his article "The Purpose of the Polemic of a Pauline Fragment," *NTS* 8 (1961) 317-332. Recent authors in favor of unity are Luke Johnson, *The Writings of the New Testament: An Interpretation* (Philadelphia: Fortress, 1986) 338-339 and W. J. Dalton, "The Integrity of Phil." *Bib* 60 (1979) 97-102.

[2]This odd Greek construction is idiomatically translated "circumcised on the eighth day." The literal rendering brings out grammatical parallels with the other clauses.

[3]*genos* refers to physical descent and to groups united by descent.

seem to derive from his Pharisaism. 1. His adherence to the Pharisaic mode of interpreting the law led him to attack a group which had mounted a major challenge to the Pharisaic way of life. As some of the Pharisees had challenged and plotted against Jesus (according to the gospels,) so Paul the Pharisee attacked the followers of Jesus who threatened the Pharisaic influence on Jews and who more and more taught a significantly different understanding of Torah and the Jewish way of life.[4] The Pharisees and followers of Jesus especially clashed on the importance of purity laws, tithes and other "boundary mechanisms" for maintaining the integrity of God's people. 2. Paul kept the law as one was supposed to and achieved the righteousness from law which was proper to it. Paul is not referring to a highly complex doctrine of works righteousness vs. grace righteousness, but simply saying that he lived a good life according to the rules. Paul's point is that he was humanly acceptable according to the ordinary Jewish norms for proper behavior toward God and fellow Jews; he had lived up to the expectations of society's code of behavior and could not be rejected as a disgruntled failure.

Paul's description of his life as a Pharisaic Jew refers to the past. In following Jesus, Paul rejected the Jewish system of community norms and replaced them with Jesus' teaching and resurrection as the basis for a new code of behavior. Since Paul's honor and integrity is being attacked, he defends himself as a conscientious Jew who followed the Pharisaic interpretation of the law. Paul's reference to Pharisaism implies that it is well known and accepted as a legitimate and strict mode of living Jewish life.

Two other cases, in which Paul refers to his Jewish heritage without specific reference to law and Pharisaism will help to fill in his view of Judaism. In 2 Cor 11:21-33 he defends himself against opponents, who claim to be greater than he, by "foolishly" boasting that he too is a Hebrew, an Israelite, a descendant of Abraham (11:22), and of course a servant of the suffering Christ. In Romans 11:1 he refutes the notion that God has rejected Israel by pointing out that he is "an Israelite, a

---

[4] See the details of this persecution below.

descendant of Abraham, a member of the tribe of Benjamin." In both these passages Paul points out that he is permanently Jewish by birth and in the second that God continues to love Jews because God has loved him. These passages contrast with Philippians where the value of the law was in question. In 2 Corinthians and Romans Paul affirms that he is a Jew loved by God but in Philippians he rejects the normal understanding and practice of Judasim.

Paul's very brief description of his Jewish way of life as a Pharisee partly fits the view of the Pharisees found in Josephus. Both Josephus and Paul say that the Pharisees had an interpretation of the law, though neither says what it is, and both refer to the Pharisees as a well known group which, unfortunately, does not need detailed identification. Like Josephus, Paul does not tell us of the inner organization of the Pharisees. Both Paul and Josephus say that they were Pharisees once, but never again refer to this as part of their Jewish identities. Perhaps both habitually thought of themselves as Jews against the larger horizon of the Greco-Roman world where inner Jewish distinctions, such as membership in the Pharisees, were largely important.

Paul's Social Context

Though Paul's letters say nothing else about the Pharisees, a few things concerning them can be deduced with some probability from Paul's life and activities. It is likely that the Pharisees and their influence extended into Palestine and adjacent areas in Syria and Cilicia. In Josephus Pharisees only appear in Jerusalem. The limited information in Paul's letters agrees with Acts in suggesting that much of Paul's life before he became a follower of Jesus took place in Syria-Palestine and neighboring Cilicia which contained Tarsus, his home according to Acts. He had persecuted the churches in Judea (Gal. 1:22-23) and implies that he had his vision of Jesus in or near Damascus because after it he went to "Arabia" (Gal. 1:17), by which he probably meant the Nabatean kingdom in greater Syria and trans-Jordan. (Only Acts makes Damascus the place of Paul's instruction and baptism). He claims that he went to Jerusalem only three years after his conversion (Gal. 1:18) and he never resided there as a follower of Jesus.

Paul never says where he made contact with Pharisaism, in Tarsus, Syria or Jerusalem. Since he never refers to Pharisees as his opponents nor as leaders in the Jewish community in any of the letters addressed to communities in Asia Minor and Greece, it is very probable that Pharisees were not found in those communities. Since Paul lived and worked in the greater Syrian area as a Pharisee, it is somewhat probable that Pharisaism had some influence there and that some Pharisees lived outside Jerusalem and Judea. However the evidence that Pharisaic teaching and influence spread beyond the Palestinian borders is very tenuous.

The evidence concerning Pharisaism is so slim that we do not know how Paul came to know about Pharisaism, why he was attracted to it and what being a Pharisee entailed. Pharisaism, as depicted by Josephus, the New Testament and rabbinic writings, concerned itself with Palestinian Jewish political and social issues and with a certain style of Jewish life which included tithing and ritual preparation of foods especially suited to life in Jewish villages and towns. Since Paul uses purity language metaphorically to describe and maintain the new boundaries of the Christian community, it is likely that he was familiar with Jewish and perhaps Pharisaic purity rules.[5] If this is so, Paul was consciously creating a new community with a new understanding of purity, just as the Pharisees had for Judaism.

In the diaspora it is unclear what being a Pharisee might have meant. Both Josephus and Paul claimed to be Pharisees and consciously lived in the larger world of the Roman empire. Perhaps they found the Pharisaic view of how to live Judaism a viable response to the intellectual and spiritual challenge of the Hellenistic world view. Though we do not know the teachings of the Pharisees in any detail (despite later rabbinic texts and some New Testament allusions which imply a sect-like way of life), they probably brought Jewish practices into daily life and created a conscious way of life which answered the questions and crises

---

[5]For the early purity rules, see ch. 10. For Paul's use of purity language, see Jerome Neyrey, "Body Language in 1 Corinthians: The Use of Anthropological Models for Understanding Paul and His Opponents," *Semeia* 35 (1986) 129-170.

felt by some Jews when confronted with the Greco-Roman world. Neither says how one became a member of the Pharisees nor what kind and intensity of commitment was required. Possibly neither joined a clearly defined group, but rather identified loosely with the Pharisaic way of life because it fitted or could be adapted to fit their needs as Jews living in a largely Greco-Roman world.

Paul was not a Palestinian nor a member of the governing class. Though Paul does not say where he was born in his letters, Acts (21:39; 22:3) says that he came from Tarsus in Cilicia. His reasonably good Greek in his letters and his life and work in the diaspora make it very likely that he was a diaspora Jew. According to his own testimony he worked as an artisan while on his missionary travels (1 Thes 2:9; 1 Cor 9:6). The work must have been some sort of urban craft and Acts says that it was tentmaking, which was a form of leatherworking (18:3). Thus, Paul is unlike the Pharisees who appear in Josephus as retainers linked to the governing class in Jerusalem and as a Palestinian political interest group with goals which included renewal or reform of Jewish society according to their norms and under their influence and power.

As an artisan Paul was in principle a member of the lower classes. Artisans were not an independent middle class, but a subservient class who were limited by their ability to produce only a small amount of work by hand. Though some artisans became wealthy or powerful because of the quality of their work or their ability to organize other artisans in workshops, most were firmly lower class, like the peasants. Hock gives a detailed and dramatic account of the hours of hard labor required to work with leather in making tents and argues that artisans achieved very low social status because manual labor was demeaned in antiquity and because their work resembled that of slaves.[6] Thus, when Paul refers to his hard life as a Christian missionary in order to support himself, he is not engaging in rhetorical flourishes. While traveling, Paul probably made his first contacts in the leather workers' quarter and may even have used the workshop as a place for mission preaching and instruc-

---

[6]Ronald Hock, *The Social Context of Paul's Ministry* (Philadelphia: Fortress, 1980) 20-27, 31-37.

tion.[7] Though the pauline churches contained members from all stations in life, Paul's urban audience was mainly the lower classes who formed the major part of ancient society.[8] Paul's status as a lower class artisan would have been a help in contacting these groups.[9]

Paul could have enlisted a patron, as did Josephus, and joined the ranks of the educational and religious retainers who served the governing class and the needs of a complex society. In Paul's case that would have meant attaching himself to the house of a wealthy convert to Christianity and working within the community under his aegis. But for the most part Paul refused patronage and kept his independence by supporting himself.[10] Thus, in his profession and in his Christian ministry Paul chose to be a member of the lower classes, an artisan.

Though Paul's letters present him as an artisan, some facts about Paul's life suggest that he had connections with the upper classes and was more than an uneducated, powerless artisan. That he was a city dweller does not mean that he was educated or influential, though the city did not exlude the possibility as rural areas usually did. His letters, written in fundamentally good, but not highly literate Greek, testify that Paul received basic education in grammar. His familiarity with and interpretations of the Bible show that he had received a solid Jewish education.[11] It is likely that he spoke and read Hebrew and/or Aramaic. Paul, like many artisans in antiquity, travelled; as an artisan he could find employment in cities and large towns.[12] In the account of his life in Galatians, he says he persecuted the church of God. Acts locates this activity in Jerusalem, Judea, Palestine and southern Syria, but Paul's own letters leave this vague. Nor do the letters say why Paul had left his home in the

---

[7] Hock, *Social Context*, 37-42 and Meeks, *Urban*, 29.

[8] See Gerd Theissen, *The Social Setting of Pauline Christianity: Essays on Corinth* (Philadelphia: Fortress, 1982)

[9] See Meeks, *Urban*, for an extended analysis of Paul's urban context as a Christian preacher.

[10] Hock, *Social Context*, 50-59; Meeks, *Urban*, 27 and 202, n. 63.

[11] The claim in Acts that he had been a student of Gamaliel may be an exaggeration. See below.

[12] Hock, *Social Context*, 9 for the locations of artisans.

first place or what his relationship to Jewish authorities in Jerusalem and elsewhere were before he followed Jesus. Because he constructed the concise account of his life in Galatians 1-2 in order to defend his independence and the truth of his gospel, it is incomplete and slanted toward the point Paul wanted to make, that he was called by Jesus and that his gospel and his ministry are independent of any other apostle, especially those in Jerusalem. In recounting his early relations with followers of Jesus, Paul admits that he persecuted and tried to destroy the church of God (Gal 1:13). Here (see also 1:23), in Philippians and in 1 Cor 15:9 Paul makes a point of admitting he persecuted the church. He stresses his past hostile activity to show God's mercy toward him and the power of Jesus' revelation and call.

Of his life in Judaism Paul says enigmatically, "I advanced in Judaism above many of my own age among my people, being extremely zealous for my paternal traditions" (Gal 1:14). Paul does not say how or where he persecuted Christians nor does he describe how he was advanced and zealous beyond his fellows in relation to Judaism. Because Paul was involved in Judaism more than the ordinary and persecuted Christians, it is likely that he was involved with Jewish leadership, in Jerusalem or elsewhere, and that he had better than ordinary knowledge of Jewish traditions. This is not to claim that Paul was a rabbi (an anachronism so early in the first century) or that he was a community official. Since the divisions between classes were not sealed and especially since there was much downward mobility in addition to some upward mobility, that Paul would have been on the border of the upper and lower classes is quite possible. The fact that he is literate and learned in Jewish traditions argues that he received some education in addition to apprenticeship to a leather worker.

Paul's letters leave his social standing unclear, perhaps because his stress on Jesus' humility and death led him to deemphasize social standing as a criterion in the Christian community. Though Paul was a Pharisee, it is not clear how much education he had, how or where he made contact with the Pharisees, what if any group commitment he made as a Pharisee and what role he had in the Jewish community when he persecuted the early followers of Jesus.

Acts

In Acts Luke turns Paul into a highly educated, well connected and active Jewish Pharisee who belonged to the retainer class. According to Acts, Paul was a Roman citizen (25:11), and so must have come from a family which had at some time achieved distinction in the service of the empire and been part of the retainer or military classes. He had travelled to Jerusalem and had been educated by Gamaliel (22:3) and he had enough access to the high priest to ask for letters of introduction to the Jewish community in Damascus (9:1-2; 22:4-5; 26:12). He was involved enough with community leadership to take strong initiatives in opposing the new Jesus movement. In doing so he functioned as a low level community leader, dependent on the governing class. This portrait is very unlikely. Neither Paul's letters nor his activities suggest that he was a Roman citizen, that he was educated in Jerusalem or that he was a Jewish community leader. He does admit that he persecuted the Christians, but the type of persecution depicted in Acts is improbable. In Acts Luke depicts Paul as engaged in violent persecution, but this type of persecution is a late first century experience for the Christian community.[13] Paul's zeal for Jewish traditions would have led him to use persuasion as well as Jewish community legal procedures and sanctions to contain the influence of the new group of followers of Jesus. Christians were to be avoided and their teachings rebutted; Jews (including Jewish Christians) who continued to cause trouble would be subjected to community discipline and expulsion. This view is supported by Paul's letters according to which the Jewish synagogues of the diaspora used the same procedures on Paul, disciplining him five times with lashes (2 Cor 11:24) and otherwise opposing him (2 Cor 11:26) and expelling him.[14]

To summarize, Paul only once identifies himself as a Pharisee, and does so in a context which indicates that he led Jewish life according to the Pharisaic interpretation. The Pharisees had a following in Palestine and probably in the immediately sur-

---

[13]See the excellent study by Arland J. Hultgren, "Paul's Pre-Christian Persecutions of the Church: Their Purpose, Locale, and Nature," *JBL* 95 (1976) 97-111, esp. 107-109.

[14]See Hultgren, "Persecutions," 101-103 and 108-109.

rounding territories, including Tarsus which was close to Antioch in northern Syria. Paul's letters indicate that he knew the Bible well and could write, but they do not show whether he gained his education as a youth or after becoming a follower of Jesus. When Paul persecuted the early followers of Jesus, he probably derived his influence and any power he had from the Jewish governing class, either in Jerusalem or in local communities. What kind of influence and status he possessed within the Jewish community is very unclear. By occupation he was an artisan, and so lower class. Certainly, when he became a Christian, he lost any influence and status within Judaism, but gained status and power in the Christian community, a position which he protected fiercely, especially when his teaching authority and Christian behavior were at stake.[15] The one reference to Pharisees in Paul's letters does not provide any direct information concerning the Pharisees, except to indicate that Pharisees taught a particular Jewish way of life which was well known in Judaism. If the Pharisaic teaching sought to reform and strengthen the Jewish community by influencing other Jews to live in a certain way, then Paul, when he began to follow Jesus, understood the new way of life in Jesus to be an alternate mode of reforming Judaism and vigorously promoted it. Paul seems to have been a member of the lower classes with some links to the governing classes. His membership in the Pharisees may have been such a link. However, it is not clear that Paul, as a Pharisee, had gained any particular education or standing in the community.

[15]For a sociological study of power in the pauline communities, see Bengt Holmberg, *Paul and Power: The Structure of Authority in the Primitive Church as Reflected in the Pauline Epistles* (Philadelphia: Fortress, 1980). For social relations in the pauline community and world at large, see Norman R. Petersen, *Rediscovering Paul: Philemon and the Sociology of Paul's Narrative World* (Philadelphia: Fortress, 1985).

8

The Pharisees, Scribes and Sadducees in Mark and Matthew

INTRODUCTION

The gospels do not easily provide information for the historical understanding of the Pharisees, scribes and Sadducees. The gospels date from the last third of the first century and thus do not give first hand witness to what happened in the life of Jesus. They often project onto the life of Jesus later controversies between the Christian and Jewish communities and may simply reflect a later author's misunderstanding of traditions at his disposal and of Palestinian society. In all cases the gospel authors have woven Jesus' opponents into a dramatic narrative which is controlled by their purposes in writing the narrative rather than by a desire to faithfully reproduce the events of Jesus' life.[1] Thus the Pharisees, scribes and Sadducees undergo mutation for dramatic and theological purposes. Finally, all the gospels attack Jesus' opponents, who included almost all the Jewish leaders who appear in the narrative.

In the analysis of the gospels special attention will be paid to the social relations which bound villagers together in a small, face-to-face world, especially the honor system, patron client relations, coalitions and factions. Mark's literary presentation, the historical facts and general social patterns will to some

---

[1]See Elizabeth Struthers Malbon, "The Jewish Leaders in the Gospel of Mark: A Literary Study of Markan Characterization," *JBL*, forthcoming, for a thorough study of the use Mark makes of Jesus' opposition.

extent confirm and augment one another.

The theory of Markan priority is assumed in this treatment of Mark and Matthew (and Luke in the next chapter). Mark and Matthew are treated together because Matthew follows Mark fairly closely and changes him in ways which can be clearly explained by his view of Judaism and Jesus. Matthew's picture of the Pharisees, scribes and Sadducees is less distinct than Mark's and it is likely that Matthew has revised Mark to fit his literary and theological purposes without providing any new first hand information. Both Luke-Acts and John, to be treated in the next chapter, have significantly different pictures of the Pharisees and other Jewish leaders, pictures which are probably not based on first hand information but which do reflect their understandings of first century society and the relations of Jesus with Jewish leadership.

The Pharisees and scribes appear numerous times in both Mark and Matthew. By contrast, the Sadducees appear only once in Mark and three times in Matthew. Frequently the Pharisees, scribes and Sadducees are allied with other parts of Palestinian Jewish leadership, including the chief priests, the Herodians and the elders. Mark has a coherent and consistent picture of the Pharisees and other leadership groups which fits his understanding of Jesus' work and place in Palestinian society. Mark's traditions probably date to mid-first century Palestine and so give an indirect account of the early community's relations with Jewish leaders and perhaps some insight into Jesus' own conflicts with the leadership.[2] It should be noted that Mark's account of the Pharisees differs significantly from that of Josephus and his sources. Some of the contradiction may be explained by the different perspectives and interests of the authors, but the conflicts will require historical analysis at the end of this study. The same is true for the accounts given by the other evangelists.

[2]R. Bultmann, *The History of the Synoptic Tradition* (New York: Harper, 1963) 52-54, argued that many controversy stories originally circulated with unnamed opponents for Jesus, such as the people and their village leaders, and that the tradition tended to insert Pharisees, scribes, etc. Morton Smith, *Jesus the Magician* (New York: Harper, 1978), Appendix A: "The Pharisees in the Gospels," pp. 153-157, esp. 157, argues that the Pharisees are anachronistic in *all* passages. The question of whether the Pharisees were found in Galilee will be taken up in detail in ch. 12.

The Gospel of Mark

The Pharisees along with the scribes are the chief opponents of Jesus in Galilee; the chief priests, scribes and elders are his opponents in Jerusalem at the time of his death; the Sadducees appear only once. The social relations which bind these groups and Jesus together in coalition and conflict will be the main focus of this treatment. Since most commentators date Mark near the war with Rome (66-70), it is unlikely that Mark is reflecting the changes in Jewish leadership in the decades following the war and it is likely that he is reflecting something of the mid first-century situation, either through his own knowledge or the data in his traditions.[3] Even if Mark is using earlier traditions, it is not certain to what extent these traditions are based on accurate and sophisticated knowledge of Judaism. Since Mark often translates Hebrew or Aramaic terms and explains Jewish customs (e.g. 7:3-5) and since he rejects ritual purity outright (7:19), it is likely that his audience is mostly gentile in background and not familiar with Judaism.

Mark mentions the Pharisees a limited number of times, less often than Matthew. They occur alone in five cases, and in all instances they are in conflict with Jesus.[4] The scribes and Pharisees are mentioned together on two occasions when they are in conflict with Jesus (2:16; 7:1, 5).[5] The Pharisees are also linked with the Herodians twice (3:6; 12:13) in more political matters. The scribes are mentioned alone on seven occasions.[6]

---

[3]Martin Hengel, *Studies in the Gospel of Mark* (Philadelphia: Fortress, 1985) has defended Mark's presentation of the pre-70 tradition. However, if Mark is in Rome, as Hengel says, or if he is elsewhere and not familiar with pre-70 Palestinian Judaism as many hold, then he may be personally ignorant and dependent on his traditions. See Michael Cook, *Mark's Treatment of the Jewish Leaders* (Leiden: Brill, 1978) who argues that Mark is ignorant of the Palestinian situation and wrongly conflates two sources without understanding that the Pharisees and scribes are the same group.

[4]2:18; 2:24; 3:2; 8:11, 15; 10:2. Mark 3:2 says "they" were watching Jesus in the synagogue in order to accuse him. Context both before this story and at the end, where the Pharisees conspire with the Herodians against Jesus, indicates that the Pharisees are meant, at least in the Markan context.

[5]Michael Cook's contention *(Jewish Leaders)* that these instances are redactional is gratuitous. A textual variant in 9:11 also links the Pharisees with the scribes.

[6]Mark 1:22; 3:22; 9:11; 9:14; 12:28, 32; 12:35; 12:38.

They are linked with the chief priests and elders five times[7] and with just the chief priests an additional four times.[8] Finally, to round out the picture, the chief priests are mentioned alone five times.[9] The chief priests, scribes and elders occur together from chapter 8 on, especially in chapters 11-15 where they are concerned with the death of Jesus.[10]

The social class and status of the Pharisees, scribes and Sadducees in Mark and their relationships to society can be determined by their geographical location and the issues they deal with.

Location

PHARISEES

Mark places the Pharisees in Galilee on all occasions except one when the Pharisees and Herodians are sent to Jesus to entrap him in Jerusalem.[11] The Pharisees meet Jesus at Capernaum and other rural towns (3:2, 6; 7:1, 5) and in many, often indeterminate, places (2:18, 24; 8:11; 10:2). In contrast with Josephus, who shows the Pharisees as closely linked with the leadership in Jerusalem, Mark sees them as active only in Galilee. They do not lack alliances and connections with other groups, for they plot with the Herodians (3:6), join the scribes in conflict with Jesus, and have some scribes in their midst (2:16). They even appear in Jerusalem once, but this may be due to the literary arrangement of Mark.[12] This does not eliminate the

[7]8:31; 11:27; 14:43; 14:53; 15:1.

[8]10:33; 11:18; 14:1; 15:31.

[9]14:10; 15:3, 10, 11, 31. The chief priests and the whole sanhedrin are mentioned in 14:55. In addition, the high priest and his household are mentioned a number of times in the passion story.

[10]For a brief review of these patterns in the gospels, see A. F. J. Klijn, "Scribes, Pharisees, Highpriests and Elders in the New Testament," *NovTest* 3 (1959) 259-267.

[11]The Pharisees are in Galilee in 2:16, 2:18, 2:24, 3:2, 3:6, 7:1 and 5, 8:11, 10:2. They with the Herodians are in Jerusalem only in 12:13. They are described in 7:3 and 8:15 in a Galilean setting.

[12]In ch. 12, just before the arrest of Jesus, Jesus meets a series of his opponents: the Pharisees and Herodians (12:13), the Sadducees (12:18), and a friendly scribe (12:28). He

possibility of the Pharisees being active in Jerusalem, but it does render Mark's testimony uncertain.[13]

SCRIBES

The scribes appear both in Galilee and Jerusalem, but more often in Jerusalem. Comments which Mark makes about the scribes indicate that their teaching and their authority were generally known to the people, so they may have been active in both places. The scribes are found in Jesus' house in Capernaum where he is teaching (2:6) and on another occasion scribes from Jerusalem make charges against him in the same place (3:22). Some scribes from Jerusalem along with the Pharisees challenge Jesus in an indeterminate place (7:1, 5) and the scribes of the Pharisees also challenge Jesus once in his home in Capernaum (2:16). Scribes argue with his disciples after the transfiguration in an indeterminate place (9:14). In addition, the disciples refer to the teachings of the scribes in a Galilean context (1:22; 9:11) and the Galilean people contrast Jesus' authoritative teaching with that of the scribes (1:22), indicating that the teachings of the scribes are well known and well accepted in Galilee. In several cases the scribes either come from Jerusalem (3:22 and 7:1) or are found in the larger towns, such as Capernaum (2:6, 16; 3:22). Later in the narrative the scribes are located in Jerusalem and frequently associated with the priests and elders. They are mentioned with the chief priests and sometimes the elders in two of the passion predictions (8:31 and 10:33) and several times in the Jerusalem narrative.[14] As an educated leadership group, the scribes seem to be associated with large centers, either Jerusalem or major towns.

then concludes with an attack on the scribes (12:35-40) and implicitly on the Temple authorities, the priests, when he says that the Temple will be destroyed (13:1-2). It is likely that Mark brings the Pharisees (and possibly the Herodians) into this context to create a complete roster of Jesus' opponents just before the arrest and crucifixion.

13 Cook, *Jewish Leaders,* argues that the Pharisees in the early part of Mark and the scribes in the latter part are really the same group called by different names in different sources. His thesis presumes Rivkin's analysis of the Pharisees and depends on a rather arbitrary source analysis.

14 11:18, 27; 14:1, 43, 53; 15:1, 31.

OTHER LEADERS

To complete the survey, the chief priests and elders are mentioned only in Jerusalem and in connection with Jesus' death. The Herodians are mentioned with the Pharisees in 3:6 in Galilee and again in 12:13 (where they like the Pharisees may have been recruited into Mark's roster of Jesus' enemies).[15] The Sadducees are mentioned only once, in Jerusalem, in theological controversy with Jesus, as part of the roster of enemies.

Issues

PHARISEES

Further information concerning the nature and social position of the Pharisees and scribes can be deduced from the issues which they discuss with Jesus. The Pharisees dispute with him over fasting (2:18), sabbath observance (2:24 and 3:2) and divorce (10:2). The scribes and Pharisees dispute with him over purification of hands (7:1) and the scribes of the Pharisees question his eating with sinners (2:16). The Pharisees also question Jesus' authority by demanding a sign (8:11). In concert with the Herodians the Pharisees try to trap Jesus in a political matter, the question of Roman taxes (12:13), and they enter into a plot with the Herodians against Jesus.

Because the Pharisees in Mark have relationships with other groups in society, enter into a political alliance with the Herodians against Jesus (3:6) and with the Herodians put Jesus to the test at the instigation of the Jerusalem leaders (12:13), they act like a well connected political interest group, of which the

---

[15]Scholars have long argued about the Herodians. A survey of positions is given in H. H. Rowley, "The Herodians in the Gospels," *JTS* 41 (1940) 14-27 and in S. Sandmel, "Herodians," *IDB* 2:594-95. Rowley is most probably correct that they are people associated with Herod's court, either as officials, partisans or men of standing and influence allied with him. This fits well our theory that the Pharisees and Herodians also are "retainers" in Lenski's categories. W. J. Bennett, "The Herodians of Mark's Gospel," *NovTest* 17 (1975) 9-14 shows how the Herodians function literarily in the Gospels and suggests that they are a Markan creation. But Rowley's philological argument, drawn from Lieberman and Jouön, shows that adherents of Herod, in some form, are likely. This does not deny their literary function pointed out by Bennett.

scribes of the Pharisees (2:16) may be the Jerusalem representatives. Since their religious views are integral to the way Jews
lived in Palestine, they sought to control or influence, as much
as possible, the political, legal and social factors which might
determine the social practices and views of the community.

Jacob Neusner has argued that the New Testament polemic
against the Pharisees' concern with ritual purity, agricultural
tithes and sabbath observance accurately reflects their program
for Judaism in the first century.[16] These issues suggest to Neusner
that the Pharisees are primarily a religious sect or table fellowship
group and not a politically active force.[17] As we have seen in our
analysis of Jewish society, however, a group with sect-like
practices need not be cut off from political life since religion is
embedded in political society. Jerome Neyrey has analyzed all
Mark's comments concerning purity using Mary Douglas' anthropological studies to show that the purity rules in Mark function
as boundary setting mechanisms for the community.[18] Thus the
Pharisees are the defenders of a certain kind of community and
Jesus challenged the Pharisees' vision of community by attacking
their purity regulations concerning washing and food, as well as
sabbath practice. The effect of Jesus' teaching is to widen the
community boundaries and loosen the norms for membership
in his community. Jesus thus created a new community outside
their control and quite naturally provoked their protest and
hostility.[19]

Jesus and the Pharisees did not argue over theological issues
which were of interest to a limited number of Jews, but rather

[16]*From Politics to Piety* (Englewood Cliffs: Prentice-Hall 1973) ch. 4. He has also
shown that the dispute over cleaning the inside or outside of the cup in Mark 7 reflects a
genuine first century controversy over ritual purity in "'First Cleanse the Inside,'" *NTS*
22 (1976) 486-95. See ch. 10 for further discussion of Neusner's work.

[17]Further analysis of table fellowship and of other data on what kind of group the
Pharisees might have been will be presented in the chapter on rabbinic sources.

[18]Jerome Neyrey, "The Idea of Purity in Mark's Gospel," *Semeia* 35 (1986) 91-128.

[19]Joanna Dewey, *Markan Public Debate: Literary Technique, Concentric Structure,
and Theology in Mark 2:1-3:6* (SBLDS 48; Chico: Scholars, 1980) 120-121; 188-190,
argues that healing and eating are two issues that link the early chapters of Mark
together and connect to the ultimate condemnation of Jesus. She thus attributes the
function of these themes to Markan redaction. These literary conclusions do not address
or deny the traditional nature of the controversies over purity nor their probability as
first century issues between Jews and the Jesus movement.

competed for control over the community. The Pharisees were recognized leaders in the Galilean community, according to Mark. This means that they had high standing in the community and influence, if not power, with the people and other leaders of the community. Jesus, who was from a lower class artisan family, did not have the social standing, honor and influence to command respect as a teacher, as his return to Nazareth shows (6:2-3). Those who knew him dismissed him as a local carpenter without any community recognition of wisdom or power. His family is an ordinary one and his new claim to teach and to a special standing in the community is rejected out of hand.[20] Mark explains the embarrassing lack of acceptance in Nazareth by the proverbial saying that "a prophet is not without honor, except in his own country, and among his own kin, and in his own house" (6:4).[21] Jesus was excluded from the society of his own town but went on to attain new status, honor and influence in the other towns of Galilee through his own work and that of his followers (see the rest of Mark 6). This provoked the attack of the Pharisees and scribes over purity regulations and control of the community in ch. 7.

SCRIBES

The issues raised by the scribes in Mark center around Jesus' teaching authority. In two instances, when the scribes of the Pharisees confront Jesus and when the scribes who came from Jerusalem along with the Pharisees question him, the issues discussed match those raised by the Pharisees. The scribes of the Pharisees criticize Jesus because he eats with tax collectors and sinners (2:16) and the scribes from Jerusalem and the Pharisees question Jesus because his disciples do not ritually wash their hands before eating (7:1, 5). Such issues of table fellowship and ritual purity are typical of the questions raised by the Pharisees

---

[20]The competition for honor and community standing in antiquity required that anyone who claimed more prestige or authority than that recognized by the community should compete for that position and defeat anyone who challenged him.

[21]Lacking honor *(atimos)* is mentioned in the gospels only here and in Mt 13:57 and honor *(timē)* is used in the Johannine version of the saying (Jn 4:44). Lk 13:33 has another version of this saying. In Mt 27:6, 9 *timē* is used in its other meaning, price.

above. In the rest of the interaction between Jesus and the scribes, the issues center more around Jesus' authority for his teaching and activity than around sectarian-like rules.

In three places Mark's narrative reveals that the people and Jesus' disciples know and recognize the teachings of the scribes. When Jesus first teaches in the synagogue in Capernaum (1:21-28) the people are astonished at his teaching because he "taught them as one who had authority, and not as the scribes." (1:22). The scribes are the point of reference for Jewish religious teaching and Mark implies that they are the ordinary teachers with whom people are familiar. Jesus, who also teaches, is contrasted with them, especially because of the way he teaches, rather than the content of his teaching. Mark, who has just shown Jesus as commissioned by God at the Jordan, now presents Jesus as exercising that authority in the way he teaches. Later in the Gospel the disciples of Jesus quote the teaching of the scribes about the coming of Elijah (8:11) and Jesus, who accepts the teaching, explains that it has already been fulfilled (9:12-13). Finally, Jesus quotes the teaching of the scribes that the Messiah must be the son of David (12:35) and refutes this contention by Scriptural interpretation, to the delight of the crowd (12:36-37). In these three cases, the teaching of the scribes is well known and assumed to be the "norm" and the beginning point of discussion. Of course, Mark shows Jesus as superior to the scribes, but even his comparison presumes that the scribes are the norm.

In three encounters with scribes Jesus' or his disciples' authority is in question and on one of those occasions a scribe accepts Jesus teaching authority. In the first of the sequence of five controversy stories the scribes were sitting with a crowd in Jesus' house in Capernaum and questioned (in their hearts) Jesus' authority to forgive the paralytic's sins because only God can forgive sins (2:6). After Jesus' transfiguration, he found the scribes arguing with his disciples because they could not cure a possessed boy (9:14). Though the content of the argument is not spelled out, it probably concerned the disciples' claim to authority and power to do works which are beyond human capability and their failure to perform. Finally, in 12:28 a scribe, who had heard Jesus disputing with the Sadducees, was impressed with his answer and so asked him a friendly question of his own in order to enter into discussion with him. The scribe and Jesus agreed on the greatest commandment and Jesus said that the scribe was near the kingdom of God (12:28-34). In the first two cases the scribes are not in direct conflict with specific teachings of Jesus, but with his exercise of authority and power. In the last case the scribe is impressed with Jesus' teaching ability and authority and questions him as a disciple would question a master or a teacher his colleague.

The scribes are described in a polemical way when Jesus attacks them while he is in Jerusalem. As he completes his teaching and controversies, preparatory to his discourse on the end of Jerusalem and the world, Jesus warns his disciples to beware of the scribes because they seek social prominence, are economically oppressive and pretentious in prayer (12:38-40). The scribes are said to wear long robes, seek recognition in the market place and the best seats in the synagogue, devour widows' houses and recite long prayers for pretense. They are assumed to be socially prominent and politically powerful and condemned for their misuse of their station. This condemnation of the scribes comes at the climax of Jesus' verbal conflicts with his opponents and just before he is apprehended and executed by the Jewish and Roman authorities. The scribes, who "devour widows' houses," are contrasted with the poor widow who gives two coins to the Temple and is praised by Jesus. Mark identifies Jesus with those out of power and rejected by society since that describes Jesus' position exactly.

The attack on the scribes speaks to their other role in the Gospel of Mark, that of community leaders along with the chief priests and elders. These three groups are mentioned by Jesus as his adversaries who will kill him in the first of the passion predictions (8:31) and the chief priests and scribes are mentioned in the third prediction (10:33). While Jesus is in Jerusalem (chs. 11-15) the scribes are associated with the chief priests and sometimes the elders in seven passages.[22] In all cases they are part of the Jewish authority structure which seeks Jesus' death.

---

[22] 11:18, 27; 14:1, 43, 53; 15:1, 31.

SADDUCEES

The Sadducees appear only once in Mark, as part of a sequence of groups in Jerusalem who ask Jesus the final series of questions before the passion (12:18-27). The point of the controversy is the Sadducees' rejection of resurrection as a legitimate Jewish belief. Their position on resurrection is found also in Josephus, is repeated in the parallel passages in Matthew and Luke and brought up in Acts. In defending resurrection Jesus puts himself on the side of the Pharisees and scribes, as is recognized by the friendly scribe who is impressed with Jesus because he answered the Sadducees well (12:28).

More important to an accurate understanding of the Sadducees is what we do not learn about them. Though they are in Jerusalem, they are not said to be members of the governing class nor is the nature of their group or their social role explained. Mark, or the tradition he used, assumes that the Sadducees are known to the reader. It may be that a description such as Josephus gives is presumed. In view of a common misunderstanding in New Testament scholarship it must be emphasized that neither Josephus nor the New Testament claim that all or most of the chief priests, elders and other members of the governing class were Sadducees, only that Sadducees, however few or numerous, were mostly drawn from that class.

The Class and Status of Jewish Groups in Mark

The relationships and interests of the Jewish leadership groups are reasonably clear. The chief priests go to Pilate because they are clearly the dominant group in Jerusalem, especially in dealing with the Romans and the larger political and social issues of the Jewish community. They object to Jesus' large following among the people and their resultant loss of control over the community as a whole and they also fear disorder from the activities of an unauthorized teacher. Their concerns are mainly political and in these interests they are joined by the elders, probably the traditional leaders of the community who were senior members of prominent families, and by the scribes, who were, as we have already seen, recognized teachers in the community. Pilate sees the chief priests and scribes as Jesus' competitors and their dispute as factional strife motivated by envy. The scribes who are associated with the chief priests had some governing authority over the community, according to Mark.

This view of the scribes, chief priests and elders is consistent with what we know of ancient society. In Judean society under the Romans it is highly likely that the chief priests and prominent citizens functioned as the governing class, restricted in their power, but responsible for the community to the imperial government. The prominent citizens would have been heads of powerful and old families, leaders of groups in the community and others recognized as leaders because of their knowledge or function in the community.[23] In Mark the (some?) scribes are seen as leaders. In this capacity they might have had legislative, judicial and bureaucratic responsibilities. Such a role fits the scribes who were a literate group educated in Jewish law and customs. Such groups typically functioned in a variety of roles such as advisors, high officials, bureaucrats, judges, teachers and low level functionaries. Scribes were in principle members of the retainer class which aided and was dependent on the governing class. However, high ranking scribes would function as members of the governing class and might even reach independent power as members of that group.

The scribes and Pharisees are described in Mark as having many interests in common. They both confront Jesus concerning his teaching and they both object to Jesus' challenge to tradition. The matters brought up by these two groups reflect slightly different specific concerns. The Pharisees speak of Sabbath and food laws and the scribes argue about teaching authority. This suggests that the scribes are officially recognized and authoritative teachers in the community and the Pharisees are a group with a specific interpretation of certain laws and practices. Both scribes and Pharisees seek influence and resultant control among

---

[23]The local leaders active in the village disputes, misunderstandings and uprisings under the procurator Cumanus and his predecessor, Pilate, have a variety of designations in Josephus. For example, in the *War* 2.12.5-6 (237-243), Josephus refers to the magistrates *(archontes)* of Jerusalem, the notables *(gnōrimoi)* of Galilee, the eminent *(dunatoi,* powerful) Samaritans, the Jewish notables, including the high priest, and the high priest with persons of the highest eminence *(dunatōtatōn),* notables and the most distinguished *(epiphanestatous)* of the Samaritans. Later the notables of the Pharisees are among the leaders in Jerusalem in the *War* 2.17.5-6 (422-429).

the people as religious experts and in this quest they compete with Jesus.

Mark differs from Josephus in placing the Pharisees and their allies the scribes in Galilee as potent political and religious forces. Since Mark writes just before or after the war against Rome, he is not anachronistically reading the later Pharisees/rabbis back into Jesus' life. His traditions reflect at least the mid-first century and the experience of the early Christian community if not the experience of Jesus. Mark's placement of the Pharisees in Galilee will be historically assessed in chapter twelve. At this point a few observations on Galilee will guide our consideration of the other sources. Herod Antipas and then Agrippa ruled Galilee as client kings of the Roman empire. The chief priests and other Jerusalem authorities had no direct political control there. Galilee itself was not a uniform province, but divided into upper and lower Galilee by topography and tradition.[24] Galilee had several major towns which served as regional centers for tax collection and security, such as Sepphoris and Tiberias. In view of the complex social and political structure of Galilee, Jesus and his opponents in Galilee, the Pharisees, scribes, Herodians, etc., must be seen as part of the larger political struggle for control during the first century. Jesus' opponents are not independent religious authorities, but members of the retainer class, involved in community guidance and leadership. As such they probably had community standing and some official role in the community. They probably functioned as unofficial patrons and brokers for the people and perceived Jesus as a threat to their power and influence. All the actors in Mark played a minor role in the national drama, especially in Galilee which was far from the center of Jewish political power in Jerusalem and where Jerusalem's influence was attenuated. Galilee should not be pictured as cut off from Jerusalem, because both in Josephus and in the gospels officials come down to Galilee from Jerusalem. However, they do not have direct power and they must struggle for influence over the people and local leaders in each case.

In Mark's Gospel, as in Josephus' history of the first century,

---

[24]See chapter five, Josephus' account of his activities there, for tensions with Jerusalem and within Galilean leadership.

the Pharisees are a religious interest group with political goals, but they are not a dominant group. Mark's Pharisees are not based in Jerusalem, contrary to Josephus, but the dominant social pattern remains. The Pharisees exercise influence on the people and compete with Jesus for control. They enter into political alliances with the Herodians and are associated with the scribes, who have some political control and a presence in Jerusalem. Even if Mark does not know much about the historical Pharisees or scribes, as M. Cook argues,[25] he does reproduce the dominant social pattern of ancient society and places the Pharisees at the edges of the governing class. Because they are a political interest group which is out of power, they are not seen as active in Jerusalem. Though we cannot be certain that Mark and his sources give us a completely accurate picture of the Pharisees as a strong community force in Galilee in the early and mid-first century, their role in Galilean society is intrinsically probable.

The Gospel of Matthew

Matthew tends to insert the Pharisees into more situations than Mark, though not in as many as Luke. He also pairs the leaders differently from Mark. The Pharisees and Sadducees, a historically opposed and thus improbable pair according to some scholars, are mentioned in two contexts (3:7; 16:1, 6, 11, 12 [bis]). The pair scribes and Pharisees, not found in precisely that form in Mark,[26] appears in a large number of places (5:20; 12:38; 15:1; 23:2, 13 [14], 15, 23, 25, 27, 29).[27] In the latter part of Mark the chief priests and scribes are a frequent pair (10:33; 11:18; 14:1; 15:31), but in Matthew the chief priests and scribes occur only three times (2:11; 20:18; 21:15). In Matthew the chief priests, scribes and elders appear together only once (16:21), in contrast to Mark who has them several times, but the chief

---

[25] *Jewish Leaders.*

[26] See Mark 2:16 and 7:1 for the only two examples of the conjunction of scribes and Pharisees, but in neither case is the formulaic designation "scribes and Pharisees" used.

[27] The order scribes and Pharisees is reversed only in 15:1 because the Markan parallel (7:1) has them in that order.

priests and elders occur frequently (21:23; 26:3, 47; 27:1, 3, 12, 20; 28:12). Finally, Matthew has the scribes alone in five passages (7:29; 8:19; 9:3; 13:52; 17:10) and the Sadducees in 3:7 and ch. 16 as well as in the Markan parallel (Mark 12; Matt. 22).

These peculiar Matthean characteristics, which are generally but not exclusively attributed to his redaction of Mark and other traditional materials, prompt questions concerning Matthew's traditional sources and purposes in writing. Recent work on the role of the Jewish leaders in Matthew has been dominated by a redactional perspective which has emphasized the dramatic and theological use to which Matthew has put these leaders and doubted that either Matthew or the traditions he passes on provide any accurate, recoverable knowledge of these groups.[28] Three explanations of Matthew's procedure, which are not mutually exclusive, have been proposed. Some argue that Matthew's view of Jewish leaders, especially the prominence given to the Pharisees, reflects the polemical confrontation between the Matthean community and the post-70 Jewish community which was dominated by the Pharisees become rabbis.[29] Others suggest that the Matthean community had separated from the Jewish community and that at least some polemical sections and views of the Jewish leaders reflect earlier (pre-70) traditions.[30] Finally, some see Matthew's characterization of the Jewish leaders as a literary and theological device for identifying the Christian community in contrast to Judaism and explaining the rejection of Jesus by Judaism.[31] According to this last view, in Matthew's narrative the leaders form a united front against Jesus and need not be precisely distinguished from one another in themselves or by specific function in the community.

---

[28]Sjef van Tilborg, *The Jewish Leaders in Matthew* (Leiden: Brill, 1972) typifies this view.

[29]See W. D. Davies, *The Setting of the Sermon on the Mount* (Cambridge: Cambridge University, 1963) and R. Hummel, *Auseinandersetzung zwischen Kirche und Judentum im Matthäusevangelium* (München: Kaiser, 1963) for classic statements of this position.

[30]See, for example, D. E. Garland, *The Intention of Matthew 23* (SupplNovTest 52; Leiden: Brill, 1979) for ch. 23.

[31]See R. Walker, *Die Heilsgeschichte im ersten Evangelium* (Göttingen: Vandenhoeck, 1967).

Scribes

Since the scribes appear alone in only five passages in Matthew and three of them come from Mark, their role can be easily established. As in Mark, the scribes are noted for their teaching authority. Their teaching authority is contrasted with that of Jesus (7:29) and their teaching concerning Elijah (17:10) is alluded to as well known and accepted in Palestinian society. In another case the issue is a judgment about how to interpret and live the Jewish tradition, a matter which requires learning. When Jesus told the paralytic that his sins were forgiven, the scribes said within themselves *(eipan en autois)*, and not to Jesus, that Jesus was blaspheming (9:3). The scribes do not accept Jesus as an equal and enter into discussion with him. Rather, they treat him as a subordinate by judging him while ignoring him. Jesus must interject himself into their deliberations, challenge their social standing, learning and condemnation of him and finally vanquish them with his teaching.[32]

In two passages scribes are associated with Jesus positively. Once a scribe says that he will follow Jesus (8:19) and while Jesus' answer points out the difficulty of following Jesus ("Foxes have holes . . ."), the scribe is certainly of good will and whether he followed Jesus is left unclear.[33] This passage is derived from Q and it is likely that the Lukan version with a man *(tis)* telling Jesus he will follow him is original (Lk 9:57-58). Thus Matthew has attributed to a scribe, who addresses Jesus as teacher, a sincere desire to follow Jesus as a disciple. The scribe accepted Jesus as a fellow learned person and as a superior from whom he can learn. At the end of the parables chapter Matthew refers to scribes who have accepted Jesus as those who have been "trained for the kingdom of heaven" (13:52) and who have both old and new to teach. It is likely that he is referring to Christian scribes in his own day. In all cases the scribes are associated with

---

[32]See Malina, *New Testament World,* ch. 2 on honor, especially 29-39. By confronting the scribes and making their judgment public, Jesus opens a conflict with them. By publicly besting them in conflict Jesus gains honor and reputation in the eyes of the people and lowers the scribes' social standing.

[33]In Matthew only non-disciples address Jesus as teacher. However, the scribe expresses a simple desire to follow Jesus without qualification, in contrast to another potential disciple (8:21) who wants first to bury his father.

learning or discipleship and because scribes are accepted as teaching authorities in Jewish society, they can also function in that way in the Christian community if they are followers of Jesus.

One additional passage gives an insight into the role of scribes as legitimate teachers in Jewish and Christian society. In his polemic against the scribes and Pharisees in ch. 23 Matthew ironically refers to scribes who had been rejected in Jewish history and perhaps to Christian scribes rejected in the present (23:34): "I send you prophets and wise men and scribes, some of whom you will kill and crucify, and some you will scourge in your synagogues and persecute from town to town."[34] This saying is from Q and the parallel in Luke has prophets and apostles (11:49). It seems that the prophets are original to this saying and part of Q's polemic against the rejection of the prophets in Judaism. Both Matthew and Luke adapted the saying so that it fits Christian circumstances in the late first century. Matthew conceives of the leaders and teachers of Christianity, and of Judaism before, as prophets, wisemen and scribes. Thus, for Matthew the office of scribe remains an important part of the community, even if he does attack some scribes for their opposition to Jesus.

Scribes and Other Groups

In all other passages where the scribes appear in Matthew, they are associated with other groups, mostly chief priests or Pharisees. When associated with the chief priests, the scribes retain their role as learned members of the community but function more strongly as authoritative leaders and spokesmen for Judaism. In these contexts they are less political than in Mark. Several times in the passion narrative Matthew drops the scribes entirely or substitutes the elders.[35] The Jewish leaders are

---

[34]See van Tilborg, *Jewish Leaders,* 128-141, esp. 140-141.

[35]D. Senior, *The Passion Narrative According to Matthew* (Louvain: Leuven University, 1975) 24-25 says that the changes made in chs. 26-27 reflect Matthew's use of standard groupings. Here we pursue the question of the sociological nature and historical probability of Matthew's view of Jewish leadership.

often identified as the chief priests and elders, a pairing preferred by Matthew (21:23; 26:3, 47; 27:1, 3, 12, 20). In three of these passages, also found in Mark, the author of Matthew drops the scribes and leaves only the chief priests and elders. (21:23; 26:47; 27:1); in one passage (21:45) Matthew refers to the chief priests and Pharisees, rather than the chief priests, scribes and elders.[36] In another passage he substitutes elders for scribes as associates of the chief priests (26:3). (To complete the picture, in one passage he uses chief priests and elders on his own [27:3] and in two others he adds the elders to Mark's chief priests [27:12-20].) Matthew conceives of the central figures in the Jewish leadership as the chief priests and elders, a view which accords with Lenski's view of the ruling classes outlined previously.[37] The ruler, in this case Rome, is supported by a governing class typically made up of the most powerful land owners, community leaders and religious leaders. The Jewish chief priests and elders fit into this class perfectly. The governing class is supported by the retainer class, who have influence and sometimes power, but are not as important as the governing class. The scribes, as learned religious functionaries, would be members of the retainer class. The chief priests and elders have a large political involvement in seeking the death of Jesus as a troublemaker and the scribes play a subsidiary political role since they are more concerned with his teaching.

In only a few places are the scribes associated with the more political aspects of leadership. In two of the passion predictions Matthew follows Mark in naming Jesus' enemies in Jerusalem as elders, chief priests and scribes (16:21) and chief priests and scribes (20:18).[38] These opponents of Jesus threaten his physical safety and Matthew follows the Markan tradition in designating scribes as opponents. The scribes appear twice in the passion narrative as part of the complete leadership of Judaism. When

[36]In 12:12 Mark has "they," with the nearest antecedent the chief priests, scribes and elders in 11:27.

[37]It should be noted that in ch. 21 the chief priests are linked to the scribes (vs. 15), the elders (vs. 23) and the Pharisees (vs. 45). While Jesus is in Jerusalem, the chief priests are the constant opposition and the other groups of leaders are allied with them at different times.

[38]The middle prediction mentions only "men" in both Mark and Matthew (Mt. 17:22-23; Mark 9:31).

Jesus is brought before Caiphas, the high priest, Caiphas is joined by scribes and elders (26:57) who are identified as the council (sanhedrin) (26:59). When Jesus is on the cross, he is mocked by the chief priests, scribes and elders (27:41). In both cases, in which Matthew follows Mark, the priests, scribes and elders symbolize the complete leadership of Judaism condemning and rejecting Jesus. Once Matthew presents the scribes, along with the chief priests, as Temple officials who challenge Jesus (21:15) concerning the appropriateness of the people's designation of him as son of David; implicitly they attack the legitimacy of Jesus as a popular leader.[39] Jesus has aroused the interest of the learned religious leadership because his new faction threatens their status and influence. Matthew is consistent in the view of scribes he projects into the infancy narrative where Herod assembled the chief priests and scribes to inquire where the Messiah was to be born (2:4). This scene is sociologically correct, though the stories are not historical. The ruler consults them because they are members of the retainer class entrusted with responsibility for the religious traditions and are available to advise him. The narrative assumes that the scribes, as well as the chief priests, possess learning, authority and social prominence.

In summary, Matthew's understanding of the scribes, when he refers to them without the Pharisees, differs somewhat from Mark's, but is not greatly different from what one would expect. The scribes are associated with learning; as learned men they have an elevated standing in the community and in association with the chief priests they are consulted by those in power and exercise some authority and community control. However, in contrast to Mark, Matthew does not present them as a major force in the events leading up to Jesus' death and consequently they are less politically involved than the scribes in Mark. This is probably because Matthew knows of Christian scribes and has a fundamentally positive view of scribalism. Only when scribes are specifically opposed to Jesus are they evil.

The scribes are associated with Jerusalem; they appear alone in Galilee only in the cure of the paralytic (9:1) and in the case of the scribe who wants to follow Jesus (8:19). (They appear with

---

[39]Jesus is not a legal or socially established leader, but a reputational leader. See Malina, *Christian Origins,* 143-153.

the Pharisees a number of times in Galilee, as will be seen below.) As in Mark, their teachings are alluded to as if known by the people (7:29; 17:10) and so they are assumed to have had contact with the people in Galilee somehow. Matthew has a couple of passages where scribes are treated positively (8:19; 13:52; 23:34) as does Mark (12:28), but generally they are opponents. Matthew's emphasis on the scribes' interpretation of the Bible and authoritative teaching of law has obvious links with scribal practices in the Near East (see ch. 11).

Scribes and Pharisees

In several passages Matthew eliminates Mark's scribes when they are opponents of Jesus and replaces them with Pharisees.[40] Mark's unusual category of the "scribes of the Pharisees" (Mk 2:16) is regularized into Pharisees (9:11). This is proper because the occasion, a challenge over Jesus' eating with sinners, fits the Pharisaic agenda of table fellowship and ritual purity. Mark's "scribes who came down from Jerusalem" and said that Jesus did his works by Beelzebul (3:22) become Pharisees in both of Matthew's versions of the story (9:34; 12:24). The group challenging Jesus in the Temple before his passion and wishing to arrest him (the chief priests, scribes and elders in Mark 11:27 and 12:12) becomes the chief priests and elders in Mt 21:23 and chief priests and Pharisees in 21:45.

Mark's friendly scribe, who asks the question concerning the greatest commandment, is transformed into an unfriendly lawyer who is a Pharisee and who introduces the question at the instigation of the Pharisees as one final test (22:34-40). The contrast with Mark's friendly scribe is striking because Mark has the scribe at the climax of a series of questions from various Jewish factions, the Pharisees, Sadducees and then scribe, and ends on a positive note with the great commandment. Matthew stresses conflict in his Jerusalem section and so eliminates this note of harmony and replaces the friendly scribe with a typically hostile Pharisee. There is one exception to Matthew's tendency

---

[40]Luke inserts the Pharisees into the material even more than Matthew.

to turn scribes into Pharisees. Matthew changes Mark's Pharisees who ask for a sign from heaven (Mk 8:11) into some of the scribes and Pharisees (12:38).

In summary usually the scribes are omitted and the Pharisees added to passages where there is confrontation with Jesus. The Pharisees are seen by Matthew as more active opponents of Jesus than the scribes. Though the scribes remain as opponents, their role both as contestants against Jesus and as Jerusalem leaders is restricted.

The scribes and Pharisees are joined together by Matthew on four occasions, in two conflict stories and in two polemics. In these four incidents, scribes and Pharisees are a set group which represents Judaism through its leadership and no clear distinction is made between the two groups. In the first polemic, the author of Matthew has Jesus summarize the requirements for the kingdom of God in the Sermon on the Mount with the saying: "Unless your righteousness exceeds that of the scribes and Pharisees, you will never enter the kingdom of heaven (5:20)."[41] The scribes and Pharisees are presented as the pious and zealous official representatives of Judaism, whose practice and interpretation of the Bible may be contrasted with Jesus' interpretation of how Christians and especially Christian leaders should lead life in the second generation of Christianity.[42] In the background of Matthew's polemic against the scribes and Pharisees are the Jewish and Christian communities in Matthew's day. The earlier followers of Jesus and of the Pharisees and scribes are conceived of as competing groups, each with their own teachings, practice and identity, a situation similar to that of the Matthean community a generation later.

The second polemic is the greater part of ch. 23 in which Jesus rails against "scribes and Pharisees, hypocrites" (23:13, 15, 16, 23, 25, 27, 29).[43] Contrary to the tone of the chapter, the

---

[41]For a thorough presentation of the arguments for the redactional nature of 5:20, see John P. Meier, *Law and History in Matthew's Gospel* (AnBib 71; Rome: Pontifical Biblical Institute, 1974) 108-119.

[42]Meier, *Law,* 111-112. Note that Matthew consistently differentiates the crowd or people from the leaders. The crowd responds favorably to Jesus and is treated positively but the leaders are universally negative in response to Jesus and in presentation by Matthew.

[43]23:14 is rejected by most textual critics. It is missing from many manuscripts,

scribes and Pharisees are introduced with a pre-Matthean saying in which they are acknowledged to be the official interpreters of Biblical law who must be obeyed (23:2-3). Such approbation of the scribes and Pharisees is contrary to much of what Matthew teaches and so the author moves quickly to attack their failure to practice Judaism sincerely, guide others to live Judaism correctly, interpret the Bible correctly and attend to the major principles of the law and Jewish way of life. They are used as negative examples for how a community leader should act (23:4-7) and contrasted with Christian leaders who should not use titles and should be characterized by lowliness (23:8-12).[44]

Matthew pairs the Pharisees and scribes without regard for any differences in their interests and functions in chapter 23, in contrast to Luke who carefully separates the woes against the Pharisees and lawyers so that they are condemned for failings appropriate to their respective activities in society (11:37-52). Both groups are charged with being hypocrites and a series of examples of hypocrisy are assembled from the tradition to substantiate the case. Scribes and Pharisees are seen as corrupt leaders who reject God and fail to lead the people properly. Matthew has provided a traditional list of improper attitudes and activities with which he accuses both the opponents of Jesus and the adversaries of his own community, both internal and external. The list is so polemical and the Pharisees and scribes so identified with one another that little reliable historical information can be gleaned from it.

The competition between Jesus and other Jewish groups becomes explicit in the two conflict stories. The scribes and Pharisees address Jesus as teacher and challenge him for a sign, presumably to authenticate his teaching authority and show the source of his power (12:38).[45] The challenge by the scribes and Pharisees is preceded by a passage (thematically similar to 3:7-

---

interrupts the topical arrangement of the woes and increases the number of woes from seven to eight.

[44]See Garland, *Matthew 23,* 53-54.

[45]Matthew has a second version of this challenge in 16:1 in which the Pharisees and Sadducees challenge Jesus. Mark has the Pharisees only (8:11) and Luke has indeterminate people (11:16, 29). It is likely that there were two versions of this story, one in Mark and one in Q.

10, John the Baptist's polemic against the Pharisees and Sadducees) in which Jesus addresses them as a brood of vipers and refers to their fruits. In another conflict story the Pharisees and scribes clash with Jesus over purity rules (15:1). The story and the order of the opponents (Pharisees before scribes, here only in Matthew) comes from Mark 7:1. Mark has only the scribes come from Jerusalem because he does not associate the Pharisees with Jerusalem; Matthew does to some extent so both Pharisees and scribes are said to come from Jerusalem. Thus, Matthew sees the Pharisees as official representatives of Judaism to a greater extent than Mark. In this passage the Pharisees and scribes defend the tradition of the elders (*tēn paradosin tōn presbuterōn*) and Jesus defends the more important commandments of Gòd. Even though Pharisees and scribes are joined in a defense of the tradition, the Markan and Matthean association of the Pharisees with purity laws appears in a redactional passage at the end of the dispute (15:12) when Jesus' disciples warn him that he has scandalized the Pharisees (the scribes are not mentioned).[46] The disciples' warning implies that the Pharisees have standing in the community and that to offend them is dangerous.

In the four passages where scribes and Pharisees are combined, they join forces to oppose Jesus (or are pictured as a single group of Jewish leaders). The distinction between their interests found in Mark, authority for the scribes and purity, food, sabbath rules for the Pharisees, is obscured in places. But passages such as 15:12, in which the scribes are dropped in a discussion of purity, show that the author of Matthew knows and maintains, albeit imperfectly, the distinction between the Pharisees and scribes, a distinction which will become clearer in the passages where Pharisees are treated alone or with other groups.

Pharisees and Sadducees

In two places Matthew has what many have considered the unlikely combination of Pharisees and Sadducees uniting to

---

[46]See van Tilborg, *Jewish Leaders,* 99-104.

oppose Jesus.[47] Commentators have cited these passages as evidence that Matthew lumps all Jewish groups and sees no distinctions. But it is possible and even probable that the Pharisees and Sadducees, as interest groups within Judaism, might have common interests in how Judaism was lived and might unite against a new faction centered around Jesus.

In the first instance John the Baptist attacks the Pharisees and Sadducees who come to him for baptism with a standard warning of judgment and an exhortation to bear good fruit (3:7-10). Luke has John address the *people* and probably is following the text of Q, but, since Matthew favors the crowd, he has inserted the Pharisees and Sadducees as the object of John's attack. Matthew presumes that the Pharisees and Sadducees are well known Jewish groups (as does Josephus) and part of the Jewish leadership which articulates and promotes a view of Jewish life in competition with Jesus and John. Their presence to be baptized is not taken seriously because John immediately attacks them as a brood of vipers (see 23:33 where the scribes and Pharisees are addressed this way).

The Pharisees and Sadducees are also seen as teachers who are in competition with Jesus when they ask Jesus for a sign (16:1-12). Jesus, building on the symbol of bread in the feeding of the five thousand (ch. 15), warns his disciples about the leaven of the Pharisees and Sadducees which is interpreted as the teaching of the Pharisees and Sadducees. In Mark the leaven is that of the Pharisees and Herod (8:15) and its meaning is not specified. In Luke it is the leaven of the Pharisees (12:1) which is hypocrisy. Matthew uses both leading groups in Judaism, the Pharisees and Sadducees, as symbols for erroneous teachers who are in conflict with Jesus.

The Pharisees

Matthew expands the role of the Pharisees as opponents of Jesus, in comparison with Mark. The Pharisees are the most constant opposition to Jesus in Galilee and are concerned with

[47]Mark and Luke have the Sadducees only once in their gospels, when the Sadducees question Jesus concerning resurrection (Mark 12:18-27; Luke 20:27-40).

the same agenda as Mark's Pharisees, sabbath observance, food rules and purity.[48] The Pharisees in Matthew have a wider role and are less distinct from the scribes than in Mark. They challenge Jesus' authority as a religious and social leader by assaulting its sources (9:32-34; 12:22-30) and argue with him concerning divorce (19:3-9 in Judea). In chs. 21-22 after Jesus attacks the Pharisees with a series of parables which they perceive as directed against them (21:45-46), they plot against Jesus (22:15). Thus they are active in the Jerusalem leadership, in contrast to Mark's Pharisees. The hostility of the Pharisees brackets the crucifixion, in which they take no direct part. A lawyer of the Pharisees asks the last hostile question (22:34-35) and the Pharisees join the chief priests in asking for a guard for Jesus' tomb (27:62-65). The Pharisees are not only part of the local leadership whose influence over the people and power over social norms are being challenged and diminished by Jesus; they are also in direct contact with the more powerful forces of the Jerusalem leadership.

A review of some passages will bring out Matthew's particular view of the Pharisees. Jesus disputes with the Pharisees (and John the Baptist's disciples) concerning the importance of food rules. After the call of Levi the Pharisees challenge Jesus' disciples because Jesus eats with unclean people (9:6-13).[49] Jesus' answer appeals to righteousness, understood in the new way presented in Matthew, as the ground for his eating with sinners and still remaining acceptable, that is, honorable.[50] Jesus and the Pharisees are in conflict over the community boundaries and the criteria for acceptance. Factional conflict over boundaries is evident in the next incident in which John the Baptist's disciples challenge Jesus because his disciples do not fast the way they and the Pharisees fast (9:14-17). Again, food rules are determinative for the behavior and identity of groups within

---

[48]9:6-13; 9:14-17; 12:1-14.

[49]Matthew regularizes Mark's unique group, the scribes of the Pharisees (Mark 2:16; Mt. 9:11), into Pharisees because purity concerns are normal to them. Luke 5:30 changes Mark's odd phrase into the Pharisees and their scribes.

[50]Leland J. White, "Grid and Group in Matthew's Community: The Righteousness/ Honor Code in the Sermon on the Mount," *Semeia* 35 (1986) 61-90.

Judaism.[51] Jesus' followers are different from the Pharisees, the followers of John the Baptist and the later Christian community because they do not fast.[52] Jesus and his followers are more part of society in this story and the effect of the story is to change the social rules so that fasting is contingent on Jesus, the arbiter of all rules.

Matthew's Pharisees are also concerned with the source of Jesus' power in two versions of the healing of a dumb demoniac (9:32-34 and 12:22-30). In Mark 3:22 it is scribes who come from Jerusalem who challenge Jesus' authority, but Matthew blurs the distinction.[53] The accusation that one's rival is possessed is typical of factional disputes and struggles for influence and social status. Such claims are a type of witchcraft accusation used by groups which are trying to maintain their boundaries and identities against a more powerful, outside social force. In this case Judaism is struggling to maintain itself within the Roman empire. Such a concern also underlies the two conflicts over sabbath observance (plucking grain and curing the man with the withered hand) which are taken over from Mark in 12:1-14.

Though Matthew eliminates the political connections of the Pharisees with Herod and the Herodians in Galilee, he pictures them as a secondary political force in Jerusalem. When the Pharisees plot how to destroy Jesus (12:14), Matthew omits the Herodians from their plotting (cf. Mark 3:6) and later Matthew substitutes the Sadducees for Herod in the saying about the leaven (Mark 8:15; Mt. 16:6). But, as Jesus enters Judea (ch. 19), the Pharisees explicitly test Jesus and take a more aggressive stance toward him by plotting and making alliances with others. The first test concerns the lawfulness of divorce, another issue which is typical of the Pharisees' agenda. The increased hostility of the chief priests and Pharisees is met, in chs. 21 and 22, with a

---

[51]In Mark the people ask Jesus about fasting (2:18) and in Luke "they" (5:33), presumably the Pharisees and their scribes from the previous incident (5:30), ask him.

[52]A minority religious interest group usually fasts to appeal to God for reversal of its oppressed status and to seek group identity through pious practices which mark it off from others. See Bruce Malina, *Christian Origins,* ch. 9 for a study of fasting, esp. p. 202. But for the disciples, Jesus is with them and gives them a special standing before God and strong identity in Jesus.

[53]In Luke some of the people challenge Jesus (11:15).

series of parables attacking them for not believing in Jesus. In 21:45-46 the chief priests and Pharisees perceive that the vineyard parable is about them. At the end of the series of parables attacking Jews for unbelief in chs. 21-22 Matthew concludes that "the Pharisees went and took counsel how to entangle him in his talk" (22:15). As a result of their plotting, they send their disciples with the Herodians to ask Jesus about paying tribute to Caesar. The presence of the Herodians signals a different type of conflict between the Pharisees and Jesus, one less factional and more political. It should be noted that in ch. 21 the chief priests are linked to the scribes (vs. 15), the elders (vs. 23) and the Pharisees (vs. 46). While Jesus is in Jerusalem, the chief priests are the constant center of political opposition to Jesus and the other groups of leaders are allied with them at different times. Matthew includes the Pharisees among the groups plotting against Jesus in Jerusalem, contrary to Mark who sees them almost exclusively as a force in Galilee.

Matthew's sharpening of the political opposition in Jerusalem is clear in the question concerning the greatest commandment. Mark's friendly scribe is changed into an unfriendly lawyer who is a Pharisee and who introduces the question at the instigation of the Pharisees as one final test (22:34-40). The contrast with Mark's friendly scribe is striking because Mark has the scribe at the climax of a series of questions from various Jewish factions, the Pharisees, Sadducees and then scribe, and ends on a positive note with the great commandment. Matthew ends on a note of hostility and continues that tone into the rest of the chapter and the great polemic against the scribes and Pharisees in ch. 23 (treated above). For Matthew Jesus concluded his conflicts with the Pharisees, his major opponents (and with all others as well, since no one dared ask him any more questions) by stating the main teaching of his program, the love commandment (22:34-40), and by establishing his own status as messiah. (22:41-46). Jesus is depicted as victorious over his opponents in the sphere of factional dispute, challenge and riposte. He cannot be overcome by verbal conflict and his status as teacher and honored leader who knows the law and interprets it authoritatively is established. He can only be overcome by physical, political power in the hope that his influence will be negated.

The passion narratives in Mark and Matthew are alike in that the Pharisees do not have a role in the accusations and judicial proceedings against Jesus. Matthew differs from Mark in having the Pharisees active in Jerusalem before Jesus' arrest (above) and after his death when the chief priests and Pharisees appeal to Pilate for guards at Jesus' tomb so his disciples will not steal his body and claim he is risen (27:62-65). It is expected that the chief priests deal with Pilate, but anomalous that the Pharisees accompany them rather than the elders or scribes. However, the point at issue, resurrection, fits perfectly the Pharisees' theological position and explains why Matthew used them in this story. The chief priests' position on resurrection is not known,[54] but we may assume that they were interested in quieting the crowd and putting Jesus behind them. The chief priests' political interests are clear when they (without mention of the Pharisees) bribe the guards to change their account of how the tomb came to be empty (28:11-15).

Class and Status of Pharisees, Scribes and Sadducees in Matthew

Matthew places the Pharisees both in Galilee and in Judea, in contrast to Mark who restricts them almost exclusively to Galilee. In his view they dogged Jesus footsteps everywhere. They were sometimes allied with officials in Galilee and Jerusalem, but most often they were allied with the scribes. For Matthew both the scribes and Pharisees were the learned groups par excellence. The Pharisees' and scribes' specific agendas are not as sharply defined and differentiated as they are in Mark though the same general topics are covered, that is, sabbath observance, food laws, ritual purity, and Jesus' teaching authority. The scribes appear in Jerusalem with the chief priests, though less often than in Mark. In Galilee, as in Mark, they are less constant and powerful members of the leadership of Judaism than the Pharisees.

As in Mark, both the scribes and Pharisees seem to be

---

[54] Many assume the chief priests were Sadducees and did not believe in resurrection, but we have no firm evidence identifying all the chief priests as Sadducees.

members of the retainer class who served the governing class of the nation (that is, those with wealth and direct political power) and allied themselves with them and other groups to promote their own programs for Judaism. In Galilee, they were not the top level of leadership, but influential in the local village leadership, according to Matthew's account. They were a middle level of leadership between the governing class and people and sometimes acted as brokers for the people with their higher contacts. Whether they were themselves paid officials is unclear, though the Pharisees seem to be such and the scribes by their very title probably were. The Sadducees are hardly mentioned. Matthew puts them in alliance with the Pharisees on a couple of occasions. This is possible in the shifting coalitions of Jewish political and religious life, but no hard proof of such an alliance can be derived from Matthew.

It is clear that to Matthew, as well as to Mark and Josephus, the Pharisees and Sadducees were well known groups in first century Judaism. Each had certain teachings for which it was noted and some influence and authority in the community. Matthew sometimes favors the scribes since he wishes to promote a certain kind of acceptance of Jewish law among Christians and supports the office of Christian scribe. But, the scribes are also opponents of Jesus and part of the political alliance against him. The Pharisees are the day to day opponents of Jesus par excellence. They oppose his teachings on sabbath, purity and other issues and they try to destroy his reputation and influence with the people. As in Mark, the exact roles of the Pharisees in society are not clear, but in Matthew they are a constant presence in Galilee and they are a minor force in Jerusalem. We know little about the Sadducees because of lack of evidence.

Many have charged that Matthew had no knowledge of Jewish society in Jesus' time and was projecting the post-Jamnia situation of Judaism and Christianity back on the life of Jesus. This position is most probably overstated. The social positions and functions assigned to the scribes and Pharisees, and also the Sadducees, chief priests and elders, are sociologically probable and fit first century Jewish society as we know it from Josephus, other New Testament books and later rabbinic sources. The lines which marked off the scribes and Pharisees from other groups and from each other have become somewhat blurred, but the groups are not simply identified with one another.[55] It is likely that Matthew was working with older traditions and lacked a lively appreciation of the exact nature and social role of the Jewish groups. Consequently, he is not totally consistent in his portrayal of Jewish leadership and opposition to Jesus. But, it does not seem that he is reading the late first century situation back into the life of Jesus on a grand scale.[56] The opposition of the scribes and Pharisees to Jesus is reasonable and expected, for they and the Jesus' movement were leadership forces trying to shape Jewish life and piety and trying to defend Jewish society from the many non-Jewish political and social pressures which surrounded it. Matthew's placement of the Pharisees in Jerusalem and linking of them with Sadducees is not found in Mark. Whether Matthew was basing himself on reliable historical knowledge or just meeting the dramatic requirements of his narrative is unclear. Josephus places the Pharisees in Jerusalem, so their presence is not improbable. The conflicts between the Pharisees and Sadducees have been overdone by some scholars to the point where their alliance is thought to be impossible. But both groups were varieties of Judaism and contestants for power within the same system, not mortal enemies. Finally, the Pharisees' presence and influence in Galilee is derived from Mark and not found in Josephus. But Josephus was not interested in village life; he did note that the Pharisees were very popular and influential among the people and Matthew's sketch of them is consistent with this. A final judgment on the probability of Pharisees in Galilee will be reserved for chapter twelve.

---

[55]The Gospel of John merges all opponents into the Pharisees much more thoroughly than Matthew.

[56]Matthew is usually said to derive from Antioch in Syria or from east of Antioch, but the evidence for this is slim. If Matthew is in contact with Pharisees after 70 A. D. or has traditions concerning them, his gospel may derive from Galilee and reflect the (continuing?) presence of Pharisees after the destruction of the Temple.

9

The Pharisees, Scribes and Sadducees in Luke-Acts and John

The Pharisees, scribes and Sadducees appear very differently in Luke-Acts and John from the way they appear in Mark and Matthew. The Pharisees are independent leaders, essentially part of the governing class in Galilee and in John and Acts they have power in Jerusalem as well. The scribes do not appear in John and are indistinct from the Pharisees in Luke. In none of the works do we learn much about the Sadducees, beyond their rejection of resurrection.

Luke

The Gospel of Luke is notable for adding the Pharisees a number of times.[1] Many have claimed that the author has a less hostile attitude toward the Pharisees both in the gospel and especially in Acts.[2] The situation is not simple, however, for in the gospel Luke inserts hostile Pharisees into several situations but removes them from some places where Mark and Matthew portray them as hostile.[3] Whether Luke is less hostile to the

---

[1] In the gospel Luke increases the number of mentions of the Pharisees as follows: alone 7:36; 13:31; 14:1; 16:14; 17:20; 18:10-14; with scribes 11:53; with lawyers or teachers of the law 5:17; 7:30; 14:3.

[2] See J. A. Ziesler, "Luke and the Pharisees," *NTS* 25 (1978-79) 146-157 for a recent study of the problem.

[3] Jack T. Sanders, "The Pharisees in Luke-Acts," in *The Living Test: Essays in honor*

Pharisees will not be our main concern here. It is clear that Luke is not unreservedly friendly toward the Pharisees and has his own specific and limited complaints about them.[4]

A brief survey of Luke's view of the Pharisees, scribes, lawyers and Sadducees will precede a more detailed analysis. Some aspects of the Pharisees in Luke-Acts are unique. Three times Jesus dines with Pharisees.[5] The Pharisees are community leaders (14:1), involved with wealth (16:14) and politically active and informed (13:31). Though Luke follows Mark in locating the Pharisees in Galilee and not in Jerusalem, they are more ubiquitous and powerful than in Mark or Matthew. Along with the scribes, they are a leadership group with power and wealth in the Galilean villages (cf. 5:17-26, 30-32; 6:7-11; 11:37-53; 14:1-3; 15:2). Finally, the Pharisees seem sympathetic to Jesus and Christians on several occasions (Lk 13:31; Acts 5:34-39; 23:6-9). Acts especially treats the Pharisees well because the Pharisees accept resurrection (even though they don't accept Jesus).[6] Secondly, Jesus and his followers, who were presented as a group over against Judaism in the Gospel, are now seen (along with Judaism) as a small part of the larger and more diverse Greco-Roman world. Finally, the positive view of some Pharisees toward Christianity and one reference to Christian Pharisees (Acts 15:5) fit Luke's theme of continuity between Judaism and the church.

Luke's presentation of the Pharisees and other Jewish leaders is part of a theologically motivated, literary inversion of ordinary society. The leaders of the Jews, the rich, the other established citizens, and sometimes Israel itself are pictured as rejecting Jesus and thus rejecting God and ultimately losing out on salvation. By contrast, the poor, sinners, outcasts like tax collectors and non-Jews accept Jesus and salvation from God and become Israel. This new community is gradually outlined

of Ernest W. Saunders, (eds.) D. Groh and R. Jewett (Lanham/NY/London: Univ. of America, 1985), pp. 141-188, esp. 149-154.

[4]Luke T. Johnson, *The Literary Function of Possessions in Luke-Acts* (SBLDS 39; Chico: Scholars, 1977) 116-117 correctly cautions that Luke's friendliness to the Pharisees should not be assumed.

[5]7:36; 11:37; 14:1.

[6]Sanders, "Pharisees," 182-187, concludes that because the Pharisees reject Jesus Luke judges that they are not and cannot be true Christians.

and formed in the narrative and the Pharisees, scribes and other leaders serve this overarching narrative theme.[7]

From a sociological viewpoint, the Pharisees function as rich and powerful patrons of the peasants within the village society and as brokers for the peasants in their relations with the outside world. Luke's objection to them is that they do not care for the poor who depend on them and have a claim on their patronage, especially their generosity and reciprocal, just relations. Luke also complains that the poor, because they are judged to be unclean and outsiders to the social order, are deprived of justice. The Pharisees' use of purity regulations to maintain social order leads to unjust relationships. In response Luke defines true uncleanness as a moral, not ritual, deficiency and thus opens Christianity's group boundaries to the outcasts, Gentiles and sinners.[8]

Because the Pharisees are the key opposition group for Luke, the scribes are less prominent. They occur alone in Luke-Acts only in two gospel passages (20:39, 46). Otherwise, they are associated with other leaders, namely the Pharisees in Galilee and the chief priests and elders in Jerusalem. Luke also introduces a new group of opponents, the lawyers *(nomikoi)*. This group, often identified with the scribes, should be understood as a group learned in and involved with law, not as legal advisors and advocates in the modern mode. Finally, the designation "teacher of the law" is used on two occasions (Lk 5:17; Acts 5:34).

The Sadducees appear in the gospel once, questioning Jesus about resurrection (cf. Mark 12:18-27). In Acts they appear several times as a party connected to the high priests and, as in the gospel, they are characterized by not believing in resurrection (Acts 4:1; 5:17; 23:6-8).

These materials shall now be subjected to a literary, historical and sociological analysis to discover the social class and status of these groups, their roles and functions in society and their relationships to other groups. Luke-Acts most directly shows us

[7]Johnson, *Possessions,* 112-115; 140 and passim.

[8]This description of the Pharisees in Luke is indebted to the unpublished manuscript by Halvor Moxnes of Oslo, provisionally entitled "The Pharisees were Lovers of Money: Social and Economic Relations in Luke's Gospel."

how Luke and his sources envisioned the social fabric of Jewish society in the empire; its value as a historical source is debatable.

The Gospel

In comparison with Mark, Luke more uniformly makes the Pharisees the Galilean opposition to Jesus and disconnects them from politics. In the early sequence of conflict stories (Lk 5:17-6:11) Luke inserts the Pharisees into the story of the paralytic (5:17, 21). In addition, Luke makes explicit their presence in the story of the man with the withered hand (6:7). In all the other disputes, the Pharisees appear in the stories just as they did in Mark. Luke regularizes Jesus' opposition and sees the Pharisees as the key and central opponents to Jesus. However, he differentiates among the Pharisees and has only *some* of them challenge Jesus concerning the plucking of grain (6:2).

Significantly, Luke separates the Pharisees from the Herodians. At the end of this sequence of conflict stories (6:11), Luke does not charge that the Pharisees and Herodians are plotting how to destroy Jesus, as does Mark (3:6). He refers vaguely to "they" (the closest antecedent is the scribes and Pharisees in 6:7) and says they were furious with Jesus and discussed what they might do to Jesus. Luke also eliminates the Pharisees from the other passage in Mark where they and the Herodians appear together (12:13).[9] Though Luke certainly does not see the Pharisees as friendly to Jesus, he does not see them as politically hostile and in league with the highest authorities. The Pharisees make common cause with Jesus against the authorities in a later passage, found only in Luke, when they warn Jesus to escape because Herod is seeking him (13:31).[10] One further passage deserves consideration and may manifest the same attitude. As Jesus is being praised during his entry into Jerusalem, Luke has the Pharisees, rather than

[9]This is the only passage in Mark where the Pharisees appear in Jerusalem. In Luke they are at Jesus' entry into Jerusalem (19:39) only, and not in Jerusalem at all.

[10]This warning does not seem to be an attempt to get rid of Jesus. Rather, it fits the role of Pharisees as middlemen between the people and the government. See Sanders, "Pharisees," 145-146.

Matthew's chief priests and scribes, tell Jesus to rebuke his disciples (Lk 19:39-40). Note that in Matthew (21:15-16) the place of the rebuke is in the Temple after Jesus has entered the city and gone to the Temple. It is not clear whether the Pharisees are worried about the political dangers of Jesus' acclamation or scandalized by the type of praise being given him. Though the latter is more probable, the Pharisees are not presented as politically in league with the leaders in Jerusalem. Their intervention is independent and disconnected from any other political party.[11] Luke's view of the Pharisees who oppose Jesus is consistent in that their activity is limited to Galilee and not connected to the highest governing circles in Jerusalem.

Jesus interacts with Pharisees in Galilee more constantly and more closely than in the other Gospels. Luke pictures the Pharisees as the local leaders who are engaged in a contest with Jesus for influence and control in Galilean society. For example, three times Jesus eats with Pharisees (5:36; 11:37; 14:1) and in each case the Pharisees are watching him and a conflict erupts. The Pharisee who invites Jesus in 14:1 is a local Pharisaic leader *(tinos tōn archontōn [tōn] pharisaiōn)*. Finally, when the Pharisees scoff at Jesus' teaching concerning the dishonest steward and mammon, Luke makes the startling assertion that they were "lovers of money" (16:14). This saying, found only in Luke, has a strong theological connotation in context;[12] it presupposes that the Pharisees' social station includes access to wealth, either independently or by dependence on the rich. Thus according to Luke the Pharisees in Galilee are members of the governing class and are competing for wealth as well as influence and power. Luke uses wealth, power, etc. as symbolic of rejection of Jesus by society's leaders and as a catalyst for the formation of a new Christian society.

Much more than in Mark and Matthew the Pharisees in Luke have an important social station in Galilee and their relations with Jesus show that they considered him and his leadership of the people as a threat to their position and thus

---

[11] Johnson, *Possessions,* 112, argues that 19:39 40 completes the pattern of rejection of Jesus by the Jewish leaders and acceptance of him by the people.

[12] See J. Fitzmyer, *The Gospel According to Luke* (AB 28-28a; Garden City: Doubleday, 1981, 1985) 1111-1113, and Johnson, *Possessions,* 141.

rejected him. Luke's attitude toward the Pharisees is complex and cannot be simply characterized as friendly or hostile. Luke's problem with Pharisees is that they do not accept Jesus. This does not mean that there is no contact or that all relations are hostile, but their resistance to Jesus' authority is intimately tied up with their social position, according to Luke.

Luke's view of the Pharisees' social position in brought out in several passages where the Pharisees keep their distance from social outcasts. The contrast of the Pharisees with tax collectors and sinners is typological for Luke and symbolic of the paradoxical rejection of Jesus by Judaism and acceptance of him by the Gentiles. The Pharisees are presented as the guardians of the normal social boundaries against Jesus who seeks to change the boundaries and reconstitute the people of God. After Jesus eulogizes John the Baptist, Luke comments parenthetically: "When they heard this all the people and tax collectors justified God, having been baptized with the baptism of John; but the Pharisees and lawyers rejected the purpose of God for themselves, not having been baptized by him" (7:29-30). Luke's judgment is substantiated in the story of the woman who anointed Jesus' feet when he was eating at a Pharisee's house. The woman was a sinner and the Pharisees think that Jesus should have known this and not let her touch him (7:36-39). Jesus answers their objection by discussing the forgiveness of sins and also by pointing out that the woman is fulfilling the acts of courtesy omitted by the host, Simon the Pharisee, by washing his feet, kissing him and anointing his head with oil (7:40-47).[13] The parables of the lost sheep, coin and prodigal son are prefaced by the objection of the Pharisees and scribes that Jesus eats with tax collectors and sinners (15:1-2). Finally, the parable of the Pharisee and tax collector (18:9-14) is spoken against those who "trusted in themselves that they were righteous and despised others." Two themes run through these incidents. First, the Pharisees (and presumably the majority of the people) who reject those usually considered to be social outcasts, such as sinners and tax collectors, are contrasted with Jesus who initiates a new community which includes the outcasts. More importantly

---

[13]The Pharisees are pictured as denigrating those of lower social station, including Jesus and sinners.

for our analysis here, Luke pictures the Pharisees as also separating themselves from the people and from Jesus. Luke sees them as claiming another and higher social status and he criticizes them for it. The Pharisees have demarcated sharp and tight boundaries for society and have excluded the normal outcasts and also Jesus and in some cases the people. When Jesus refuses to accept their boundaries, they challenge his legitimacy and enter into a contest with him for control over society.

Luke emphasizes the hostility and rivalry between the Pharisees and Jesus in several more passages not found in Mark and Matthew. After the woes against the Pharisees Luke summarizes their hostility by saying that the scribes and Pharisees began to provoke Jesus to catch him in something he said (11:53-54). Immediately after this Luke identifies the leaven of the Pharisees as hypocrisy (12:1). Luke also repeats a variant of an earlier healing-conflict story (Lk 6:6-11; Mk 3:1-6), set this time in a Pharisaic ruler's house (14:1-6). In 17:20-21, a passage unique to Luke, the Pharisees ask Jesus when the kingdom of God will come and he answers that it is already among/ within them. The exact meaning of this enigmatic answer is debated, but it at least indictes that the kingdom is all around them and they are missing it.[14]

The final passage to be considered in the gospel is a major attack on the Pharisees and lawyers which includes instruction concerning the ritual washing of hands before dinner and then three woes against each group (11:37-54). Some of the material is found in Matthew, ch. 23, so Luke has probably composed this chapter using materials derived from Q. In its present form and in its narrative setting, a dinner at a Pharisee's house, it reflects Luke's judgment of the Pharisees. The three woes against the Pharisees and the discussion of ritual washing concern the contrast between outward observance and inner attitude and between important commands concerned with justice and lesser ones concerned with ritual observances. Luke does not say that the Pharisaic observances are wrong in themselves, but he does

---

[14]Johnson, *Possessions,* 110-11, argues that the Pharisees' question in 17:20 begins a section of the gospel (until 18:4) in which the Pharisees are attacked for their misunderstanding, especially of the place of outcasts in the kingdom.

qualify their importance to such an extent that the Pharisees and their way of life are seen as a bad influence on society.[15] The agenda attributed to the Pharisees, purity and tithes (as in Mark), differs from that attributed to the lawyers and shows that Luke is sensitive to the distinction between Pharisees and lawyers, in contrast to Matthew who puts scribes and Pharisees together in several of the woes.

The historicity of Luke's presentation of the Pharisees is questionable in many particulars. Luke presented them as Jesus' Galilean opponents par excellence and inserted them into several incidents where Mark did not include them. Luke pictured them as important, influential and even powerful community leaders in Galilee. In limiting them to Galilee, he followed the tradition he found in Mark, and perhaps elsewhere. In seeing them as an active political force in Jewish society with influence and control among the people he is consistent with Josephus. (In Acts the Pharisees are active in the Sanhedrin in Jerusalem, as they are in Josephus.) The Pharisees have often been treated as creatures of Luke's literary composition and narrative needs, a type of Jesus' opposition. Though they do function as a stereotyped opposition to Jesus, they also fit Jewish society historically and sociologically in some ways. However, it is doubtful that the Pharisees were the community leaders in Galilean agricultural villages. The elder leaders of the traditionally prominent families, mostly large landowners, would have been the rural leadership. Though it is possible that some Pharisees flourished in alliance with them, Pharisees would not have had the numerical and political dominance which Luke assigns them.

SCRIBES

The scribes are mentioned a number of times in Luke, but they do not have a distinct and independent role. Their social place and roles are conflated almost totally with those of the Pharisees and of the chief priests and elders. The scribes appear alone only twice in Luke's gospel. Once they approve the answer which Jesus gave to the Sadducees' challenge to his belief in the

---

[15]See Fitzmyer, *Luke,* 943-45, who interprets this passage more positively.

resurrection (20:39) and so are presented positively as in agreement on the question of resurrection (see Acts also). On the other hand, Luke takes over from Mark (12:37-40) Jesus' warning against the scribes who seek public recognition and devour widows' houses. The charges brought against them are similar to those brought against the Pharisees elsewhere (16:14). In all other cases the scribes appear either with the Pharisees (5:30; 6:7; 11:53; 15:2) or with the chief priests, and sometimes the elders, (9:22; 19:47; 20:1, 19, 46; 22:2, 66). In all passages where they appear with the chief priests Luke is following Mark. When linked with the Pharisees, the scribes do not have a distinct identity to differentiate them from the Pharisees, but are seen simply as an allied group opposed to Jesus.

In summary, the scribes are not a very distinct group in Luke. They are like the Pharisees in their belief in the resurrection and join with the Pharisees several times in opposition to Jesus. Luke has no clear idea of their role or function and they are made an appendage of the Pharisees, who are the dominant group. In addition, Luke takes over from Mark several references to the scribes as part of the leadership group in Jerusalem, along with the chief priests and sometimes the elders. Since the term scribe designated a skill and occupation with varied roles and statuses in the Greco-Roman world, Luke probably did not conceive of the scribes as a distinct political and social group the way Mark did. Thus, the author tends to merge the scribes with the Pharisees.

LAWYERS

Luke also introduces a new category of opponent to Jesus, the lawyer *(nomikos)*. A lawyer appears alone once, when he asks Jesus about eternal life in order to test him (10:25). In Mark, in a different context (12:28), the questioner is a scribe. Mark's scribe is more friendly than Luke's lawyer, though both the scribe in Mark and the lawyer in Luke answer correctly and have their answer approved by Jesus.[16] In all other cases they are closely associated with the Pharisees, in a way similar to the

---

[16]In contrast, in Matthew the question is asked by a hostile Pharisee who is a lawyer.

scribes. In 7:30 Luke judges that both the Pharisees and lawyers reject God's purpose for them. In 11:45 and 14:3 lawyers are present in the houses of Pharisees who have invited Jesus to dinner and in 11:46-52 Jesus denounces the lawyers with three woes. The content of the woes fits the activities of lawyers (and scribes) who are publically active and have official positions. They are chided for placing unreasonable legal burdens on others, indulging in public display and protecting their own authority to the detriment of God's.

Some evidence suggests that Luke uses lawyer as an alternate for scribe.[17] Immediately after the woes against the Pharisees and lawyers in ch. 11 he has the Pharisees and *scribes* seek to entrap Jesus (11:53-54). In 10:25 he changes Mark's scribe to lawyer. Since Matthew has a lawyer who was a Pharisee in the parallel passage (22:34-35), this usage may come from Q. However, Luke is not consistent in his usage since he retains the scribes in many cases and even inserts them in places unique to him. He does not insert lawyer simply as an aid to his gentile audience because scribe *(grammateus)* is as comprehensible to his audience as lawyer. The proper question concerns Luke's understanding of scribes and lawyers and his purpose for bringing lawyers into the narrative. Certainly, Luke does not mean by lawyer a legal advocate in the judicial system. Lawyers in Luke are experts in Jewish law whom people might consult and perhaps a group zealous for the law.[18] It is likely that in the author's world lawyers rather than scribes functioned as author-itative experts in social and religious law and custom, officials and guardians of community norms. As such they fit into the narrative better than scribes.[19]

The three woes against the lawyers provide the most infor-mation concerning their nature as Luke sees it.[20] The first charge, that they put heavy loads on the people, could have been

---

[17]Fitzmyer, *Luke,* on 7:30; Sanders, "Pharisees," 172.

[18]Sanders, "Pharisees," 169, 172; P. Parker, "Lawyers," *IDB,* 3:102.

[19]It is unclear whether Luke conceives of some of the lawyers as being Pharisees. Fitzmyer, *Luke,* 947, interprets the lawyers in ch. 11 as being lawyers among the Pharisees.

[20]Sanders, "Pharisees," 173-174.

made of the Pharisees too.[21] But the lawyers are treated as authorities who have a special power to control the people's way of living Judaism and a concomitant special obligation to help the people. In the next woe they are accused of having approved the killing of the prophets and thus being responsible for it in the way leaders and judges are. Implied, of course, is their rejection of Jesus and responsibility for his death. The final woe charges them with refusal to understand and impeding others from doing so. In context this saying refers to understanding the Bible and especially prophecy. Just as their ancestors rejected and killed the prophets, so the lawyers do not understand the prophetic writings and so reject the latest in the line of prophets, Jesus. In the woes the lawyers are presumed to be learned, custodians of the Bible, responsible for teaching the people, influential leaders and powerful opponents of past and present messengers sent from God.

One final term used by Luke is teacher of the law *(nomodidaskalos)*. It describes a certain degree of learning rather than a social role or group. In the first controversy story (5:17) the Pharisees and the teachers of the law were sitting around Jesus but later in the story the scribes and Pharisees challenged Jesus. Consequently, Luke understood the scribes to be "teachers of the law." However, in Acts Gamaliel the Pharisee is said to be a "teacher of the law" (5:34). Thus Luke understood this title as referring to any learned and accepted teacher, and not to a distinct sub-group within Judaism.[22]

Acts

New aspects of the Pharisees, scribes and Sadducees appear in Acts. Pharisees appear as members of the Sanhedrin twice. Gamaliel, a Pharisee and a member of the Sanhedrin, had enough wisdom, respect and influence to be able to overcome the Sanhedrin's rage and counsel prudent caution in dealing with the apostles (5:33-40). Because Gamaliel helped the apostles

---

[21]See Acts 15:10, where Peter argues against putting the load of the law on the Gentiles.

[22]This word occurs in one other place in the New Testament, 1 Tim 1:7.

and because he was open to the possibility that their teaching might come from God, Luke's attitude toward him was positive.[23] Whether the presentation of Gamaliel in Acts is historical can be questioned because as a literary figure he serves Luke's purpose of showing Christianity's continuity with Judaism. When Paul appeared before the Sanhedrin, he declared that he was a Pharisee, the son of a Pharisee. His claim of Pharisaic membership disrupted the proceedings against him by provoking an argument over resurrection between the Pharisees and Sadducees within the Sanhedrin (Acts 23). According to that story, some of the scribes of the Pharisees contended that Paul might have received his message from a spirit or angel, beings whose existence was denied by Sadducees. Thus, Luke, like Josephus, claims that the Pharisees and Sadducees disagree on their teaching about resurrection and the existence of angels. Because Paul believes in resurrection and is a Pharisee he enters into a very temporary alliance with the Pharisees against the Sadducees in their competition for power in the Sanhedrin and presumably in Jewish life.

Some Jerusalem Christians, as well as Paul, are identified as Pharisees by Luke, At the meeting of the Jerusalem community with Paul "some believers of those from the school *(hairesis)* of the Pharisees" claimed that Gentile believers had to be circumcised and instructed to keep the law of Moses (15:5). This zeal for the law of Moses fits Luke's idea of the Pharisees in both the gospel and Acts and it is consistent with his picture of Paul when Paul later claims that he lived Judaism according to the strictest school *(hairesis),* the Pharisees (26:5). The author of Acts uses the same word as Josephus to describe the Pharisaic group and identifies them by the strict way of life they lead according to their interpretation of the Biblical law. In a way similar to Josephus Luke presents the Pharisees as a political force in Judaism, noted for its program for Jewish life. Acts also agrees with Paul's own characterization of Pharisaism in Phil 3:5 where he implies that the Pharisaic way of life is a recognized, demanding and accepted way of living Jewish life.

---

[23]Luke has Paul cite his study with Gamaliel as an honored and important part of his activity as a Jew in Acts 22:3 and thus testify to Gamaliel's importance and honored place in Judaism.

A word must be said about the historicity of Luke's account of the Pharisees. That some were members of the Sanhedrin and competed for power in Jerusalem is likely. However, Luke's idea that Paul could be a Pharisee and a Christian and that there were Christians who remained Pharisees is very unlikely, especially granted all the conflicts with Jewish authorities and teaching recounted in Acts and alluded to in Paul's letters. The Pharisees were a political interest group with a program for living Judaism and any interpretation of Christianity, no matter how Jewish, would have found itself in conflict with them. In trying to establish the continuity between Christianity and Judaism Luke maximizes their agreements in teaching and common interests. He lumps together the Jews who were strict in observance of the law (Pharisees) with the Jewish Christians who wished to remain faithful to the Mosaic law. Luke correctly perceives many things about the Pharisees, but he probably overemphasizes their positive relations with the early followers of Jesus.

SCRIBES

The scribes appear in several passages in Acts, but they do not differ from the scribes in the gospel. The scribes are associated with the rulers, elders and the high priests Annas and Caiphas in examining Peter and John (4:5). They function in relation to the apostles as they did in relation to Jesus; they are part of the official opposition. When Paul is before the Sanhedrin some scribes are said to be of the party *(meros)* of the Pharisees and to support Paul because of his belief in resurrection (23:9). Finally, members of the Freedmen Synagogue stirred up the people, elders and scribes against Stephen and then brought him before the Sanhedrin (6:12). The scribes in Acts, as in the gospel, are recognized and learned leaders of the community who are politically active in protecting the Jewish community.[24]

---

[24]In Acts 19:35 the scribe of Ephesus brings the town assembly to order and presides. He is a city official, such as a city clerk or secretary of the assembly. See ch. 11 for more examples of this usage.

SADDUCEES

The Sadducees, who are mentioned only once in the gospel (as in Mark), appear three times in Acts. In all cases they are associated with the highest Jerusalem leadership. Peter is arrested in Solomon's portico within the Temple precincts by the priests, the captain *(stratēgos)* of the Temple and the Sadducees (4:1). The apostles are arrested by the high priest and all those with him, "that is the school *(hairesis)* of the Sadducees" (5:17). Finally, in a scene we have already examined, the Sadducees are a part (or party [*meros*]) of the Sanhedrin who do not believe in resurrection or in angels and spirits. The beliefs of the Sadducees and their association with the governing class fit the description of the Sadducees given in Josephus, who also calls them a school and party.

Conclusion

Luke's view of the Pharisees, scribes and Sadducees is difficult to evaluate historically. His view of Jewish society is coherent in many respects and in agreement with Josephus on some matters. But he clearly stereotypes Jesus' opponents, especially the Pharisees. Too little information is given on the scribes and Sadducees to present a rounded picture. The scribes are a group dependent either on the Pharisees or on the Jerusalem leaders, as is appropriate for learned functionaries within the leadership system. Luke agrees with Josephus that the Sadducees are closely connected to the rich and powerful leadership and that they do not believe in resurrection and angels. The Pharisees in Acts are influential in Jerusalem, as they are in Josephus. In the gospel they are influential in Galilee, as they are in Mark.

The Pharisees in John

The Pharisees function both as government officials and as the learned doctors of the law who are interested in Jesus' teaching and dispute its truth; neither the Sadducees nor the scribes are mentioned in John.[25] The presentation of the Pharisees in John differs greatly from that in the synoptic gospels, though a few common features remain. In both Galilee and Jerusalem the Pharisees are an ominous presence, "ever watchful and suspicious adversaries of Jesus, who keep the people under surveillance and influence it with their propaganda."[26] They compete with Jesus for influence with the people and attempt to undermine his teaching. All through the gospel the Pharisees are allied with the chief priests in taking official action against Jesus, especially on his trips to Jerusalem. In addition, the Pharisees, either alone or with other officials, control the synagogue and the judicial processes for removing those whom they oppose. This picture of the Pharisees as an officially powerful group has significant features in common with Josephus' presentation of them during the Hasmonean period. According to both accounts they attained real political power, even though it was derived from the governing class which they served. That they are not the highest authorities is clear in the account of Jesus' condemnation to death, during which the Pharisees drop from view (just as in the synoptic gospels).

The Pharisees are first mentioned in connection with a delegation sent from Jerusalem to the Jordan to investigate John the Baptist (1:19-28). The Jews sent priests and Levites to John to ask him who he was. The Jews are, of course, the "authorities" generically understood, who oppose Jesus all through the gospel.[27] Since this is the only place in the gospels where priests

---

[25]The scribes appear in 8:3 (the woman caught in adultery) but the passage is a non-johannine pericope, missing in the best manuscripts and characterized by non-johannine language. The Pharisees in John fill the roles of the Markan scribes and Pharisees. Cf. C. H. Dodd, *Historical Tradition in the Fourth Gospel* (Cambridge: Cambridge University, 1963) 264.

[26]R. Schnackenburg, *The Gospel According to St. John* (New York: Herder, 1968) I:293.

[27]The word Jew occurs about seventy times in John and has a number of meanings. See Urban C. von Wahlde, "The Terms for Religious Authorities in the Fourth Gospel: A Key to Literary Strata?," *JBL* 98 (1979) 233-34 for a summary of the usages and recent bibliography. When "Jews" refers to opponents of Jesus, it always means the authorities, except in 6:41 and 52 where it means the people. These latter two passages may come from a redactor. See Urban C. von Wahlde, "The Johannine 'Jew': A Critical Survey," *NTS* 28 (1982) 44-46. Raymond Brown, *The Community of the Beloved*

and Levites are identified as officials who deal with John or Jesus,[28] Dodd argues that it is probably an earlier, pre-70 tradition preserved in John.[29] After the priests and Levites satisfy themselves that John does not have dangerous pretensions to prophetic or messianic leadership, others question John about the meaning of his baptism and its legitimacy (1:24). The Greek text is disputed; the questioners could be some Pharisees or some people sent by the Pharisees and they could be part of the previous delegation or a separate delegation.[30] It is most likely that some Pharisees are members of the same delegation.[31] The Pharisees in the incident are located in Jerusalem, engage in official inquiry of John and are interested in his precise teaching and the authority for it. Here and often John locates the Pharisees in Jerusalem, contrary to the synoptic tradition and in agreement with Josephus' presentation. In addition, the Pharisees act as official representatives of the governing class.

The supervisory role of the Pharisees in society is further attested when Jesus' trip to Galilee from Judea (4:1) is said to be motivated by his hearing that the Pharisees know that he is making more disciples than John the Baptist. The implication is that the Pharisees will disapprove of Jesus and be a threat to him in some tangible way. The story of Nicodemus confirms this picture of the Pharisees. He is a Pharisee and a "ruler" *(archon)* of the Jews, who comes to Jesus in Jerusalem during the Passover festival, addresses him as Rabbi and recognizes

---

Disciple (Ramsey, NJ: Paulist, 1979) 40-43, points out that for the author of John and his community, late in the first century, after separation from the synagogue, Jews refers to all Jews. They are seen as the heirs of the Jewish authorities who opposed Jesus in his lifetime. Both the Jews of John's time and the Jewish authorities of Jesus' time are bitterly attacked. R. Alan Culpepper, *The Anatomy of the Fourth Gospel: A Study in Literary Design* (Foundations and Facets; Philadelphia: Fortress, 1983) 126 suggests that from a literary point of view John is using "Jews" with multiple, connected meanings. Though this is true in a broad sense, multiple meanings based on redaction cannot be overlooked.

[28]Similarly, in Josephus, *Life,* 189-198 (38-39) priests and Pharisees are sent to remove Josephus from his command in Galilee.

[29]Dodd, *Tradition,* 263-264.

[30]See Raymond Brown, *The Gospel According to John* (Anchor Bible 29; Garden City: Doubleday, 1966) I:43-44.

[31]Schnackenburg, *John,* I:292.

him as a teacher from God (3:1-2).[32] In return Jesus characterizes Nicodemus as a teacher of Israel (3:10) when he chides him for his unacceptable ignorance. Nicodemus fits the profile of the Pharisees in that he has an official capacity in Jerusalem, knows about Jesus, has a learned interest in his teaching (in this case, positive) and feels the threat of disapproval from his fellow Pharisees.[33] Nicodemus, who represents for John a partly "good" Pharisee, accepts Jesus as a fellow teacher and even his superior and so consults him and enters into educational dialogue with him.[34] That the disapproval of the Pharisees, which Nicodemus fears because of his acceptance of Jesus, is a serious social threat is clear in a later meeting of the chief priests and Pharisees in which Nicodemus speaks on Jesus' behalf (7:52) and in the comment that many Jewish leaders *(archontes)* believed in Jesus but not openly because the Pharisees would see that they were put out of the synagogue (12:42).[35]

The power of the Pharisees and the political threat they presented is clear when Jesus went to the Feast of Tabernacles secretly rather than openly because the Jews sought to kill him (7:1, 10). The kind of influence the Pharisees had and sought to preserve can be seen in what is said of Jesus in Jerusalem. When Jesus taught in the Temple, the Jews marvelled because he was learned[36] but had not studied. Just what type of study or legitimation was required is unclear, but community norms for learnedness and teaching authority are common. Most probably what is meant is a familiarity with law and custom recognized

---

[32]Brown, *John,* 130, suggests that Nicodemus was specifically a member of the Sanhedrin, though the term Sanhedrin is not used here and is used only once in the whole gospel (11:46).

[33]S. Pancaro, *The Law in the Fourth Gospel* (Studia Neotestamentica 42; Leiden: Brill, 1975) 86, suggests that the description of Nicodemus here and in 7:50 and 19:39 is stereotyped and as such gives us further knowledge of the author's view of the Pharisees. This is certainly true of Nicodemus, as well as of all johannine characters, but Culpepper is right in arguing that Nicodemus is both representative and also subtly individual (*Anatomy,* 134-136).

[34]In John teacher and rabbi are used of Jesus only. The one exception to that usage is Jesus ironic designation of Nicodemus as a teacher in Israel who does not understand (3:10).

[35]In 9:22 the Jews have decided to expel anyone who confesses Jesus. The Pharisees may be implied as the Jewish authorities, or John may just be imprecise.

[36]Literally, he "knew his letters."

by the people and peers, like the Pharisees, rather than an office legitimized by law.[37] The results of Jesus' teaching show what the Jewish leaders, including the Pharisees were trying to prevent. Because many believed Jesus, some Jerusalemites tried to kill him (7:30-31) and others engaged in debate (literally, murmuring) over him. The dispute led to a confrontation with the Pharisees, who are once again portrayed as interested in Jesus' teaching. In this case they with the chief priests take official political action by sending subordinates[38] to arrest Jesus (7:32). When those sent to arrest Jesus returned without Jesus because they were awed by him (7:44-46), the Pharisees suggested that they were being led astray by Jesus (7:47).[39]

The criteria for rejecting Jesus as a teacher are revealing: none of the authorities *(archontes)* or Pharisees have believed in him and the people who have believed do not know the law and so are accursed. The Pharisees manifest their customary interest in what Jesus teaches and does and their emphasis on learning as a criterion for leadership. Note also that the leaders (probably the chief priests and other political authorities) are distinguished from the Pharisees, even though (some of?) the Pharisees are linked with the chief priests in exercising power.

Usually the Pharisees do not legitimate Jesus by treating him as an equal.[40] Rather, they maintain a superior position based on social recognition of their learning, their influence with the people and their political power in conjunction with the chief priests. Only once do the Pharisees directly debate Jesus, in contrast to the synoptic gospels in which conflict stories abound. A disconnected discourse in the Temple treasury (8:13-20) begins with Jesus' claim that he is the light of the world and the Pharisees' objection that he bears witness to himself, invalidly

---

[37]See Malina, *Christian Origins,* 144-153.

[38]*hupēretai* are servants or ministers. They have been interpreted as officials, Temple police, officers, etc.

[39]The chronological sequence in ch. 7 is confused. They seem to be sent out when Jesus is speaking in the middle of the feast (7:14, 32) and return after Jesus has spoken on the last day of the feast (7:37). The dramatic sequence and Jesus' effect on the officers within the narrative is clear and is the main point of the author.

[40]Malina, *The New Testament World,* ch. 2 on honor. One enters into challenges and contests for honor and community standing only with one's equals. One ignores one's inferiors or sends subordinates to deal with them.

according to the law. This leads to a brief discourse on Jesus' authority and the correct interpretation of the Law with a further question from the Pharisees. The subject matter is typical of the Pharisees.

The story of the cure of the man born blind (ch. 9) and the controversy following it reveal much about the Pharisees and most probably about the situation of the author of the gospel of John and his community.[41] When the man born blind has been cured and returned to his neighborhood in Jerusalem, those who knew him sought an explanation for his cure. The people did not wish the good order of the community disrupted and were anxious about an exercise of power by someone they did not know. Upset by this change in the physical and social order, they took the man to the guardians of community order and custom, the Pharisees, for an evaluation of the situation. The Pharisees questioned the man and upon discovering that Jesus had mixed clay on the sabbath, dismissed him as a sinner who broke the sabbath rest (9:13-17). In this narrative the Pharisees are leaders concerned with teaching, order and the exercise of power in the community. They use their socially accepted role as accurate interpreters of the tradition to condemn Jesus according to the laws and customs which give the community its identity and shape. What is especially noteworthy is that the people turn to them as the local officials concerned with public order and community norms.

The dialogue with the blind man's parents reveals that the Jews had decided that anyone who confessed Jesus to be Christ would be expelled from the synagogue (9:22). R. Brown,[42] says that the Pharisees (13, 15, 16 and 40) are the same as the Jews (18, 22) in this narrative. This interpretation is consonant with 12:42 which says that many authorities believed in Jesus secretly but "because of the Pharisees they did not confess (it) lest they be expelled from the synagogue."[43] This is acceptable if all the

---

[41]See J. Louis Martyn, *History and Theology in the Fourth Gospel* (rev. ed.; Nashville: Abingdon, 1968) 24-62, who sees in ch. 9 a reflection of the situation of the johannine community in the late first century when it was expelled from the synagogue by the rabbis, the successors of the Pharisees.

[42]*John*, 373.

[43]See 16:2 also for expulsion from the synagogue.

Jewish leaders are being lumped into one opposition group or if the close association of the Pharisees with other Jewish leaders is assumed. However, it is equally possible to read the text as referring to a second investigation by other officials, called generically, the Jews. In this case, the Pharisees share authority over the synagogue with other Jewish officials, a more likely historical situation both before and after the destruction of the Temple. Both the Pharisees and the Jews functioned as community leaders with authority to summon and question members of the community and with enough standing to be consulted by and exert control over the people and an important institution of the people, the synagogue.

When Jesus spoke to the blind man for the last time, he linked blindness and sight with faith. The Pharisees, who were somewhat artificially within hearing, asked whether *they* were blind and Jesus expanded the metaphor by telling them that since they claimed to have seen, they were not blind and innocent, but guilty. In an ironic twist the Pharisees' claim to knowledge and truth is turned against them. They, like Nicodemus (3:10), are teachers who have no excuse for ignorance.

As in the story of the man born blind, so in the story of Lazarus, many believed in Jesus (11:45), but some went and reported what Jesus had done to the Pharisees. In both cases the Pharisees are the community leaders to whom people turn when there is disruption of the ordinary. But as a result of this complaint, the official action moved to a new level. The chief priests and Pharisees gathered a council (sanhedrin)[44] to discuss what to do about Jesus (11:46). The presence of the chief priests and the official nature of the meeting lead toward the plot against Jesus and his eventual condemnation. In Mark the scribes and elders appear with the chief priests as the official, political opposition and in Matthew either the elders or scribes join the chief priests in opposition. Neither scribes nor elders occur in John; rather the Pharisees are the associates of the chief priests and the roles of both scribes and elders are incorporated into them.

---

[44]This is the only occurence of *synedrion* in the gospel, though the body seems to be alluded to elsewhere, e.g., 7:45.

The concerns articulated by the council are typically political. They feared that all the people would believe in Jesus and thus disrupt civil order, with the consequence that the Romans would destroy their place and nation (11:47-48).[45] Consequently, they planned from that day on how to put Jesus to death (11:53) and sought to find Jesus in order to arrest him (11:57). The chief priests are also said to plan the death of Lazarus (12:10) because his popularity and presence caused people to believe in Jesus.

The opposition and concern of the Pharisees were manifested twice during Jesus' last trip to Jerusalem. When Jesus entered Jerusalem triumphally and was witnessed to by those who had seen Lazarus raised from the dead, the Pharisees complained that they could do nothing because the world *(kosmos)* had gone after Jesus (12:19). They feared losing their social status in the community as recognized leaders and their influence over the beliefs and behavior of the people and expressed frustration that they were losing the competition with Jesus.

The Pharisees appeared a final time when they sent some subordinate officials with Judas in order to arrest Jesus (18:3). From then on the high priests Annas and Caiaphas, the chief priests and their subordinates took over and the Pharisees were not mentioned. In this the johannine passion narrative is similar to those in the synoptic gospels: the priests rather than the Pharisees play a leading role in Jesus' condemnation and execution. The Pharisees are not the ultimate governing authority, but they have some direct power.

The Pharisees are conceived of as having either direct power or decisive influence in determining who is recognized as a Jew in good standing many places in the gospel. This function is made clear in the summary which ends the first half of the gospel (12:36-50). Many believed, including leaders *(archontes),* but did not admit it because of fear of the Pharisees who might put them out of the synagogue (12:42-43). The designation of

---

[45]See Richard Horsley, "High Priests and the Politics of Roman Palestine," *JSJ* 16 (1985) 23-55 on the role of the elite who cooperated with the Romans and on their overriding interest in preserving the status quo. The links between Roman provincial officials and native aristocracy and the tendency of the aristocracy to cooperate with the Romans to their own benefit and sometimes to the detriment of their own people is brought out by Richard P. Saller, *Personal Patronage Under the Early Empire* (Cambridge: Cambridge UP, 1982) 145-194 for the case of North Africa.

membership in the synagogue as decisive for being a Jew seems more characteristic of the diaspora than of Palestine. In Palestine, especially before 70, one was a Jew by living Jewish life within a Jewish village or town.[46] In the diaspora Jews had to maintain Jewish identity by active membership in a Jewish community and organization, that is, in a synagogue. The emphasis on synagogue as decisive for one's good standing may fit Palestine after the destruction of the Temple when Jewish leaders may have used the threat of expulsion or some sort of ban or ostracism in the village as a strategy for strengthening Judaism and protecting it against Christianity.[47] Since efforts to protect and give shape to the Jewish community are amply witnessed in Jewish and New Testament literature, community sanctions were probably an early experience of the followers of Jesus, though the formulation "expel from the synagogue" fits the diaspora especially well.

Conclusions

In the Gospel of John the Pharisees, along with the Jews and the chief priests, are the most important opponents to Jesus and have an integral role in the plot of the gospel. Dramatically they further the action of Jesus' life and death and rhetorically they represent the opponents of the johannine community in the time of the author.[48] A sociological analysis of the johannine portrait of the Pharisees can help us to assess its historical probability.

In John the Pharisees play a much more official role than they do in the synoptic gospels. The absence of scribes and elders, who are found in the synoptic gospels and were certainly members of the Jewish leadership in the first century, argues to a simplified and unhistorical view of Jewish leadership in John.[49]

[46]See chapter four.

[47]Dodd, *Tradition,* 409-410, points out that Christian traditions about being brought before sanhedrins (Mark 13:9; Mt. 10:17) and synagogues (Luke 21:12) are common to all traditions, probably early and so perhaps reliable descriptions of what happened to the followers of Jesus. These early traditions could stem from Palestine or Syria. The term sanhedrin can refer to something as small as a local village council and a synagogue to the local Jewish community assembled.

[48]See Culpepper, *Anatomy,* 129 and his citation of Fortna.

[49]Culpepper, *Anatomy,* 129.

Many scholars argue that the Pharisees took over the leadership of Judaism after the destruction of the Temple in 70 and that the Pharisees in the narrative are symbols for the emerging rabbinic leadership in the late first century, a group with which the johannine community had serious conflicts.[50] This position is oversimplified. It is doubtful that the rabbis dominated Judaism by the end of the first century, especially in the diaspora where John was finally edited. In addition, the rabbis emcompassed more than former Pharisees in their ranks.[51] Jewish leadership after the destruction of the Temple probably remained with the traditional elders and community leaders, including some Pharisees and scribes, and only gradually during the second century and even into the third did the "rabbis" become the dominant force in the community.

The Pharisees, as presented in John, may partly reflect the Palestinian situation in the middle of the first century. The commentators are correct in seeing that John combines all Jesus' opponents, except the chief priests, into one category, the Pharisees. But John's reinterpretation of history must not be exaggerated. That the Pharisees were historical opponents of Jesus is well attested in the New Testament and Dodd has shown that John often preserves reliable early traditions.[52] John's overview needs to be corrected by Josephus because the Pharisees were only one of a number of groups in first century Judaism competing for social influence and power and so were less prominent than the johannine narrative would lead one to believe.[53] Granted this adjustment in focus, the johannine picture of the Pharisees as active in Jerusalem and competing with Jesus is sociologically probable and consistent with other sources.

The Pharisees were a learned group who had influence with the people because they were accepted by them as guides in Jewish behavior and belief. As such they were community leaders, perhaps with some direct power in both the synagogue and government council in Jerusalem, and certainly with great

[50] Martyn, *History,* 72-75; 84-89 and passim.

[51] See chs. 6 and 10.

[52] This is the thesis of his study, *Traditions.*

[53] Martyn, *History,* 84-89 exaggerates when he claims that John presents the Pharisees as the power behind all the other Jewish groups in the gospel.

influence in conjunction with the chief priests and other community leaders ("the Jews"). Like Josephus, John emphasizes those Pharisees (probably only a small leadership core) who were in Jerusalem and participated in direct leadership of the nation. In contrast with the synoptic gospels, John emphasizes the Pharisees' leadership role in the community. They kept watch over Jesus and over how people reacted to Jesus. They were the ones the people consulted or reported to when they were disturbed or confused by Jesus. They discussed Jesus' teachings and authority to teach, but except in one case, they did not directly challenge Jesus. Rather, they acted as established leaders should; they kept their distance from the newcomer and schemed to blunt his influence and preserve their own. When they took official action, it was with the cooperation of the chief priests and other officials. They were not the main political leaders, for the chief priests took over as the main opponents of Jesus in the passion narrative, just as in the synoptic gospels. This argues that both John and the synoptics drew on traditions which agreed that the Pharisees were not major factors in the crucifixion.

In summary, John's view of the Pharisees fits much of what we know about societies embedded in the Roman empire. Religion is part of the political and social structure. The leaders of society are traditional, in this case the chief priests, supported by retainers who fulfill various functions in society and compete for influence on those who have power. John pictures the Pharisees as the most successful and influential group; this is probably an unhistorical simplification because the Pharisees were only one among many political and religious forces in first century Judaism. John's view of the Pharisees probably fits his community's experience of Judaism and of the Pharisees in the mid-first century. The Pharisees were a major opposition group for the johannine community because some Pharisees had great influence in Jerusalem and so some control of who was accepted as a Jew in good standing and allowed into the assembly (synagogue).[54] Other sources, as well as John, make clear that

---

[54]The early experience of the johannine community was in Palestine; the final edition of the gospel comes, probably, from Asia Minor. See Brown, *The Community,* 25-31.

the Pharisees were an established force in interpreting Jewish law and life, had great influence on the people and competed against Jesus and the early Christian community to maintain their position.

10

The Pharisees and Sadducees in Rabbinic Literature

Most studies and textbook treatments of the Pharisees and Sadducees cite the rabbinic sources extensively because they provide much more information than Josephus and the New Testament and because they are assumed to be less biased than Josephus and the New Testament. But these reconstructions of Pharisaism and Sadducaism have been based on an uncritical reading of a wide range of later Jewish sources, loosely designated as rabbinic literature. These collections, from the Mishnah about 200 C.E. through the Talmuds in the fifth and sixth centuries and on to early medieval midrashic collections, have usually been culled for the few passages which spoke of Pharisees and Sadducees, for the more numerous laws, sayings and stories attributed to the sages who dated from before the destruction of the Temple, and for anonymous passages which seem to refer to pre-destruction society. These materials, taken out of context, have been treated as historically accurate first century traditions and patched together into a narrative.[1] Though studies frequently refer to the problems of dating and efforts are made to discern

---

[1]For a frank and polemical review of Pharisees scholarship, see the Bibliographical Reflections in Jacob Neusner, *The Rabbinic Traditions about the Pharisees before 70* (Leiden: Brill, 1971), Vol. 3, pp. 320-368. Classic and influential reconstructions of the Pharisees are found in George Foot Moore, *Judaism in the First Centuries of the Christian Era* (Cambridge: Harvard UP, 1927), vol. 1, pp. 56-92; Jacob Lauterbach, *Rabbinic Essays* (New York: Ktav, 1973); R. Travers Herford, *The Pharisees* (New York: Macmillan, 1924).

earlier from later traditions, they generally treat the scattered texts as historically reliable unless proven otherwise.

In this study the rabbinic sources will be read with the same kind of critical methodology used on Josephus and the New Testament. The Pharisees will not be assumed to be like the later rabbis, nor will texts from later documents be automatically accepted as accurate first century sources. Because each of the rabbinic sources tells stories of earlier times to accomplish its own religious purposes, these stories cannot be taken as history. If they are, they produce an illegitimate and unhistorical retrojection of second through seventh century rabbinic Judaism on the first century. Such an uncritical reconstruction invites prejudicial readings. For example, when such a reading has been coupled with an uncritical acceptance of the negative New Testament evaluation of the Pharisees, the traditional and inaccurate image of "legalistic" Pharisees has emerged. The Sadducees are seldom mentioned and then always pejoratively.

Since the uncritical reading of the rabbinic sources has produced a welter of arbitrary reconstructions of the Pharisees and Sadducees which still abound in even the best literature, reference will be made to the more recent misinterpretations of some of this evidence and the limits of what we know will be stressed. Credit must be given to the work of Jacob Neusner, who, in a series of studies of the Pharisees, the early sages and the Mishnah has laid the foundations for a critical evaluation of rabbinic literature and for understanding the development of early Judaism and the place of the Pharisees in that development.[2]

A full analysis of all the texts dealing with the Pharisees, and early sages and reputedly early laws in rabbinic literature is impossible here because the texts number in the hundreds and each must be analyzed literarily within its context and then evaluated historically for the data it gives and the purposes it

---

[2]The major works of Neusner, besides *Pharisees* mentioned above are *The Development of a Legend: Studies on the Traditions Concerning Yohanan ben Zakkai* (SPB 16; Leiden: Brill, 1970) and *Eliezer ben Hyrcanus: The Tradition and the Man* (SJLA; Leiden: Brill, 1973), 2 vols. These works Neusner now designates as the beginning of the critical enterprise. His later works analyze independent rabbinic documents both internally and in relation to others parts of the rabbinic canon. See his forty-three volume *History of the Mishnaic Law* (SJLA; Leiden: Brill, 1974-1985), covering five of the orders and his synthetic conclusions in *Judaism: The Evidence of the Mishnah* (Chicago: University of Chicago, 1981).

serves. Materials in rabbinic literature which may be helpful in understanding the Pharisees are of three kinds: sayings and stories from or about pre-70 sages, anonymous laws attributed to the pre-70 period, especially if they seem to fit pre-destruction society, and texts which mention the Pharisees and Sadducees by name. *First,* sayings and stories concerning a number of sages who date from before 70 C.E. as well as the disputes between the houses of Hillel and Shammai do not explicitly identify the sages as Pharisees, even though they are treated as the predecessors of the rabbis and as a powerful force in Jewish society. Since Gamaliel is identified as a Pharisee in Acts 5:34 and his son Simeon is identified as a Pharisee at the time of the war in Josephus' *Life* 190-194 and since rabbinic teaching seems continuous with what is attributed to the Pharisees in the New Testament and Josephus, the early sages are assumed to have been Pharisees and the rabbis to have been an extension of the Pharisaic tradition.[3] But Pharisaism is a phenomenon of the second Temple period. The later way of life and historical views of the rabbis are very probably related to the phenomenon of Pharisaism, but not simply an extension of it. Consequently, the rabbinic stories of the second Temple period will be read here not as history but as the later rabbinic movement's reconstruction of its earlier history.[4]

The *second* body of evidence is the anonymous laws attributed to the pre-70 period, especially those laws which apply to second Temple society. The usual reconstruction of the development of the Mishnah, the first written body of rabbinic law, assumes that traditions were gradually accumulated from the time of Ezra and began to take shape in mishnaic collections in the first and second centuries. The debates between the houses of Hillel and Shammai are seen as typical of Pharisaic legal discussion which continued into the rabbinic period.[5] However, the Mishnah has been thoroughly edited and no linguistic criteria can reliably

[3]See the brief discussion and reference to Cohen, "Yavneh," 36-41 in ch. 1.

[4]Even if these stories were taken as historically accurate, they are so sparse as to prevent any adequate historical reconstruction of the development of Pharisaism and its ways of life without great flights of imagination to fill in the gaps.

[5]See Jacob Neusner, *From Mishnah to Scripture: The Problem of the Unattributed Saying with Special Reference to the Division of Purities* (BJS 67; Chico: Scholars, 1984) for a study of this problem.

differentiate earlier sources. Neusner's analysis of the attested traditions of the pre-70 sages and of the logic of argument in the Mishnah has isolated a small body of legal subjects which are probably prior to traditions developed at Jamnia after 70 C.E. because the content in these traditions is presumed by later laws and disputes and thus their existence is assumed and indirectly attested.[6] Though one cannot prove historically that a law is first because it is logically prior (the historical development of cultures and religions is too varied for this),[7] Neusner's analysis may give us an insight into pre-70 thinking in Pharisaic schools. Even these pre-70 traditions cannot be securely attributed to the Pharisees nor do the pre-70 strata of the Mishnah fit the Pharisees as we know them particularly well, so other groups are not excluded as creators of early laws.[8] Judaism in the first century did not consist of the four philosophies listed by Josephus (the Pharisees, Sadducees, Essenes and Revolutionaries). Most probably Jewish society was filled with groups, coalitions, factions and interest groups which varied in practice, viewpoint and strategy on major social issues.

A *third* relatively small body of evidence concerning the Pharisees and Sadducees is found in the texts which mention them by name. Since most of these texts date from beyond the first couple of centuries, all treat the Sadducees in a polemical way and some treat the Pharisees pejoratively. They reflect a later reinterpretation of the Pharisees and must be used with great caution. Use will be made of the careful work of Ellis Rivkin on these texts,[9] though his overall interpretation will be contested because he reads texts from many times and sources as one body of evidence. His control texts from the Mishnah

[6]See a recent summary of his earlier findings in *The Mishnah Before 70* (BJS 51; Atlanta: Scholars, 1987)

[7]On the problems with this approach, see Jonathan Smith, *Map is Not Territory* (Leiden: Brill, 1978) 258.

[8]Neusner, *Evidence,* 70-71. While the Mishnah certainly takes up some Pharisaic teaching, it also deals extensively with priestly and Temple matters, civil order and property rights pertaining to village landowners and farmers. The post-70 rabbis most probably included priests, scribes and other influential Jewish leaders along with Pharisees (Neusner, *Evidence,* 230-256).

[9]"Defining the Pharisees: The Tannaitic Sources," *HUCA* 40-41 (1969-70) 205-249; see also *A Hidden Revolution: The Pharisees' Search for the Kingdom Within* (Nashville: Abingdon, 1978) esp. ch. 3, pp. 125-179.

and Tosefta, that is, those texts which contrast the Pharisees and Sadducees, number only seven and are too incomplete to define the Pharisees.[10] Many of the later texts reflect nothing concerning the first century Pharisees because the term Pharisee is no longer understood and has been applied to later sectarian phenomena.

The first century, C.E. sages shall be treated first because rabbinic literature contains relatively more stories and sayings concerning them than earlier sages. (The relatively sparse materials concerning the sages during the second and first centuries, B.C.E. will be omitted because of lack of space and because these traditions are even more historically difficult to use than materials concerning the first century.) The late first century and second century origins of the rabbinic patriarchate shall be examined as a context for understanding the Mishnah and later rabbinic literature. Though space does not permit a review of second century sages, the Mishnah and Tosefta, the earliest and most reliable source of their teachings, will be critically reviewed as an historical source. Finally, texts which explicitly mention the Pharisees and Sadducees will be critically examined with special reference to the recent work of Ellis Rivkin.

Attention will be given to the social situation implied by the texts and by some of their traditional interpretations. Rather than reliable historical evidence for the first century, the sources provide direct and reliable insight into the interests and agenda of the second through sixth century rabbis. The evidence in the texts, interpreted by the sociological models developed in earlier chapters and the information offered in Josephus and the New Testament, can provide a historically probable sketch of some aspects of the Pharisees and their contribution to the development of the rabbinic movement.

---

[10]Jack Lightstone, "Sadducees *Versus* Pharisees: The Tannaitic Sources," in *Christianity, Judaism and Other Greco-Roman Cults: Studies for Morton Smith at 60.* Ed. Jacob Neusner. (Leiden: Brill, 1975) Vol. 3, pp. 206-217. See the discussion below.

The Sages in the First Century C.E.

HILLEL AND SHAMMAI

Of all the pre-70 sages, only Hillel has a large body of sayings and stories attributed to him.[11] Because the talmudic rabbis conceived of Hillel as their founder and major teacher, they consistently depicted him as an appealing, wise and patient person and surrounded his legal teachings with an array of wise sayings, stories of his origin and status, and accounts of his disciples.[12] Hillel is even made the ancestor of Gamaliel and Simeon his son and thus a founder of the patriarchal house, though there is no evidence for this in either Tractate Abot or the Babylonian Talmud.[13] The stories about Hillel in the later rabbinic sources fit the interest of the later patriarchal house, such as his rise to power, his wisdom, his moral teaching and the dominance of his positions on matters of law. He is pictured as a leader of great influence and power in all areas of life, in contrast to the earlier sages whose teachings concerned internal Pharisaic matters such as tithing, purity, and sabbath observance.

The Hillel of these rabbinic sources is not simply historical

[11]See Neusner, *Pharisees,* II: 185-302 and III:255-272 for a literary and historical analysis of the traditions. Using Neusner's calculations, which can only be approximate because of the nature of the materials, the sages before Hillel taken together have only 75 traditions in 173 pericopae but Hillel alone has 33 traditions in 89 pericopae. See Jacob Neusner, "Three Pictures of the Pharisees: A Reprise," *Formative Judaism: Religious, Historical, and Literary Studies. Fifth Series* (BJS 91; Chico: Scholars, 1985) 65. This article (pp. 51-77) is a concise summary of Neusner's position.

[12]Neusner, *Pharisees,* II:294.

[13]M. Abot 1:16-18 with Gamaliel and Simeon are added to the original chain of tradition which includes the pairs up to Hillel and Shammai. Another sequence of names is given in b. Shabbat 15a. In neither case is Hillel said to be related to the patriarchal dynasty, but such a conclusion could be later deduced from the sequence. The search for legitimacy through descent reaches its peak in the later claim of the patriarchal house that Hillel was a descendent of David (j. Taan. 4:2). H. Strack, *Introduction to the Talmud and Midrash* (New York: Harper, 1965), 109, expresses the older consensus by saying that Gamaliel was "probably the son of Hillel." J.N. Epstein, *Mevo'ot le-Sifrut ha-Tannaim* (Jerusalem: Magnes; Tel-Aviv: Dvir, 1957), 31 expresses the more critical judgment that we know of no relationship between Hillel and Gamaliel. Neusner, *Pharisees,* II 294-95 and 375-76, notes that neither the Hillel nor the Gamaliel materials claim a relationship. In addition, the Gamaliel materials show no intrinsic relationship with the Hillel materials nor with those of Hillel's school.

any more than the Jesus of the gospels is. The only evidence for Hillel is in rabbinic sources, and they show with relative certainty only that he was a dominant Pharisaic teacher at the turn of the era whose influence was felt after his death. When he was adopted as the originator of the Pharisaic and later rabbinic patriarchate, he was turned into a larger than life figure and even compared to Moses.[14] Most of the stories about Hillel come from the mid-second century and later and attest to the rabbis' self-understanding rather than to the history of Hillel. What are most likely historical among the Hillel materials are the rules concerning tithes, purity and agriculture since these matters were discussed by the other early sages and form the earliest stratum of the Mishnah, as will be shown below.

Shammai, Hillel's opponent, appears almost entirely among the Hillel materials[15] and does not now stand apart from them. The rabbis claimed Hillel as their own and did not independently preserve Shammaite material nor did they present a fair picture of him and his teachings.[16] Teachers accepted into the tradition have their rulings recorded in a standard legal form, but Shammai lacks such rulings and is depicted in stories and biographical sayings. The Mishnah and Tosefta show Shammai accepting the dominance of Hillelite positions and thus coopt him for one of its purposes, convincing all Jews to accept its own interpretation of Jewish life.[17] The Palestinian Talmud and midrashim are less hostile to Shammai than the Babylonian Talmud which totally stereotypes him. Some of the texts suggest that the later rabbinic writers conceived of Shammai as having been dominant during his lifetime. This explains the number of stories in which they attack Shammai and also the stories of the eventual victory of Hillel and ascendancy of his party.

[14]Sifre Deut #357.

[15]Neusner, *Pharisees,* II:184-211, analyzes all the texts on Shammai and in II, 303-340 all the texts which have Hillel and Shammai opposed to one another.

[16]Neusner, *Pharisees,* II:196; the majority of stories are hostile, II:208.

[17]The Mishnah does this with many figures, for example, Akabya ben Mahalaleel. See Anthony J. Saldarini, "The Adoption of a Dissident: Akabya ben Mahalaleel in Rabbinic Tradition," *JJS* 33 (1982) 547-556.

THE HOUSES OF HILLEL AND SHAMMAI

The materials attributed to the Houses of Hillel and Shammai outnumber all materials attributed to pre-70 sages, even those of Hillel. Using Neusner's rough count, 219 traditions in 300 pericopae belong to the houses out of a total of 371 pre-70 traditions found in 655 pericopae.[18] The houses materials are highly stylized and reflect a large measure of redaction which Neusner places at Jamnia after the destruction of the Temple.[19] Since the attributions of materials to particular rabbis cannot be presumed to be accurate, rules and disputes can only be reliably dated if they are assumed or referred to in materials attributed to sages in a later generation. For example, if the Jamnian (70-130) or Ushan (140-170) sages know of a teaching or dispute, then it existed at that time and probably came from the previous generation. The rules attributed to the houses mostly concern tithes, purity and sabbath observance and not other wider concerns characteristic of the later second century. Thus, the second century sages seem to have had a group of disputes which came from the first century and which they preserved as part of their teaching.

The houses disputes do not give us a full or first hand view of the first century Pharisees. The formulation of the legal materials attributed to the houses of Hillel and Shammai is so stereotyped and pithy that they are surely literary constructions and neither the record of lively debate from the middle of the first century nor the verbally exact repetition of teachings from that period. Rather, the substance of the questions and solutions alluded to and presumed by the next generation probably derived from the pre-70 period but was reformulated in a regular and manageable way by the later generations.

THE BEGINNING OF THE PATRIARCHAL HOUSE

Little more is known about the first century sages following Hillel. A number of named authorities are mentioned, but not

---

[18]Neusner, "Three Pictures," 65. This count does not include many pericopae found in the Talmuds. See Neusner, *Pharisees*, II:5.

[19]Neusner, *Pharisees*, III:315.

many traditions are assigned to them and they are poorly understood. The major figures of the first century are Gamaliel I (the elder), Simeon his son, and, after the destruction of the Temple, Gamaliel II.[20] Although later sources see Gamaliel as a son of Hillel and thus Hillel as founder of the patriarchal dynasty, there is no evidence that Gamaliel was related to Hillel. The claim of relationship with Hillel and of Hillel's relationship to the house of David are typical dynastic claims to establish authority and legitimacy.

Gamaliel the Elder is represented by twenty-six traditions in forty-one pericopae, according to Neusner's count. Simeon his son has only seven traditions in thirteen pericopae. The corpora of both patriarchs are marked by stories about them and allusions to them, rather than the standard legal rulings assigned to post-70 sages. The agenda of Gamaliel the Elder is broader than that of earlier sages and its scope is consistent with the station and duties of a member of the Sanhedrin, a role assigned him in Acts 5:34-41.[21] Simeon is known from Josephus where he was active in the Jerusalem leadership during the war.[22] It seems likely that Gamaliel and his son were members of a prominent family who were also Pharisees. Since rabbinic sources identify Gamaliel II, son of Simeon, as a Shammaite, it is probable that they were not Hillelites, but nevertheless were leaders in the Pharisaic movement.[23]

AFTER THE DESTRUCTION OF THE TEMPLE

Stories of the sages following the destruction of the Temple and through the second century are much more numerous than those concerning the pre-destruction period. Though these stories had often been accepted uncritically as historically reliable and used to construct the early history of the rabbinic movement,

[20]B. Shab. 15a has a Simeon before Gamaliel the Elder and Tractate Abot 1:16-18 does not have a clear sequence. This has led to much speculation.

[21]See Neusner, *Pharisees,* II:376.

[22]See the section on Josephus' *War.*

[23]The place of Hillel and Shammai in the chains of tradition has been subject to some editing. It may be that Shammai was dominant during his life and that the Hillelites only gained power after the war. That is the reading that Neusner gives the evidence.

much as Acts was used in previous generations of New Testament scholarship, recent studies have shown that all these stories reflect the eras in which they were formulated and the context in which they were collected. Limitations of space prevent a review of the sages of this period and their connection to Pharisaism. The phenomena observed with earlier materials continue to limit the reliability of these materials as historical data. Johanan ben Zakkai, Gamaliel II, Akiba and others surely exercised a decisive influence on the incipient rabbinic movement but many of the stories about them date from the period after the defeat of Bar Kosiba by the Romans in 135 and reflect a late second century rabbinic interest in the origins of its movement.

The midrashic and talmudic documents give the impression that the sages were immediately recognized as teachers and leaders of the Jewish community. However, only well into the talmudic period do the rabbis have community control and even then they were still struggling for control of the Jewish community and attempting to convince the majority of the Jewish population to adopt their way of living and understanding Jewish life. It is likely that the towns and villages retained their traditional and varied customs and understandings of Jewish life after the destruction of the Temple and only gradually adopted the peculiar and powerful interpretation of the Biblical laws and covenantal demands embodied in the Mishnah and other rabbinic literature. Diaspora Judaism, whose diversity is testified to in inscriptions, literature and archaeology, probably took longer to accept this new way of life.

The power of the Jewish patriarchs was most probably very limited. The wars with Rome in 66-70 and 132-135 disrupted Palestinian Jewish life and led to Roman dominance in Jewish affairs. All Jewish leaders, including the rabbinic leadership, suffered during the Bar Kosiba war in the mid-second century. Only with Rabbi Judah the Prince, around 200, does rabbinic literature portray a wealthy, influential and powerful leader with the resources and personnel to dominate, though not completely control, the Palestinian community. The political situation during the second century was extremely complex. As was noted in chapter six, the evidence that the Gamaliel II was recognized as the leader of Judaism by the Romans is slim and highly ambiguous, rendering this often repeated claim historically uncertain.[24] Though the Romans characteristically recruited local leaders as their proxies, there is no conclusive evidence that they recruited Gamaliel rather than other traditional town leaders after the war. Even if they did recognize Gamaliel as the representative of the Jewish community, he and his associates (rabbis) would have had only limited control over how Jewish life was lived at first. Michael Goodman suggests that the power of the patriarch was insecure in the second and third centuries, with its power dissipated after the Bar Kosiba war, consolidated by Judah the Prince and gradually expanded to the secular sphere in the third century. Goodman connects this expansion of power with the increasing importance of intellectuals in the second sophistic period and the relative neglect of Palestine by the Roman authorities.[25] Only in the late fourth century do Roman sources recognize a patriarch with wide powers.

FIRST CENTURY FACTIONS AND COALITIONS

The nature of the "Houses" of Hillel and Shammai is a matter of some dispute. In Hebrew the term "house" has a wide range of meanings which can include a family, group, association or place. The houses of Hillel and Shammai, like Pharisaism itself, have often been understood as religious sects or schools of thought within Pharisaism. However, given the interpenetration of religion with politics and the rest of society, it is doubtful that the picture of the houses as sectarian debating societies is accurate.[26] Since the two groups identify themselves by the

[24]Schwartz, "Josephus," 167-168. For a cautious argument that the Romans appointed Gamaliel and his successors heads of the Palestinian community, see David Goodblatt, "The Origins of Roman Recognition of the Palestinian Patriarchate," [in Hebrew] *Studies in the History of the Jewish People and the Land of Israel.* Vol. 4 (Haifa: University of Haifa, 1978) 89-102. Goodblatt shows that stories about Gamaliel make sense if he was appointed by the Romans but the case is far from certain.

[25]M. Goodman, *State and Society in Roman Galilee, A.D. 132-212* (Totowa, NJ: Rowman, 1983) 115-117.

[26]Rivkin, *Revolution,* 135. Goodman, *State,* 114-115, says that Judah the Prince in 200 was mainly a religious intellectual gradually gaining power. He uses the category "religious intellectual" with the connotation of separation from secular society, a usage which is very problematic in the light of the structure of society outlined in ch. 3. However, if Judah and his predecessors are understood as continually interested in the control of society, even when they lacked any power, his analysis makes sense.

name of a leader or founder, they can be better understood as factions, that is, temporary associations of disparate people grouped around a leader.[27] Later after the death of the leaders, these factions may have become institutionalized into formal, corporate groups and provided part of first century social structure.

Factions thrive when society's central authority is weak, disorganized or unaccepted by much of the population, exactly the sociological conditions pertaining in first century Palestine. Judaism was subordinate to Rome and many popular movements, violent and non-violent, arose in response to this situation, as Josephus attests. The priests and leading families strove to keep the populace quiet, but ultimately they failed with catastrophic results for the Jewish nation. Amidst this maelstrom of activity many groups carved out their own ways of living Judaism to preserve their identities as Jews. Those factions which persist for a long time and outlive their leaders become a formal group with an organized, self-perpetuating leadership and defined social identity. The late first century and early second century accounts of the houses suggest that they were this type of group, and as such, one of many organizations of zealous Jews which provided a program for defending and reforming Judaism in the face of Roman and Hellenistic pressure. Hillel, Shammai, Judas the founder of the fourth philosophy, Jesus the preacher of the kingdom of God, Simon bar Giora the messianic pretender and others were very common in first century Judaism and easily gathered modest groups of enthusiastic followers who strove to convince other Jews to join them in seeking influence and power over social policy. Later, the early leaders of the rabbinic movement most probably did the same. During the second century the emerging sages probably lacked power and were striving to develop their program for Judaism and gain adherents among the people .This struggle for control would continue for the next few centuries

These very partisan and fragmentary rabbinic texts require interpretation in the context of the whole of Jewish society. The Pharisees and their leaders such as Hillel and Gamaliel were no more in control of Jewish society during the first century than

---

[27]See chapter four above.

were the patriarchs and sages in the second. They were one of a number of groups competing for power and influence and struggling to forge an identity for the people in the face of increasing pressure from Rome and the need to adapt Jewish life to new circumstances. Note that all the pre-destruction sages are connected with Jerusalem, the center of Jewish society, power and religion. Those sages about whom there are a number of traditions are pictured as influential in society and in contact with the high priest and other authorities. To some extent these rabbinic sages are similar to the Pharisees in Josephus. The rabbis, as might be expected, see their forebearers as politically and religiously dominant while Josephus keeps them within more probable historical bounds as a small group of limited influence. They agree that the Pharisees were a political, religious group which sought power and influence in Palestinian Judaism.

Very limited evidence in Josephus and the New Testament suggests that Gamaliel and Simeon his son were prominent leaders of the Pharisees with substantial influence in the Jerusalem high councils of Judaism. (It is noteworthy that Hillel did not come from this prominent family and is not recognized as an important social force outside of rabbinic literature.) The broad agenda of laws attributed to Gamaliel and the later emergence of this family as the leaders of Palestinian Judaism who eventually received Roman recognition make it likely that he came from a prominent family and was a Pharisaic leader.

Internally, the Pharisees had their own vision of how society should be but rabbinic literature also indicates that they had many disagreements within their small and diverse movement. Just how they were organized is not completely clear, but their endurance in society for over two centuries and their eventual emergence as a power in Jewish society during the second and third centuries argues to a coherent program and determined policy. Theories concerning their internal organization will be considered after a review of the first century legal agenda reflected in the Mishnah.

The Legal Agenda of the First Century

As was noted earlier in this chapter, many reconstructions of the Pharisees have assumed that parts of rabbinic law in the Mishnah, Tosefta and Talmuds had their origin as far back as Ezra and were passed on by the Pharisees and others to the rabbis. In addition, laws concerned with the Temple and other pre-destruction institutions and many anonymous laws have been assumed to be authentic testimony to the first century and earlier. Since the Mishnah and all subsequent rabbinic collections have been integrally composed and edited to communicate the views of their authors, such a simple appeal to supposedly early traditions is not acceptable in a critical history of Pharisaism.

Jacob Neusner has argued that material assigned to the pre-70 period must be established either by attestations (in which a law is presumed in an argument by a named authority) or by the logical development of the mishnaic law (in which a fundamental principle or generative concept is anterior to a later law).[28] Neusner's analysis claims that literary criteria can yield no comprehensive, reliable results because the Mishnah has been so thoroughly edited and historical criteria cannot give a social context because the laws have been placed in a timeless, ideal synthesis of Jewish life which appeals to the imagination and heart but ignores the social complexities of its time.[29] While his results cannot be completely proven, they are cogently argued and a necessary starting point for reconstructing the first century

---

[28]See *Pharisees*, III:180-238 for the traditions in sages names and *Evidence*, 45-75, for the mishnaic legal agenda which is logically prior to 70 C. E.

[29]Most recently David Weiss Halivni, *Midrash, Mishnah and Gemara: The Jewish Predilection for Justified Law* (Cambridge, MA: Harvard UP, 1986) 52-53, has argued, based on his earlier, detailed analyses of portions of Mishnah and Targum, that the Mishnah was "exerpted from earlier sources." Weiss Halivni's book theorizes that midrash preceded halakic formulations and that the midrashic collections and Mishnah as we have them are based on earlier oral and written sources. Neusner's work argues that all rabbinic sources have been so thoroughly edited that earier sources cannot be isolated and further that the shape and argument of Mishnah and the other sources is best explained as a product of the later sages, not as remnants of earlier generations. Weiss Halivni's hypothesis concerning the development of the law is based on a highly intuitive and subjective determination of which parts of rabbinic literature are early and which late. Neusner's work, based on a wholistic analysis of the texts and on commonly used historical and literary criteria, is more persuasive, though many problems remain unsolved and some interpretations are controversial.

Pharisees. The materials isolated by his method are more probably typical of the first century and a surer basis for historical and sociological reconstruction than isolated talmudic stories and enigmatic proverbial sayings from Tractate Abot.

When the Mishnah and Tosefta are analyzed using Neusner's criteria (the logic of Mishnah's argument and the attested attributions), by far the largest body of law which can be somewhat reliably assigned to the early and mid-first century concerns ritual purity, tithes and other food laws and sabbath and festival observance. These laws set out an agenda of holiness for the land and people which was a fitting response for a powerless people dominated by the Romans because these laws pertain to the parts of domestic life which can be controlled by people out of power in their own society: food, sex and marriage. Food and reproduction within the household rather than the public cult at the Temple and the governance of society are within the grasp of a subject people. We do not know for certain who developed these laws dating from before the destruction, but the usual hypothesis that it was the Pharisees who bequeathed these laws to the first generation of rabbis after the destruction of the Temple is most probable, based on the gospel evidence of Pharisaic interest in purity and food and on Josephus' claim that the Pharisees had their own interpretation of some Jewish laws. Still, we must remain cautious because we do not know directly the authors of these laws.

Neusner has often argued that the legal agenda of the Pharisees, centered around food laws and festivals, bespeaks a sectarian table fellowship which was not part of the political struggle of first century Palestine.[30] However, Neusner has also noted that this identification is hypothetical because the group who developed the early agenda of the Mishnah is not certainly known for a number of reasons. First, the Mishnah does not indicate that the group which formed its earliest laws was the Pharisees. Second, the emphasis on priestly purity could come from a group of radical priests or from lay people wishing to act

---

[30]Jacob Neusner, "The Fellowship (*Ḥaburah*) in the Second Jewish Commonwealth," *HTR* 53 (1960) 125-142; "Two Pictures of the Pharisees: Philosophical Circle or Eating Club," *Anglican Theological Review* 64 (1982) 525-528; "Three Pictures."

like priests or from a combination of the two.[31] Such a group could be loosely defined as a holiness sect,[32] but in the end Neusner says cautiously that even calling the first century framers of Mishnah's early rules a "sect" is too specific for the knowledge we have.[33] Such caution is appropriate, for reconstruction of a group from a limited literature like the early stages of the Mishnah is hazardous indeed. Our own reconstruction of the Pharisees will use wider sociological categories in order to give greater precision and probability to hypotheses concerning the nature of the Pharisaic group.

Neusner has argued that the absence of a coherent body of laws concerned with civil law and sacrifice in the Temple, though an argument from silence, suggests that the Pharisees were not in control of the Temple cult or the dominant force in society. Talmudic stories which depict the Pharisees as rulers of society are later retrojections of third to sixth century rabbinic power onto the Pharisees of the first century. As has been argued in the chapter on Josephus, the Pharisees were one of a number of groups competing for power and influence in the first century. They owe their later prominence not to their supposed great power, but to two later historical developments, the Christian interests in them as opponents of Jesus and the rabbis' adoption of them as their predecessors.

In contrast to Neusner's characterization of the first century Pharisees as a non-political sect, we have argued in our earlier chapters on the sociology of Palestine and Josephus that a distinction between the Pharisees as a political group and as a religious table fellowship is inappropriate. Because religion and politics are integrally connected, they are both at all times. The admittedly sparce and indirect first century evidence and the sociological probabilities both suggest that the Pharisees still desired influence and power but attained less of it in the first century than in Hasmonean and even Herodian times. This is a likely situation since the Romans were expert in siphoning off power and influence to themselves and their proxies (the high priest and most prominent families).

---

[31]Neusner, *Evidence,* 50, 70-71.

[32]Neusner, *Evidence,* 50, 71.

[33]Neusner, *Evidence,* 71.

How then is the "sectarian" agenda of the pre-70 sages to be explained sociologically? *First,* the stress on strict tithing, on observance of ritual purity by non-priests and on a certain observance of Sabbath and other festivals probably reflects the Pharisees' internal rules and program for a renewed Judaism. The articulation of this group program and the recounting of disputes among various factions is common in the literature of political and religious social groups. Thus, interest in their own program and silence concerning their external relations do not necessarily indicate separation from the larger society. *Second,* rules concerning food, purity, and group practices are typical boundary building mechanisms as analyzed by anthropologists.[34] Though such groups with their own identity and practices are often conceived of by modern commentators as withdrawn monastic groups, such factions, movements and coalitions' were most often intimately involved with society, even if partly in an adversary position.[35] Internal rules, such as food rules, kept the intimates of the groups united to one another and distinct from gentiles and even from other Jews with whom they constantly had to interact and with whom they competed. Neusner, in his study of the Mishnah, has correctly noted that the presence of rules which decree separation of the first century Pharisees from others in society suggest constant contact with the larger society and a vigilant attitude against the dangers of that contact.[36]

Thirdly, a complete account of the first century Pharisees' beliefs, rules, customs and commitments does not emerge from rabbinic literature. Their own internal literature would presume the fundamental beliefs and practices of Judaism, acceptance of the Bible and other major characteristics of Judaism. They most

[34]See the works of Mary Douglas, especially *Purity and Danger* (New York: Pantheon, 1966) and *Natural Symbols* (London: Routledge, 1970). Ethnic groups in the Roman empire were strong groups, low grid and thus needed to maintain strong boundaries in order to keep the larger Hellenistic-Roman society and culture from absorbing them.

[35]Bryan Wilson, *Magic,* has shown that even in modern third world countries sects are politically and socially involved much more often than not. See the discussion of sects in chapter four.

[36]Neusner, *Evidence,* 75. In a recent work Neusner acknowledges the ambiguity of the Pharisees' social role by referring to them as "a group of indeterminate classification (political cult?)" ("Three Pictures," 51).

probably concentrated on those (often minor) points of law and practice which distinguished them from other Jewish groups or which were in dispute among different factions. *Fourthly,* while the precise mode of living Judaism is distinctive in these laws, the tradition of using priestly laws concerning purity, food and marriage in order to separate, protect and identify Judaism goes back to the priestly tradition in the Exile and the regulations for Judaism championed by Ezra and Nehemiah in the restoration period. The Pharisees, or whoever developed the laws concerning purity and related matters, stood in a long and well accepted Jewish tradition and were probably one of a number of groups, such as the Essenes, adapting the Jewish tradition to changed circumstances.

Ḥabûrôt (Associations) and the People of the Land

Associations or fellowships, mentioned a number of places in rabbinic literature, have often been identified with or compared to the Pharisees. The associates in Tractate Demai who are devoted to maintaining the rules of ritual purity and tithing are the best known. Other associations in Jerusalem seem to be devoted to good works of various types, especially burial rites.[37] What is unclear in all these cases is what exactly is meant by the term "associate," how the texts differ from one another in their use of the term and whether it is even a technical term at all. The Hebrew words *ḥabûrāh* (association, fellowship) and *ḥabērîm* (associates) are common words which simply refer to one's fellows, that is, one's townsfolk or social familiars, with no technical meaning or special organization implied. Thus, the tendency of scholars to gather together all the citations of *ḥabēr* and *ḥabûrāh* and create a single historical group is misguided.[38]

The Pharisees have often been identified with the associates who appear in Mishnah Tractate Demai because both groups are associated with tithing and ritual purity. The associates

---

[37]This term also appears in a few other places, but these scattered references will not be considered here.

[38]Cohen, "History," 50 and Porton, "Diversity," 71 both caution that we do not really know what these associations were. Cohen notes that our lack of knowledge of Jewish social structure impedes understanding.

promised one another to tithe the food they eat and reliably to observe certain kinds of ritual purity. A brief review of these texts and their varied interpretations will further elucidate the problems faced in understanding the Pharisees.

The rules for the associates are contained in m. Demai 2:2-3 and t. Demai 2:2-3:9, the latter of which is a "length essay" and "a beautifully-constructed, sustained commentary" on Mishnah.[39] The associate must be trusted by his fellow associates to tithe his food properly and to keep it and everything connected with it ritually pure.

> He who undertakes to be trustworthy tithes what he eats, and what he sells and what he purchases and does not accept the hospitality of an am ha-aretz.... He who undertakes to be a *ḥābēr* does not sell to an am ha-aretz wet or dry produce and does not purchase from him wet and does not accept the hospitality of an am ha-aretz and does not receive him as his guest while he is wearing his own clothes.[40]

This rule means that the associates can confidently buy and sell to one another and also eat together without fear of breaking any of the laws they wish to keep. By contrast, they must take great care in their dealings with the people of the land, the am ha-aretz, because the people of the land do not keep the special priestly laws of purity and do not tithe properly and fully. Their food has not been properly sanctified and cannot be eaten by associates and must be tithed if it is acquired. The passage concerned with associates in Tosefta (t. Demai 2:2-3:9) deals with rules for accepting one as an associate, with stages of initiation (which are unclear and have provoked numerous disputes among scholars),[41] with doubtful cases of reliability

[39]Richard Sarason, *A History of the Mishnaic Law of Agriculture. Section 3. A Study of Tractate Demai.* Part 1 (Leiden: Brill, 1979) 72, 75. For detailed comments on these passages, see pp. 65-107.

[40]M. Demai 2:2-3, translation adapted from Sarason. There is a major controversy about whether the one who is trustworthy and the one who is a *ḥābēr* is the same person or whether these are two separate categories.

[41]Neusner, "Fellowship," 129-135, among others, tries to reconcile the texts into a coherent pattern. This text has often been compared with the Community Rule of the Qumran community.

within the family and marginal cases in relations with the am ha-aretz.

Some interpreters have attempted to place the associates of Demai in specific historical contexts and roles. The $\d{h}ab\bar{e}r\hat{i}m$ (associates) have been understood as Pharisees, as a group which included Pharisees or as a group allied with the Pharisees. Neusner earlier held that all the associates were Pharisees, but that all Pharisees were not associates.[42] Freyne allows for associates who were not Pharisees but sees an overlap between Pharisees and associates, with some belonging to both.[43] Scholars have adopted such positions because of the manifest similarities between the Pharisees' interests in purity and tithing and those of the associates. As a consequence the associates' avoidance of the am ha-aretz has led to reconstructions of the Pharisees which picture them as politically uninvolved and separate from society at large. Such positions are not supported by the texts concerning the Pharisees nor by Josephus and the New Testament.

Other theories concerning the associations have abounded. A. Guttmann is moved by the presence of the associates in tannaitic documents to place them in the post-70 period and identifies them as successors to the Pharisees and as including some rabbis.[44] He stresses the hostility of the associates to the am ha-aretz and suggests that this led to a separation of leaders and people overcome only in the Amoraic period with the passing of the associates from the scene. A strikingly different interpretation of Demai comes from S. Spiro who assigns the associates the role of tax (tithe) collectors in the Hasmonean period.[45] Spiro holds that the Mishnah, Tosefta and Talmuds had only a vague idea of what the associates were because that institution was already out of date in their time. The associates were not a

[42]"Fellowship," 125. Clearly Neusner's recent work has modified the method he uses in this article, but the article is often quoted and Neusner still favors the interpretation of the Pharisees as a table fellowship, though for different reasons and with more caution.

[43]Sean Freyne, *Galilee from Alexander the Great to Hadrian 323 B.C.E. to 135 C.E.* (Wilmington: Glazier/Notre Dame: Notre Dame UP, 1980) 307-310 and 322.

[44]Guttmann, *Rabbinic Judaism,* 173-174.

[45]Solomon J. Spiro, "Who was the *Haber?* A New Approach to an Ancient Institution," *JSJ* 11 (1980) 186-216, esp. 199, 202-203 and 211-216.

sect-like group, but an institution, a council of administrators, set up for the centralized collection of tithes. Changes during the reign of John Hyrcanus broke down the older system of tax collection and led to the formation of a new institution which collected tithes by force. Spiro gathers together diverse texts and harmonizes them using the hypothesis of Hasmonean tithe/tax collection. However, his hypothesis is not supported by any direct evidence and his exegesis of the rabbinic texts is forced in many cases and improbable in others.

The problems faced by the interpreter of these Mishnah and Tosefta passages are many. The structure of the Mishnah and Tosefta here is highly articulated and sophisticated and reflects the hands of the final editors. There is no way to show literarily or form critically that this material dates from the first century. Even were it proven to be from the second Temple period, the associates are not identified as Pharisees.[46] Granted the diversity of first century Judaism, it is better to keep groups, even nameless groups like the associates, separate from one another, rather than trying to identify them with known groups. Even if associates who kept ritual purity and tithed faithfully were similar to the Pharisees, it is sociologically probable that many such similar groups existed in the first century. The Qumran literature and other Jewish writings of this period evince a strong interest in particular interpretations of Jewish law, including purity and agricultural laws, as a way of life and mode of asserting Jewish identity and independence in the face of oppression.

Other rabbinic texts, most notably t. Megilla 4:15 refer to associations which were in Jerusalem. These texts have recently been interpreted by A. Oppenheimer and P. Peli as referring to groups which engaged in good works and which functioned like Greco-Roman burial societies.[47] Though the texts indicate that these groups went to feasts, funerals, weddings, etc. and though the presence of such social welfare groups has a certain probability in the Greco-Roman world, both authors draw texts

[46]Though it is probable that the mishnaic rabbis saw the associates as Pharisees, this does not mean that they were.

[47]A. Oppenheimer, "Haberot shehu birushalayyim," in *Jerusalem in the Second Temple Period* (Abraham Shalit Memorial), ed. A. Oppenheimer, et al. (Jerusalem: Yad Izhak ben-Zvi, 1980) 178-190; Pinchas H. Peli, "The Havurot That Were in Jerusalem," *HUCA* 55 (1984) 55-74.

from a variety of sources, accept them uncritically as historical and weave them into an elaborate but insubstantial tapestry.

All the attempts to contextualize the associates in history, from Neusner's modest theory that they were a group devoted to ritual purity to Spiro's intricate transposition of the texts to another era suffer from fatal weaknesses. They take various texts out of context and treat them as historically accurate accounts. They then create a context for these accounts so that the associates become historical figures with defined social roles. They also identify the associates with other groups known to have existed. All this reconstruction, including bringing together various pieces of evidence from one or another historical period, is unsupported by historical probability. Many of the suggestions are possible, but the hundreds of possibilities of history must be reduced to what happened or at least to what was probable. In the end the exact nature of these associations remains unknown to us. The willingness of the mishnaic and talmudic authors to speak of such groups argues to their acceptibility and presence in Jewish society and supports the view that the Pharisees were a typical group among many in Jewish society.

The Names Pharisee and Sadducee

A number of passages in rabbinic literature mention the Pharisees and Sadducees, but the characteristics assigned to each group are not consistent throughout rabbinic literature. It is evident that texts from different eras and places have different understandings of what the Pharisees and Sadducees are.

PHARISEES

The designation Pharisee is relatively infrequent in rabbinic literature and the texts using that term, which derive from several centuries of rabbinic literature, use it in different and sometimes pejorative senses. The etymology of Pharisees is disputed.[48] The name seems to come from the Hebrew and

---

[48]For a review of scholarly positions see A. I. Baumgarten, "The Name of the Pharisees," *JBL* 102 (1983) 411-412.

Aramaic root *prš* which means "separate" and "interpret." The most common etymological interpretation of Pharisees is "separate ones," though separate from whom or what is disputed. In a good sense this would mean people who separated themselves from normal Jewish society or from gentile society in order to observe Jewish law (purity, tithing?) more rigorously. In a negative sense it would mean sectarians or heretics, that is, people who separated themselves illegitimately from society at large because of beliefs and practices judged illegitimate.[49] Rabbinic literature uses the term in both senses. Another possible meaning of their name is "interpreters"; this meaning would fit with the observations in Josephus and the New Testament that the Pharisees had their own interpretation of Jewish law and were considered accurate interpreters of the law.[50] The two senses of the root could imply that the Pharisees separate themselves from the priestly or dominant interpretation of Jewish law. No decisive evidence or arguments have solved this issue.

No Jewish group refers to itself as Pharisees. The authors of rabbinic literature referred to themselves and their forebearers as "sages" (*ḥakāmîm*) and after the destruction of the Temple, used the title "rabbi" for sages. They have no name for their movement, but call themselves Israel because they consider themselves to be simply proper Jews. It is common for groups to have an internal name for themselves and to be called by another name by outsiders. The name used by outsiders may be pejorative, or a popular designation which grew by chance, or descriptive name more readily understandable to outsiders. The name Pharisees is a name used by outsiders, such as Josephus (taking the stance of a Hellenistic historian) and the New Testament. The sages do not customarily identify themselves or their predecessors as Pharisees, except when they implicitly ally themselves with the Pharisees in disputes with the Sadducees.

Later in this chapter the texts which mention Pharisees and Sadducees will be examined. Here brief notice will be taken of some texts which refer to the Pharisees in a pejorative or neutral manner and clearly have a different understanding of the word

---

[49]See Guttmann, *Rabbinic Judaism,* 173.

[50]Baumgarten, "Name," 411-428, uses *accuracy* of interpretation as the key for understanding the Pharisees.

than most of the texts normally cited.

In m. Sotah, the treatise concerning the ordeal to be endured by a suspected adulteress, one of the mishnayot contains advice by Ben Azzai that a father ought to teach his daughter Torah. His position is immediately attacked by Rabbi Eliezer who says that teaching Torah to a woman is like teaching her lechery and then by Rabbi Joshua who uses a stereotypical proverb depicting women as lecherous and a second proverbial saying which attacks four categories of people including a woman *perûš āh* (pharisee). In both sayings the root of the word Pharisee, *prš*, is played upon.

> Rabbi Joshua says: A woman desires one measure (*qab*) [of food] with lechery to nine measures [of food] with self-restraint (*perîšût*). He used to say: A foolish pious man, a cunning wicked man, a woman Pharisee (*'iššāh perûšāh*) and the wounds of the Pharisees (*perûšîn*), these are wearing out the world. (M. Sotah 3:4).

The first proverb is found in b. Ketubot 62b and seems to be a well known saying. It suggests that women desire illicit or frivolous sexual activity so much that they will choose poverty to achieve it, and consequently that they lack "self-restraint," a Hebrew word which also comes from the root *prš*. In the second proverb, the pious fool and the "wise" evil person are a typical sapiential contrasting pair. The nature of the second pair is obscure, but both are characterized by the root *prš* used in a pejorative sense. The Palestinian Talmud[51] interprets the woman *perûš āh* as one who quotes a Biblical text (e.g., Gen. 30:16) in a sexually suggestive way. Finkelstein suggests that the term "separated" woman refers to a wife who treats normal marital relations as immoral or impure.[52] The wounds of the Pharisees or separated ones could refer to almost anything. The Palestinian Talmud gives two examples in which cunning tactics are used to deprive needy people of their due. In the first Rabbi Eleazar advises a deceased man's heir how to keep his widow from

---

[51]J. Sotah 3:4 (19a).

[52]Louis Finkelstein, *The Pharisees* (3 ed.; Philadelphia: Jewish Publication Society, 1962) 837, n. 52.

consuming the estate, but she in turn charges Eleazar with depriving her of her maintenance as a widow. The second concerns a poor disciple of Rabbi Judah the Prince who is tricked out of his eligibility for financial assistance. In this case Rabbi, in an equally cunning manner, sees to it that the student is once again made legally eligible to receive charitable contributions.

The explanations in the Palestinian Talmud offer no evidence that they know the original meaning of the Mishnah. The root *prš* is not central to the talmudic interpretations of the "woman Pharisee" and the "blows of the Pharisees" and the terms are not explained. The Mishnah does not seem to be using *prš* to mean Pharisee and the women and the Pharisees in this proverb do not have the same characteristics. Both are interpreted conventionally, the woman as lascivious and the men as scholars who lack integrity.

The Babylonian Talmud quotes the well known list of seven types of Pharisees as a comment on m. Sotah 3:4.[53] The list does not elucidate the meaning of the two uses of *prš* in the Mishnah, but it does show that Pharisee has multiple meanings, some of them pejorative. Clearly the first five names are meant pejoratively and in the subsequent discussion in the Babylonian Talmud the last two, those who have motives of love and fear in studying Torah, are rejected as well in favor of the study of Torah for its own sake.

> There are seven types of Pharisee, the *šykmy* Pharisee, the *nyqpy* Pharisee, the *qwz'y* Pharisee, the *mdwky'* Pharisee, the Pharisee (who says) Let me know my duty and I will do it, the Pharisee from love, the Pharisee from fear.[54]

---

[53] The Palestinian Talmud cites the list twice, but in other contexts. See the next note.

[54] The Talmud explains the first five types based on etymology. It is most interested in the discussion of the relative merits of love and fear. The list also appears in j. Ber. 9:5 (13b) and j. Sot. 5:7 (20c) where identical explanations, differing from the Babylonian ones, are given. The list appears with variations and no explanation in the Fathers According to Rabbi Nathan, Version A, ch. 37 (Schechter, 109) and Version B, ch. 45 (Schechter, 124). In j. Ber. the list of seven types of Pharisees occurs in a discussion of Akiba's martyrdom and the seven names seem to denote seven motives for martyrdom and the asceticism which accompanies it. See S. Fraade, "Ascetical Aspects of Ancient Judaism," in *Jewish Spirituality From the Bible Through the Middle Ages,* ed. A. Green (New York: Crossroad, 1986) 271.

Lack of space and the obscurity of the names prevent a full interpretation of each of the names. In context both the Babylonian and Palestinian Talmuds are interested in the correct motives for obeying Torah and in rejecting hypocritical behavior. Several of the names are made to refer to hypocritical behavior or obedience to the law from imperfect motives. The Babylonian Talmud ends this section with a saying of King Yannai (Alexander Jannaeus) who warns his wife against those "painted ones" who pretend to be Pharisees.

Since these lists are found for the first time in talmudic sources, they probably do not give accurate information about first century Pharisaism. By the fifth and sixth centuries Christianity had attained a position of power in the empire and since both the New Testament and early Christian writings contained attacks on the Pharisees as hypocrites, these lists may be a response to Christian polemics in which the talmudic authors defuse Christian criticism by agreeing with their attack on hypocritical Pharisees and separating some Pharisees and themselves from those being attacked.

Tosefta Berakot (3:25), speaking of the prayer of the Eighteen Benedictions, says that one should include the heretics (*minîm*) among the separated ones (*prwšyn*). According to this text, the twelfth benediction, usually designated as the benediction against the heretics on the basis of a Geniza text, was originally against the "separatists." According to Lieberman, "separatists" referred to those who separated themselves from the Jewish community in time of oppression and trouble.[55] Thus, "Pharisees" here is used descriptively for Jews who are not faithful to the Jewish way of life. In another passage "Pharisees" is used as a descriptive term for another group of whom the rabbis did not approve, those who mourned the loss of the temple by not eating meat or drinking wine.[56] This group had separated itself from ordinary society by ascetical practices of which the rabbis did not approve.

"Pharisee" is used positively of one who observes purity rules.

[55]Saul Lieberman, *Tosefta Ki-Fshutah.* Order Zeraim, Part I (New York: Jewish Theological Seminary, 1955) 54.

[56]T. Sotah 15:11-12; b. B. B. 60b and elsewhere. See also E. E. Urbach, "Ascesis and Suffering in Talmudic and Midrashic Sources," [in Hebrew] *Yitzhak Baer Jubilee Volume* (Jerusalem, 1960) 48-68.

Even a Pharisee who has venereal disease, which renders him impure, is not to eat with an am ha-aretz who has venereal disease, according to the school of Shammai, though the school of Hillel permits it.[57] It is unclear whether the term *prwš* in this context refers to the Pharisees as an organized group or is descriptive of a person who tithes and keeps ritual purity with special rigor and thus "separates" himself from the ordinary people. The purity of the Pharisees or separated ones is referred to as a well known category in m. Toh. 4:12. The mishnaic author seems to be citing a well known degree of cleanliness proper to the Pharisees. Interestingly, the author does not identify himself as a Pharisee but may be talking about the past.[58] In another place, perhaps implicitly referred to by M. Tohorot, the purity of the Pharisees is part of a sorites on degrees of purity. In this list the Pharisees rank above the am ha-aretz, but below three classes of priests.[59]

This brief survey does not cover all the texts which mention the Pharisees/*perûšîm*. It does, however, show the wide variety of usage associated with the word which is also used for the first century group, the Pharisees. Though the word was used as a proper name for a group, it retained its more generic meaning of "separated ones" with its many connotations.

SADDUCEES

The Greek name Sadducees and the Hebrew *Saddûqîm* (with variant forms) do not give any real insight into the group. Two explanations of the name have been proposed. The more popular explanation recently has been to connect the term Sadducee with the Sadokites, the high priestly family which traced its ancestry to David's high priest, Sadok. Thus Sadducees would be either (some of?) the Sadokite priests or partisans of the Sadokites. However, the forms of the name extant in Greek, Hebrew and Aramaic do not give clear support to this hypothesis. The other hypothesis is that the name is descriptive

---

[57] T. Shab. 1:15, b. Shab 13a.

[58] In the previous mishnah he speaks of scribes.

[59] M. Hagiga 2:7.

and characterizes this group as the "just" or "righteous," either as a positive or ironic description. No explanation has been definitively proven.[60]

Though no literature from the Sadducees has survived and the sources tell us little, the Sadducees were an established and recognized first century Jewish group because they were described and alluded to by both Josephus and the gospel writers. The little available historical information can lead to a minimal interpretation of what they were or at least were not and a sociological analysis can help us to visualize their place in Jewish society.

The Sadducees are mentioned a moderate number of times in rabbinic literature, but the references are scattered over various types of literature from different periods. Thus the historical reliability of all these passages is suspect.[61] In the Mishnah and Tosefta texts, the earliest available, the Sadducees and Pharisees disagree over practices or teachings. Since the rabbinic authors saw themselves as heirs of the Pharisees, the Sadducees are always bested in argument and usually pictured as subordinate to the Pharisees.

Several other problems impede the study of the Sadducees in rabbinic literature. In a number of places Sadducees have been inserted into the text in place of the original "heretics" (*minîm*) and "gentiles" (*gôyîm*) through either the intervention or fear of medieval Christian censors.[62] In many parallel versions of stories and laws Sadducees are found in one version and Boethusians in another. (See below for the Boethusians.) The Boethusians occur especially in the Tosefta (while appearing only once in the Mishnah). Both Sadducees and Boethusians were probably first century groups but by the third century when the Mishnah and Tosefta took shape, the two names were confused with one another and to some extent interchangeable. This has led many to merge the Sadducean and Boethusian texts into one group and use them to describe the Sadducees,[63] but such late conflation and confusion suggest that the authors of the rabbinic

[60]LeMoyne, *Sadducéens,* 155-163.

[61]See LeMoyne, *Sadducéens,* 321-27 and passim for critical problems.

[62]See LeMoyne, *Sadducéens,* 97-99.

[63]See Rivkin, "Defining," for example.

works did not understand the first century realities and thus throw doubt on the reliability of all the texts about the Sadducees and Boethusians. In addition, some parallel texts have differing opponents for the Sadducees, including the Pharisees, the sages, and an anonymous "they." These variations indicate that the Sadducees became stereotyped in later rabbinic literature as the "opponents" of rabbinic Judaism, rather than treated as a real first century group with its own identity and understanding of Judaism. In the Babylonian Talmud the Sadducees occur often in the role of opponents, and in a midrashic passage they are charged with despising the word of the Lord, presumably because they opposed the rabbinic understanding of Judaism.[64] Such passages are clearly not historical, but an indication of the roles Sadducees played in rabbinic literature.

THE IDENTITY OF THE BOETHUSIANS

The Boethusians, who appear only in rabbinic literature and who are usually identified with the Sadducees, are a more knotty problem than the Sadducees or Pharisees. They appear only from Herodian times on and their name appears only once in the Mishnah but many times in the Tosefta. The name is variously spelled in the literature and its origin is not certain.[65] Boethusians appear occasionally in the Palestinian Talmud; the Babylonian Talmud has Sadducees instead of Boethusians. It is clear that the Sadducees and Boethusians were gradually understood to be the same group,[66] but in the first century these groups were most likely separate, though the origin and nature of the Boethusians is far from certain.[67] The family of Boethus

---

[64]Sifre Num. 112 (on 15:31).

[65]LeMoyne, *Sadducéens*, 332.

[66]LeMoyne, *Sadducéens*, 101-102. The Fathers According to Rabbi Nathan, Version A, ch. 5 (to be treated below), gives them a common origin consistent with the later view of them in rabbinic literature, but the historicity of this account is doubtful.

[67]LeMoyne reviews several theories of the origin of the Boethusians' name and argues that, because they appear in rabbinic literature at the time of Herod, they probably owe their name to an Alexandrian Jewish priest named Boethus whose son Simon was made high priest by Herod in 22 B.C.E. (*Sadducéens*, 336-337). See Josephus, *Ant.* 15.9.3 (320).

may be the same one condemned by Abba Saul[68] and Boethus may have also have been the father or ancestor of Matthias, a person active at the time of the Great War.[69] Because of the close ties among Herod, Boethusians and Sadducees in the sources, LeMoyne suggest that the Boethusians were a sub-group of the Sadducees and may have been identical with the Herodians. This hypothesis is very doubtful.

Most hypotheses assume that groups associated (or confused?) with one another in the sources should be identified, but it is far better to keep groups with distinct names separate, even if we know little about them. The preservation of the name, even though the Boethusians have no known significance for the rabbinic authors, suggests that the name was known, but that later generations knew little about them and gradually assimilated them to the Sadducees. It is also likely that the Boethusians were a priestly group or associated with the priests and other Jewish leaders. As such they would have been one of many factions and interest groups competing for power and influence in Jerusalem during the Roman period. They may have had special teachings and interpretations of Jewish life, but none have been preserved distinct from those of the Sadducees.[70] References to them in the Talmud are often hostile, for example, that they hired false witnesses to deceive the Pharisees about the new moon,[71] and so untrustworthy as historical sources.

RIVKIN'S INTERPRETATION OF THE PHARISEES

Ellis Rivkin's analysis of rabbinic texts which contrast the Pharisees and Sadducees lay the groundwork for his thesis that the Pharisees are not a sect-like association concerned with ritual purity, but a "scholarly class dedicated to the teaching of the twofold law ... and to the dissemination of their belief in

---

[68]T. Men 13:21. See also b. Pes. 57a.

[69]Josephus, *War* 5.13.1 (527).

[70]LeMoyne, *Sadducéens,* 177-198, draws together a number of texts concerned with the Boethusians and liturgical law. The evidence is fragmentary and the reconstruction very hypothetical. A full consideration of the evidence would lead us away from our main subject here.

[71]T. Rosh Hashanah 1:15; b. Rosh Hashanah 22b; j. Rosh Hashanah 57d.

the world to come and the resurrection of the dead."[72] For Rivkin the Pharisees' position represented a profound internalization of Judaism, promising individual life beyond death and effectively combating the threatened dissolution of Jewish life in the Greco-Roman period. They were so successful that they succeeded in attaining enormous influence and power in Jewish society. Rivkin then interprets Josephus and the New Testament in a way consistent with his thesis.

Rivkin has provided the most acceptable alternative to Neusner's thesis, but despite his methodological care, he has interpreted rabbinic texts and ultimately the New Testament and Josephus uncritically. Since there is no space to critique his treatment of the New Testament and Josephus in detail, a couple of examples must suffice.[73] Mt. 23:2 says that the Pharisees sit on the seat of Moses and their teaching authority must be respected. Josephus says that the Pharisees were very influential with the people, as we saw in chapter six. Rivkin takes these passages and some others as historically reliable indicators of the Pharisees' political and social power in society. But Mt. 23 is a polemic against the Pharisees, who for Matthew are the major opponents of Jesus. In addition, Matthew contains many early traditions whose provenance and meaning in the pre-70 period are difficult to ascertain. Josephus does not say that the Pharisees were in charge of society permanently, but that they had great influence under Alexandra and occasionally at other times. Even his general observation that they were influential on the people does not show that they had a dominant influence on Jewish society, but only that they were one of many competing groups in society which met with varied success at different times.

Rivkin's procedure in working with rabbinic texts is an improvement over previous impressionistic essays filled with disconnected references. He correctly notes that the designation Pharisee has different meanings in some texts and is ambiguous in others. His procedure is to analyze first those texts where Pharisees are explicitly contrasted with Sadducees and thus are

---

[72]*IDBS,* 657; see *Hidden Revolution,* esp. ch. 3, pp. 125-179 and "Defining."

[73]See the critical review of Rivkin's interpretation of Josephus by Shaye J. D. Cohen in *JBL* 99 (1980) 627-629.

certainly the same Pharisees found in Josephus and the New Testament. On the basis of the Pharisees-Sadducees texts he eliminates those texts which mention the Pharisees in a way inconsistent with the control texts. Finally he analyzes ambiguous texts in a way congruent with the Pharisees-Sadducees texts.[74]

Though this method is an improvement over previous analyses, it fails because of several difficulties. First, the texts grouped together by Rivkin come from rabbinic sources spanning several centuries. His analysis takes each Pharisees-Sadducees text as historically reliable and takes no account of the kind of collection it comes from, nor place, nor date. No allowance is made for the possibility that a third or fourth century talmudic author may have written or changed a story to fit his *idea* of what the Pharisees and Sadducees were.[75] He assumes that when the Pharisees and Sadducees are contrasted, the categories have the same meaning in all sources including Josephus in the first century, the Mishnah in the second century and the Babylonian Talmud three centuries later and many miles away. He ignores category changes in different sources and the effect of later rabbinic views of the first century. For example, when the Boethusians appear in the Tosefta he takes them to be Sadducees because some of the teachings attributed to Boethusians in the Tosefta are attributed to Sadducees in other sources. By similar procedures he identifies sages (*ḥakāmîm*) as Pharisees in some texts where they oppose the Sadducees.[76] The problems with the identity of the Boethusians have been dealt with above. The change in terminology from Pharisees to sages probably reflects the later rabbinic sages' identification of themselves as Pharisees, but it casts doubt on the historical reliability of the texts in which it happens. Yet, the question of the texts' reliability as first century sources remains.

---

[74]"Defining," 207-208.

[75]For example, in t. Hag 3:5 he assumes that the Pharisees had direct power over the cult because they are said to have dipped the menorah in water to render it ritually clean, against the position of the Sadducees. But the passage is a highly rhetorical attack dating almost a century and a half after the destruction of the Temple and hardly reliable history. It also assumes that enough Pharisees were priests that they could control the Temple cult, a very late and improbable view of them indeed.

[76]"Defining," 209-217 and passim.

It is more likely that such texts transmit later rabbis' views of what they understood the Pharisees and Sadducees to be rather than the first century reality.

The earliest and most reliable Pharisee-Sadducee texts are the seven which come from the Mishnah and Tosefta.[77] Lightstone's study of this uniform but small body of texts overcomes the major difficulty in Rivkin's method, combining disparate sources (in date and type) into one amalgam. However, this homogeneous corpus of texts shows only that the Pharisees have laws, especially purity laws, which differ from the Sadducees. They do not show that the two groups had different programs for Judaism, divergent interpretations of Scripture and certainly not a dispute over adherence to the oral law. Since the earliest rabbinic sources do not yield the information usually attributed to them, the usual view of the Pharisees derived from rabbinic sources depends on an uncritical amalgamation of disparate sources, both rabbinic and non-rabbinic.

The mishnaic accounts of the Pharisees favor them greatly since the mishnaic editors adopted the Pharisees as their forebearers. In every case the Pharisees agree with the dominant position in the Mishnah because the editors' purpose was not simply to report the disagreements between the Pharisees and Sadducees but recount exemplary stories, legal precedents or polemics designed to ridicule or vilify the position taken by the Sadducees in opposition to the Mishnah's teaching. Thus from these texts no thoroughly reliable conclusions about the exact teachings of the Pharisees and Sadducees can be drawn; even if everything were accepted as reliable, the texts do not give a rounded picture of their agendas. A few of the texts in which Pharisees and Sadducees appear will be analyzed in order to show the limits of our knowledge in this area.

Pharisee-Sadducee Texts

In the Mishnah and Tosefta most of the disputes concern purity and most are controversies in which the Sadducees come

---

[77]Lightstone, "Sadducees *versus* Pharisees," above. For other problems with Rivkin's method, see ch. 1.

out second best.[78] In m. Yadaim the Sadducees and Pharisees disagree over whether Scripture renders the hands unclean, about what kind of bones render a person unclean and about the uncleanness of several types of water. The complaints of the Sadducees against the Pharisees and the retorts of the Pharisees and Johanan ben Zakkai in m. Yadaim 4:6-7 are rhetorical and polemical.[79] Another purity dispute concerns whether Sadducean women keep proper menstrual cleanness according to the teaching of the sages (m. Niddah 4:2; t. Niddah 5:2-3).[80] The Sadducean women who do not follow mishnaic custom are contrasted with Israelite women and thus are treated as less than good Jews, like Samaritans. In a minority opinion Rabbi Jose held that Sadducean women were presumed to be clean unless they explicitly followed Sadducean customs. Rabbi Jose's opinion assumes that the mishnaic sages dominated society to such an extent that all, even Sadducees, would act according to their understanding of the law. This assumption is not borne out by what we know of the first century.

In the dispute over whether immersion alone will render one clean without waiting for sunset (m. Parah 3:7; t. Parah 3:8) the Temple is pictured as having a place of immersion so that mishnaic law can be followed and the priest who is preparing the red heifer can be immediately purified, contrary to the Sadducean ruling which held that one had to wait until after sundown to be cleansed.[81] This text implies that the Pharisees were in charge of the Temple, a claim which has no historical foundation. T. Hagiga 3:35 presents another case that implies Pharisaic control in the Temple, a dispute concerning whether the menorah at the Temple must be immersed in order to be

---

[78]For a lengthy and detailed consideration of the rabbinic texts, see LeMoyne, *Sadducéens*, 198-317 as well as Rivkin, "Defining." LeMoyne treats all the rabbinic sources together. Here we shall stress the earliest collections, the Mishnah and Tosefta. For a traditional treatment of twenty-three controversies between the Pharisees and Sadducees in rabbinic literature, see Finkelstein, *The Pharisees*, 637-761.

[79]See t. Yad. 1:19/2:9; 2:20; b. Bab. Bat. 115b. The Babylonian Talmud has Johanan ben Zakkai as the disputant instead of the Pharisees in the last exchange in this series.

[80]In the Mishnah the Sadducees are opposed to the anonymous sages of the Mishnah; the Talmud sharpens the conflict and identifies the sages with the Pharisees.

[81]The Babylonian Talmud (b. Hag. 23a) sharpens the conflict, as it did in the previous case, by saying that they *purposely* rendered a priest unclean in order to immerse and cleanse him and show that the Sadducees were wrong.

rendered ritually clean. This text supposes that there were many Pharisaic priests serving alongside Sadducean ones and that the Pharisaic priests were in control. While some priests might have been Pharisees and others Sadducees, most priests belonged to neither group. The division of all priests into Sadducees and Pharisees in the Tosefta is stylized and unhistorical.

The Mishnah also contains two disputes over civil law and one over sabbath law which involve the Pharisees and Sadducees (or the sages and Sadducees). The Sadducees, in a sequence of disputes concerning purity, "cry out" against the Pharisees' contention that a master is not responsible for his slaves' injurious actions (m. Yad. 3:7). The Pharisees claim that the slaves' exercise of intention absolves the master from responsibility, a position which accords with the mishnaic emphasis on intention.[82] In the second dispute (m. Makkot 1:6) the Sadducees and sages disagreed about when a perjured witness in a capital case could be executed, a dispute based on the interpretation of Scriptural phrases rather than the type of behavior or its effects. Finally, Sadducees held their own views about the *erub* which allowed movement around town during the Sabbath.[83] The mishnaic authorities (they are not called Pharisees) must claim the courtyard before a Sadducee does and set up their erub to let them move around a common courtyard. In this text the Sadducee is treated as a Jew with different customs who would not agree to mark out the courtyard as common space and thus restrict the ability of the sages to make the courtyard common.

In the Mishnah and Tosefta most of the disputes between the Sadducees and Pharisees (and others) concern interpretations of the laws of ritual purity.[84] If the Pharisees based much of their program for Jewish life on a revised understanding of the purity laws and an application of them to all Israel, as has been argued above, then the conflict between the Sadducees and Pharisees on this issue is comprehensible and probably historical in its

[82]See Howard Eilberg-Schwartz, *The Human Will in Judaism: The Mishnah's Philosophy of Intention* (BJS 103; Atlanta: Scholars, 1986).

[83]M. Erub. 6:2.

[84]The centrality of purity to recorded Sadducean teachings is noted by LeMoyne, *Sadducéens,* 362 and by Gary Porton, "Sects and Sectarianism During the Period of the Second Temple," [unpublished paper] p. 7.

general content. The application of purity laws to the people at large was a new mode of understanding Jewish life, law and Scripture and it is reasonable and even inevitable that the Sadducees or someone else should oppose them. The Sadducees had their own (probably more traditional) understanding of Judaism and promoted it against the new Pharisaic view. If many of the Sadducees were priests or supporters of the traditional priesthood, they would have had another motive to oppose the Pharisees. The priests would not want the purity practices characteristic of the Temple and priesthood to be diluted by adaptation to the multitude.

BABYLONIAN TALMUD

The Babylonian Talmud contains a number of passages with Pharisees and Sadducees in which Sadducees seem to be original and not replacements for "heretics" or "Christians." A review of a few of them will show how the Babylonian masters emphasized the opposition between the Sadducees and Pharisees. When a Pharisaic family wishes to set up an *erub* in a public courtyard so it can move around on Sabbath, it must do so before other Jews with different observances set out their belonging. If a gentile lives in the courtyard, it does not matter.[85] In the Mishnah Rabban Gamaliel tells a story which implies that the Sadducees are Jews with different beliefs, but in the Babylonian Talmud they are treated by a minority opinion as equivalent to gentiles in status. The Sadducees are also excluded from the fraternity of the authoritatively learned in an aside in b. Yoma 4a which explicitly says that the students of the sages from the students of Moses, who are to instruct the high priest concerning the conduct of the Day of Atonement, are not to be Sadducees.

The dominance of the Pharisees over the Sadducees is presumed and reinforced in the Babylonian Talmud, as has been indicated above. In another case, the Mishnah says that the Jewish court in Jerusalem is to instruct the high priest concerning his duties on the Day of Atonement (m. Yoma 1:5). The Sifra 81a-b and b. Yoma 19b argue that the Sadducees who were high

---

[85]m.Erub. 6:2; b. Erub. 68b.

priests had to follow the sages' rules concerning lighting incense, that is, they were permitted to light it only after entering the Holy of Holies on the Day of Atonement. The Talmud goes on to tell a story of a high priest who dropped dead after he disobeyed this rule. In addition, in the Talmud the sages of the Mishnah are designated Pharisees and the generalization is made that the Sadducees feared the Pharisees and so followed their interpretations of the law. This later Babylonian view is hardly historical for the first century. The contest between the Sadducees and Pharisees is carried to a fictional extreme in another case when the Talmud claims that in the preparation of the red heifer the Pharisees purposely rendered a priest unclean in order to immerse and cleanse him and show that the Sadducees were wrong in requiring that the priest wait until after sundown to attain ritual purity.[86]

Conclusion

The stories about the second Temple sages and the limited references to the Pharisees and Sadducees have often been used as the main body of evidence for reconstructing the history of these two groups. Such an historical use of rabbinic stories is illegitimate for a number of reasons and fails to produce a historically reliable account of the origins and history of the Pharisees and Sadducees. The stories concerning the pre-destruction period come from many collections of rabbinic literature, including Mishnah, Tosefta, both Talmuds and many midrashic collections. Seldom have these passages been analyzed by source, in context, in order to judge the role of the story or teaching in the work in which it appears and its congruence or non-congruence with the tendencies of the larger work. When different versions of such teachings and stories have been compared, they have usually been harmonized in order to produce a coherent account without attention to the critical question of historicity. The widely varied dates and contexts of these materials seriously impede any effort to derive a coherent whole from them.

[86]b. Hag. 23a. See also b. Zeb. 21a.

Even if the historical probability of some statements or events can be established, we are left with incomplete fragments which tell us little about the origin, development, social status, teachings and inner life of the Pharisees and even less about the Sadducees. The use of the materials concerning the pre-70 sages assumes, but does not prove, that they were Pharisees, that they understood themselves to be Pharisees and were seen that way by others. We do not know that this is so and even if we did, the texts we have would tell us little about these shadowy figures. In order to write a history of the Pharisees and Sadducees from rabbinic sources, scholars have been forced to create a whole historical and social framework for interpreting these texts. But such overviews of Jewish society have often not been based on the history and sociology of antiquity, but on later views of the rabbinic tradition.

From the rabbinic traditions we can learn a bit about the Pharisees, especially in the first century. We can deduce with some probability that Hillel was a major leader of one of the groups which made up the rabbinic movement after the destruction of the Temple. Though the stories about him make him larger than life, his influence at least on a limited group is undeniable. Because of the legendary elaboration concerning Hillel, few historically reliable specifics can be known about him. It is also highly probable that Hillel's followers formed a faction called the "House of Hillel" and were in conflict with another faction which gave allegiance to Shammai. If Neusner is correct that the earliest stratum of laws in the Mishnah concerned ritual purity, tithing and other food laws, then these concerns may have been the basis for the conflict. But these texts do not reveal the internal structure of the Pharisaic groups, how demanding membership was, what parts of society were drawn to membership, the size of the groups or many other aspects of group structure.

Because the Sadducees are mentioned so seldom in rabbinic literature, because the stories and disputes are hostile to them and because even the occurrence of their name is textually uncertain in many cases, few historically reliable conclusions can be drawn concerning them. They were opponents of the Pharisees, but this was probably not the core of their identity. They presumably had a well articulated view of how Jewish life was to be lived, but rabbinic sources tell us little about it, except for a few particulars where their views differed from the Pharisees. Even Josephus' accounts were sparse and gave no coherent picture. A full synthetic evaluation of the Sadducees will be attempted in the final chapter.

The rabbinic sources can be of limited help in reconstructing the history of the Pharisees and Sadducees if they are interpreted in conjunction with Josephus and the New Testament, sources which are closer to the time of the Pharisees, but which, as was seen above, need careful interpretation themselves. Further non-harmonizing, critical studies of stories and teachings attributed to the pre-70 period will certainly show us more about later centuries' views of the early period than about the early period itself and may even produce a few historical kernals to enlighten us about the first century and earlier.

Part III

INTERPRETATION AND SYNTHESIS

11

The Social Roles of Scribes in Jewish Society

The scribes appear as an organized social group only in the synoptic gospels, where they are associated with both the Pharisees and high priests as opponents of Jesus. Scribes are mentioned in Josephus but not as a coherent social group and in rabbinic literature the scribes are conceived of as post-exilic, pre-rabbinic teachers of Israel whose authority and teachings are sometimes invoked. In addition, scribes appear in rabbinic texts in their normal functions as copyists and teachers. Scribes are unlike the Pharisees and Sadducees in that they appeared all over the Mediterranean world and the Near East over several millennia, fulfilled many functions and had varied roles and status over time and in different places. A huge body of evidence provides a context for understanding the scattered references to the scribes in Josephus and rabbinic literature, as well as in the gospels. A survey of some of the evidence concerning scribes in antiquity will provide a context for understanding the scribes in the gospels. It will also provide some further insight into how society was organized and functioned in the Greco-Roman period.

The Hebrew word for scribe, *sôfēr,* comes from the Semitic root *spr* which referred originally to a message which was sent, that is, a written message, and then was used for writing and the writer. The Greek word for scribe, *grammateus,* comes from the word *gramma* which means something drawn and, most commonly, written letters. In various combinations this root refers to all aspects of writing and education. The word "scribe" in Hebrew, Greek and other languages had a wide range of meaning which changed over time and could denote several social roles. The closest idiomatic English equivalent is the term "secretary" which can refer to roles from a typist to a high level administrative assistant and on to a highly responsible organizational or corporate official and finally a cabinet officer at the highest level of government. In both Semitic and Greek usage the scribe was commonly a middle level government official, for example, a "secretary" in charge of the town council (Acts 19:35). In Athens major political bodies each had a scribe as one of their officers. In view of the varied meanings of the word scribe we must not assume that references to scribes in the New Testament and elsewhere imply the existence of a unified group with a common identity and role. Scribe is too diffuse a term for that.

Scribes in Egypt and Mesopotamia

Because little is known about the role of scribes and scribal training in Israel, some recourse must be made to Egyptian and Mesopotamian sources which delineate in some detail the social position, roles and education of scribes.[1] In Egypt and Mesopotamia from the third millennium on, scribes were situated in the royal court and in the temples. Their duties included administering and keeping records of tax collection, forced labor, military activities, commodities and building projects. For example, in Egypt they supervised land measurement after the annual Nile flood, drafted correspondence, contracts and treaties and at the highest level, kept the royal annals, collected laws, preserved sacred traditions, and were experts in astronomy,

---

[1]See J.P.J. Olivier, "Schools and Wisdom Literature," *Journal of North West Semitic Languages* 4 (1975) 49-60 for a review of all Near Eastern evidence, especially the Mesopotamian. Ronald J. Williams, "Scribal Training in Ancient Egypt," *Journal of the American Oriental Society* 92 (1972) 214-221 and "'A People Come out of Egypt': An Egyptologist Looks at the Old Testament," *Congress Volume, Edinburgh 1974* (Suppl VT 28; Leiden: Brill, 1975) 231-252, esp. 238-241, reviews the Egyptian evidence. For Mesopotamia, see *City Invincible*, ed. Carl Kraeling (Chicago: Chicago University Press, 1958) 94-102 and the literature cited there.

omens and other religious rites and activities. Scribes occupied high posts as royal secretaries in charge of royal correspondence and as such functioned as counsellors and high officials. The higher a scribe's place in society, the more his influence and power. In all cases the scribe derived his power from the king or member of the governing class who appointed him and thus was a retainer. It may also be that more powerful scribes occasionally established themselves as permanent members of the governing class[2] and there is some evidence that certain families were hereditary scribes.

In Egypt boys were brought to the court or temple and trained to read and write. Practice ostraca found behind one temple testify to an open air school and one text suggests that initial training took four years.[3] After training in a school, a young man was apprenticed to a scribe; more advanced young scribes were sometimes apprenticed to high officials as potential replacements. Training seems to have consisted of copying, reciting and memorizing various traditional materials. Advanced students had access to grammatical treatises, lists of idioms, catalogues of natural phenomena, and especially didactic treatises which taught them how to write, speak and behave in a correct way. It is likely that scribes in high office had to know more than one language. Students were exhorted to learn their difficult lessons both by corporal punishment and the threat that they would be transferred to a more arduous and less pleasant manual occupation.

Scribes in Israel

The scribe first appears in the Old Testament as a muster officer (Jud. 5:14). The (chief) scribe at the Jerusalem court was a high cabinet officer concerned with finance, policy and administration (2 Ki. 22; Jer. 36:10). Baruch, who recorded Jeremiah's words, was a scribe (Jer. 36:32) and as such a highly educated and influential person who moved among the top government circles. One confused text (1 Chr. 2:55) would

---

[2]For the probability of this happening in a limited number of cases, see ch. 3.

[3]Williams, "Training," 216.

suggest that there were scribal families, perhaps in the post-exilic period.[4] In other Chronicles passages, which may also reflect the post-exilic situation, Jehoshaphat is said to have sent princes, Levites and priests to the cities of Judah to teach the people the law (2 Chr. 17:7-9) and Josiah is said to have instructed the "Levites who taught all Israel" to lead the people in the celebration of the passover sacrifice (2 Chr. 35:3-6). Though the evidence for schools in monarchic times is slim, their presence is very probable, especially in major cities.[5] There is general consensus that the wisdom literature reflects scribal and school activity, similar to that found in Egypt and Mesopotamia.[6] The sheer necessity for administration in a centralized kingdom demands the hypothesis of scribal schools.

There is much more evidence for the presence and activities of scribes in the post-exilic period. However, the scattered references do not bespeak a uniform group, but a cluster of functions and social roles exercised by people in diverse social strata and groups.[7] The most well known scribe in the Bible is Ezra a priest and a "scribe skilled in the Law of Moses" (Ezra 7:6) who asked Artaxerxes, the Persian king, for permission to lead a party of Jews back to Jerusalem. The king ordered various officials to give Ezra the resources he needed (7:21-22) for the return and resumption of worship and the king commissioned Ezra to

[4]See J.M. Myers, *1 Chronicles* (Anchor Bible; Garden City: Doubleday, 1965) 12, 16. The word *soferim* in a list of personal and place names is odd and it may be an error for the inhabitants of Kiryat-sepher.

[5]See André LeMaire, *Les Ecoles et la formation de la Bible dans l'ancien Israël (Orbis Biblicus et Orientalis* 39; Fribourg: Ed. Univ./Göttingen: Vandenhoeck, 1981). See 2 Sam. 12:24-25; 2 Ki. 10:1-6; 1 Chr. 27:32; 1 Ki. 12:8.

[6]Brian Kovacs, "Is There a Class-Ethic in Proverbs?" *Essays in Old Testament Ethics* (Hyatt Festschrift), eds. J.L. Crenshaw and J.T. Willis (New York: Ktav, 1974) 171-189 notes that there is a scribal ethic implied by Proverbs. See also André LeMaire, "Sagesse et Ecoles," *VT* 34 (1984) 270-281. The problems of defining a wisdom tradition and the weakness of positing social institutions for which there is no direct Israelite evidence is reviewed and argued in R.N. Whybray, *The Intellectual Tradition in the Old Testament* (ZAW Beiheft 135; New York: de Gruyter, 1974); Gerald T. Sheppard, *Wisdom as a Hermeneutical Construct* (ZAW Beiheft 151; Berlin: de Gruyter, 1980) 1-11; James T. Crenshaw, "Prolegomenon," in *Studies in Ancient Israelite Wisdom* (New York: Ktav, 1976) 1-60, esp. 22.

[7]See the cautions of Gary Porton, "Diversity in Postbiblical Judaism," *Early Judaism and Its Modern Interpreters,* eds. Robert Kraft and George Nickelsburg (Atlanta: Scholars, 1986) 60.

appoint magistrates and judges who knew the law of God and the king (7:25-26). In Ezra 8-10 Ezra the scribe functions as the leader of the returnees in conjunction with leading priests, Levites and families. Though Ezra is of high priestly stock, he does not officiate at the cult. Rather, Ezra is pictured as priest and scribe, that is, religious leader, while Nehemiah is governor (Neh. 8-9). As such he exercised the office of teacher and priest by reading from the Law to the people, while a group of Levites helped the people understand the law, and by leading the people in prayer and sacrifice (Ezra 8). Thus he exercised the office of teacher and priest.

A number of problems beset the interpretation of Ezra-Nehemiah. Several sources have been put together into a narrative by the editor in such a way that the historical relationship of the figures Ezra and Nehemiah is uncertain. The Nehemiah sources do not mention Ezra and vice versa, except for a couple of verses which are probably redactional and meant to link the sources into one coherent account. Though the final version presents their activity as overlapping, the chronology of Ezra and Nehemiah is a matter of dispute among scholars, with some putting Ezra before, others with and others after Nehemiah.[8] In all these theories Ezra's exact office is a matter of dispute.

In a very influential study Hans H. Schaeder argued that the office of scribe was a Persian office and that Ezra was a Persian official appointed by the king to govern Judea.[9] The use of scribe as a title for a high official is possible, but difficult to prove in Ezra. K. Galling has argued that scribe is not the title of a Persian official, but an office in the Jewish diaspora community.[10] Galling's reconstruction depends on a number of uncertain interpretations of Ez. 7 and a fourth century date for

---

[8]For a review of recent work and an argument on literary and archaeological grounds that the Biblical chronology is correct, see S. Talmon, "Ezra and Nehemiah," *IDBS* (1976) 317-328.

[9]Hans H. Schaeder, *Esra der Schreiber* (Beiträge zur historischen Theologie 5; Tübingen: Mohr, 1930).

[10]K. Galling, "Bagoas and Ezra," *Studien zur Geschichte Israels im persischen Zeitalter* (Tübingen: Mohr, 1964) 149-184.

Ezra (after Nehemiah).[11] Some recent archaeological evidence suggests that Ahzai was governor when Ezra arrived in 458 and this leads Talmon to deny that Ezra was a Persian official.[12] It is very questionable, therefore, whether Ezra was governor. He was certainly a recognized authority in the Jewish community because he was of high priestly descent and also learned in the law. He had enough access to the Persian court to obtain a favor from the king and enough community standing to lead a group to Jerusalem and establish himself there. The continuing problems with intermarriage and the opposition to Ezra indicate that he was one of a number of influential and powerful forces in the Jerusalem community but that his views did not immediately predominate.

One other scribe appears in Ezra-Nehemiah, Zadok who was appointed with a priest and Levite to be a treasurer of the storehouses where the tithes were brought (Neh. 12:12-13). This text suggests that scribes were part of society and its leadership in Jerusalem.

In the post-exilic Jewish community the roles of priests, Levites, scribes and other Jewish leaders overlapped. Ezra was a priest, scribe, and community leader and possibly a government appointed leader (Ez. 7). The Levites taught (Neh. 8) and in the view of the Chronicler, which probably reflects the post-exilic situation, some Levites served as scribes.[13] The Chronicler also gave the Levites major responsibilities in the Temple and even wider responsibilities as officers and judges in the time of Solomon (1 Chr. 23:4). The Chronicler's picture of the Levites is hardly historical but it does show that what the Levites were

[11]For a critique of Galling, see Ralph W. Klein, "Ezra and Nehemiah in Recent Studies," *Magnalia Dei* (Wright Festschrift) eds. Frank M. Cross et al. (Garden City: Doubleday, 1976). R. North has argued that Ezra's function in the Bible was more religious than political (granted the overlap of these areas). Ezra did not have special civil authority, but the encouragement of the Persian king and the grant of resources. R. North, "Civil Authority in Ezra," *Studi in onore de E. Volterra* (Milan, 1971) 377-404. That Ezra was a religious leader is assumed by J.M. Myers, *Ezra-Nehemiah* (Anchor Bible; Garden City: Doubleday, 1965) LVII-LXII.

[12]Talmon, "Ezra," 325.

[13]1 Chr. 24:6; 2 Chr. 34:13. The Chronicler was interested in clarifying and establishing the roles of the Levites in the cult. See Myers, *1 Chronicles,* XXXIX. In general, the Chronicler, who wrote in the fourth century, transferred the situation in his own day back into Israel's history.

doing or what they aspired to do in post-exilic Jewish society included scribal activities.[14] What must be emphasized for our study is that scribal activity is commonly associated with priests and Levites.

Recent studies of Deuteronomy emphasize its scholastic character and its connections with the wisdom (and scribal) tradition.[15] Since Deuteronomy was probably edited before and during the exile, it implies that circles of scribes of some type existed.[16] The Book of Deuteronomy may reflect this reality when it assigns a growing role as teachers to the Levites, thus giving them a duty traditional to both priests and scribes and reflecting the overlap of roles.[17]

The Formation of the Bible

Scribal activity must be postulated in order to account for the very existence of the Bible and its many stages of redaction. The complexity of distinguishing priests, scribes, prophets and other community leaders who produced and transmitted the Biblical books, legal materials, narrative traditions, oracles and mantological interpretations has been illustrated by M. Fishbane's detailed study of the Bible's interpretation of its own traditions.[18] In Fishbane's study scribes are understood in a narrow sense as copyists and unsystematic interpreters of the Bible. As they transmitted the traditions, they did so in a living tradition of interpretation, and so they made comments and interpretations at various points in the text, some of which have

[14]For the interpretation of the varied sources on the Levites, see R. De Vaux, *Ancient Israel* (New York: McGraw, 1961) 391-394.

[15]M. Weinfeld, *Deuteronomy and the Deuteronomic School* (Oxford: Clarendon, 1972); C. Carmichael, *The Laws of Deuteronomy* (Ithaca: Cornell, 1974).

[16]See the review of evidence and presuppositions in Donn Morgan, *Wisdom in the Old Testament Traditions* (Atlanta: Knox, 1981) 94-106. Note Morgan's caution (p. 102) concerning how little we really know about the circles which produced Deuteronomy.

[17]G. von Rad, *Studies in Deuteronomy* (London: SCM, 1953) 68; G.E. Wright, "The Levites in Deuteronomy," *VT* 4 (1954) 325-330, esp. 329; LeMaire, *Ecoles,* 56 and n. 184.

[18]Michael Fishbane, *Biblical Interpretation in Ancient Israel* (Oxford: Clarendon, 1985).

been incorporated into the text as we have it. They also became authorities on the texts and their interpretations and were probably priests or closely connected to priestly circles.[19] From the scribal comments incorporated into the Biblical text it is not clear whether the scribes also belonged to the circles which produced the Biblical traditions, but certainly they had responsibility for the transmission of the tradition. Since no independent commentaries were produced in Israel until the Hasmonean period or shortly before it, scribes were probably authors, commentators and transmitters of the Biblical texts.[20]

The inner Biblical interpretation of traditions suggests a complex transmission process which included various groups in society with scribes in each group. Since the Biblical laws, narratives and prophecies have not come to us directly from jurists, prophets and other practicioners in daily life, a scholarly class produced the Biblical materials.[21] Because leaders were called on to reconcile sacred traditions with one another and law with custom and new circumstances, learned interpreters were needed. Conflicts within society produced competing interpretations of law and custom, a fact richly illustrated in the sects and groups in Hasmonean and Herodian times. Non-legal materials (narratives, sermons, rituals, prayers, hymns, prophecy, history) were also interpreted within the Bible,[22] as were prophetic oracles, dreams and visions.[23]

All the Biblical materials have been passed on in such a

---

[19]Fishbane, *Interpretation,* 78-84.

[20]Fishbane, *Interpretation,* 84-88. For the "scribal" nature of the Dead Sea Scrolls, see Malachi Martin, *The Scribal Character of the Dead Sea Scrolls* (Leiden: Brill, 1958), 2 vols.

[21]The legal topics covered in the Bible are too incomplete to be the actual code used by judges and often the punishments or other circumstances are vaguely suggested. Thus the legal codes are exemplary and meant to serve a religious, educational or other purpose (Fishbane, *Interpretation,* 91-98). This suggests that scribes, or teachers or priests or some combination of these, collected the Biblical laws which they understood as revealed by God and essential for Israel. The sacredness of the law and the Deuteronomic attempt to make the people holy, a program furthered by Ezra and Nehemiah, suggest priestly and Levitical groups in the exile and second Temple period (107-123). Note that the priests had no monopoly on teaching authority, especially in exile away from the Temple (265).

[22]Fishbane, *Interpretation,* 281-440.

[23]Fishbane, *Interpretation,* 443-524.

complex way that the activity of learned interpreters and tradents must be postulated for all of Israel's history from the monarchic period on. The diversity of materials and settings argue that no one group was responsible for passing on these traditions, but that many segments of Israelite society had their traditions and scribes skilled enough to interpret them and pass them on. Thus, scribes or people with scribal skills must have been part of priestly, prophetic, and leadership circles at all times. While it is difficult to prove historical continuity, the nature of the Biblical materials in their Near Eastern cultural setting make the hypothesis of continuous and diverse literary and interpretative traditions very likely.[24] That scribes played a part in this tradition is certain, but the nature of their roles, their social settings and their relationships to other significant groups in Jewish society remain obscure.

Greco-Roman Period

In sketching the changes brought about in Judaism by Hellenistic influence E. Bickerman posits the rise of an independent, non-priestly scribal class.[25] Since the Greeks relied on non-priestly officials and on learned individuals to serve on city councils and in local offices, they appointed learned scribes to government offices, according to Bickerman. If this occurred, scribes were probably added to, not replacements for the priests and leading citizens who were always powerful in the towns and cities of the Near East. Bickerman is probably correct, however, that the Greek tradition of councils, officials, sophists, philosophers and teachers stimulated more specialized scribal activities in Jewish society.

TEMPLE SCRIBES

Scribes of the Temple are mentioned among the Jewish leaders in Antiochus III's letter to Ptolemy, the governor of

---

[24]Fishbane, *Interpretation,* 525-527.

[25]Elias Bickerman, "Ch. 2. The Historical Foundations of Postbiblical Judaism," *The Jews,* ed. Louis Finkelstein (New York: Harper, 1949) Vol 1, pp. 99-101.

Coele-Syria.[26] Once Antiochus had gained control of Palestine just after 200 B.C.E. he reorganized his new holdings. His letter to Ptolemy affirmed Jerusalem's relative independence, made resources available for the repair and repopulation of the city and exempted certain Jewish officials from taxes.

> And all the members of the nation shall have a form of government in accordance with the laws of their country, and the senate, the priests, *the scribes of the temple* and the temple-singers shall be relieved from the poll-tax, and the crown-tax and the salt-tax which they pay.[27]

"Senate" *(gerousia)* denoted a council of elders, usually the heads of leading families, which often ruled a Greek city. Presumably the Jewish senate was composed of leading priests and citizens and may have been presided over by the high priest. The other three groups mentioned are all connected to the temple. Since earlier in the letter Antiochus allocated money for sacrifices and repair in the Temple and since the next document in Josephus' account protects the sanctity of the Temple and Jerusalem, his exemption of Temple personnel from taxes is to be expected. Though their functions are not clear, the Temple scribes were important and distinctive enough to merit explicit mention by Antiochus and exemption from taxes. We may speculate that the scribes were concerned either with the financial and organizational functions of the Temple or with the recording and teaching of sacred traditions and laws, but we cannot know for certain. That the scribes are dependent on Temple revenues and subordinate to the priests who controlled the Temple is certain and significant for understanding the scribes as they appear in the gospels for there too the scribes are located mainly in Jerusalem and allied with the chief priests.

---

[26]Josephus, *Antiquities,* 12.3.3 (138-144). The genuineness of this letter has been defended by E. Bickermann [sic], "La charte séleucid de Jerusalem," *Revue des Etudes Juives* 100 (1935) 4-35; reprinted in E. Bickerman, *Studies in Jewish and Christian History* (Pt. 2; Leiden: Brill, 1980) 44-85. Bickerman's meticulous and detailed arguments have been generally accepted, for example by the translator of Josephus, Ralph Marcus (Loeb ed., 1943; Cambridge: Harvard Univ., 1976) Vol 7. App. D, pp. 751-761.

[27]Josephus, *Ant.* 12.3.3 (142).

THE HASMONEAN PERIOD

Scribes appear once in 1 Maccabees, somehow associated with the hasideans. During the Maccabean revolt a group of "pious ones" or "hasideans" (*ḥasîdîm*) joined the Maccabees in their struggle against Antiochus IV: "Then there united with them [Mattathias and his friends] a company of Hasideans, mighty warriors of Israel, everyone who offered himself for the law" (1 Macc. 2:42). After the death of Antiochus and the accession of Demetrius I:

> "a group of scribes appeared in a body before Alcimus [the new high priest, appointed by the king] and Bacchides [the king's governor] to ask for just terms. The Hasideans were the first among the sons of Israel to seek peace from them, for they said, 'A priest of the line of Aaron has come with the army, and he will not harm us'" (1 Macc. 7:12-14).

In contrast, the Maccabees refused to negotiate with Alcimus because he was allied with the Seleucids. The author, who supported the Maccabees, makes it clear that the new governmental leaders were treacherous and that the Maccabees were correct to refuse to make any agreement. He proves his point by noting that Alcimus seized sixty of those who made peace and killed them in one day (1 Macc. 7:16).

The two sentences mentioning the scribes and hasideans follow one another awkwardly and the relationship between the two is not clear. Goldstein suggests that each pietist group had its own scribes and more than one group's scribes are implied by this passage.[28] Tcherikover identifies pietists as a special sect within the scribal class, which was composed of those learned in Torah, and Tcherikover thinks that from the time of Ezra the scribes grew in power as lay authorities, independent of the priests and allied with urban leaders who were estranged from the priests.[29] In the Maccabean period they had become the leaders of the resistance and the chief scribes.[30] Tcherikover's

---

[28]Jonathan Goldstein, *1 Maccabees* (Garden City: Doubleday, 1976) 331-332.

[29]Victor Tcherikover, *Hellenistic Civilization and the Jews* (Philadelphia: Jewish Publ. Soc., 1959) 124-126.

[30]Tcherikover, *Civilization*, 196-198.

"clerical" view of Jewish leadership is sociologically unlikely because it puts in power those without wealth, social standing or connection with the Temple. The motive for the pietists' actions, that a priest of the line of Aaron would not harm them, bespeaks a great confidence in the traditional institutions and laws of Israel and perhaps a certain interpretation of Israel's history which stressed confidence in God and the sanctity of the priesthood. However, while it is clear that the scribes are associated with the pietists and with defense of the Jewish way of life, it is not clear whether the scribes were part of the hasideans or vice versa and what social status and role they held. That they could come to Alcimus as a group and that they were the object of an assassination plot argues that they had some influence or power and were perceived as a threat by the government. It is likely that they, like the Maccabees, had some influence on the people and were perceived as an obstacle to the reassertion of control by the government and the royally appointed high priest, a struggle recounted in the rest of chapter seven. Thus, the scribes were part of the political leadership of Judaism, but in a subordinate position where they were open to the kind of oppression they suffered at the hands of Alcimus.

The nature and status of the hasideans is most uncertain also. The hasideans have most often been treated as a well defined sect or cohesive group who later spawned the Pharisees, Essenes, scribes and perhaps other second century Jewish groups,[31] but nothing in the wording of 1 Maccabees suggests this. The word for "company" is "synagogue," a Greek word with a wide range of meaning. We know only that these pious Jews were able

---

[31]For the standard view, see Martin Hengel, *Judaism and Hellenism* (Philadelphia: Fortress, 1974) 78-83; 174-247. Jonathan Goldstein follows the usual position of treating them as a sect-like group in *1 Maccabees,* 5-6. Hasid and hasideans occur in rabbinic literature. In the last century some scholars identified the pious ones with Essenes, a position amply refuted by Adolf Büchler, *Types of Jewish-Palestinian Piety from 70 B.C.E. to 70 C.E.: The Ancient Pious Men* (1922; repr. New York: Ktav, 1968). More recently S.Safrai, "Teaching of Pietists in Mishnaic Literature," *JJS* 16 (1965) 15-33, has traced an evolution of the term from the followers of the Maccabees to an austere group of sages with their own Mishnah in the first two centuries of our era on to a more general use of the term for a leading, austere sage. Safrai's argument is marred by an uncritical melding of diverse sources. The meaning he proposes for *"hasid"* in later rabbinic literature fits its use in all the sources. It is a general term used for a sage exemplary for strictness and holiness.

bodied warriors who volunteered to fight. It is much more likely that pietists is a descriptive designation of a broad spectrum of Jews who actively resisted Hellenization and defended piety, that is, their way of life, against attack from Antiochus rather than the name of a well defined group.[32]

The author of 1 Maccabees is such a supporter of the Maccabees that their opponents are polemically and incompletely portrayed. Thus, we cannot fully understand the political situation which prompted some scribes and hasideans to come to terms with Alcimus or why he killed some of them. One suspects strong rivalries and disagreements about the direction Judaism should take and a struggle for control of the populace. Clearly the Maccabees did not want to lose the power and influence they had gained. The hasideans, who took a course differing from the Maccabees, are presented as a small, naive group decimated by the government, a view deriving from the author of 1 Maccabees' pro-Maccabean and anti-pietist stand. By contrast, in 2 Maccabees, which is pro-pietist and anti-Hasmonean,[33] Alcimus the high priest, in a speech to the Seleucid king, Demetrius I, identifies all the followers of Judas Maccabee as hasideans, that is, as pious Jews who reject the government for traditional and religious reasons (2 Macc. 14:6). Such a broad generalization fits both the speech of Alcimus, in which an overview is presented to the king, and the outlook of the author of 2 Maccabees, who sees the pietists and their heroic leader Judas as the opponents of Hellenism. All genuine opponents of Hellenization were hasideans and were the preservers of Judaism against outside oppression.

The story of Eleazar, one of the leading scribes (2 Macc. 6:18) who dies for the law and as an example to younger Jews, shows that scribes were prominent leaders in Palestinian society. The account in 2 Maccabees stresses his nobility, virtue and community responsibility. It is noteworthy that the retelling of this story by a diaspora Jew in 4 Maccabees identifies Eleazar as a

---

[32]Philip Davies, "Hasidim in the Maccabean Period," *JJS* 28 (1977) 127-140, for a very effective presentation of the weaknesses of the usual hypothesis of a hasidean sect.

[33]2 Maccabees accepts Judas Maccabee as a heroic leader of the pious Jews resisting the Seleucids, but it leaves out his Hasmonean successors and is clearly hostile to the Jewish government created subsequent to the war.

priest (5:4) and stresses his learning. These texts and several others suggest that the use of scribe as a title for the learned guardians of the law was a Palestinian usage, not found in the diaspora.

Scribes in Jewish Literature

The presence of scribes in the Hellenistic period is made probable by the very existence of a wealth of Jewish literature from the period. The Enoch tradition, with its early interest in calendar and astronomical matters (1 Enoch 72-82), the wisdom books and stories (Qohelet, Daniel 1-6, Ben Sira) and the variety of literary products of this period testify to intense authorial activity and educational support for such activity. The scribal activity and separatist tendencies in the Enoch traditions were intensified later in the Qumran community's traditions and in those of many other nameless groups of the Greco-Roman period. During the Hellenistic period Judaism produced a vast amount of literature and this authorial activity argues for a strong core of educated Jews and an educational establishment, including scribes, fulfilling their normal range of duties.

BEN SIRA

The most famous description of the scribe in Jewish literature is given by Ben Sira in the early second century (38:24-39:11). Ben Sira notes that only one who has leisure can become wise (38:24) and contrasts the scribal life with the physical difficulty of other jobs.[34] He attributes to the ideal scribe all areas of knowledge, high government station and lasting fame. The wisdom of the scribe is closely linked with and dependent on God because his main source of knowledge is the "law of the Most High," the study of which leads him "to seek out the wisdom of the ancients" and "be concerned with prophecies."

[34] Ben Sira is much more generous in his description and praise of other jobs than is the Egyptian model he was following, the Instruction of Khety, Son of Duauf. See the "Praise of the Learned Scribe" in James Pritchard, *Ancient Near Eastern Texts Relating to the Old Testament* (Princeton: Princeton UP, 1950) 431-434.

He will also "preserve the discourse of notable men and penetrate the subtleties of parables; he will seek out the hidden meanings of proverbs and be at home with the obscurities of parables" (39:1-3). Ben Sira conceived of the scribe as an expert in what had by then become the three parts of the Hebrew Bible, the law (Torah), prophets and writings, especially the writings which receive special emphasis in verses 2 and 3.[35] The scribe is not simply a scholar or teacher in the modern mold, but a high official, advisor to the governing class, an international ambassador and traveler:

> He will serve among great men and appear before rulers; he will travel through the lands of foreign nations, for he tests the good and the evil among men. (39:4) They [craftsmen] are not sought out for the council of the people, nor do they attain eminence in the public assembly. They do not sit in the judge's seat, nor do they understand the sentence of judgment; they cannot expound discipline or judgment, and they are not found using proverbs. (38:32-33)

The foundation for the scribes' social leadership is not birth or wealth, but knowledge of discipline (*paideia,* education, culture), judgment and proverbs (*parabolais,* parables, similitudes).

The association of the scribe and his wisdom with God and traditional Jewish religion is strongly emphasized in vv. 5-8. The scribe prays and if God fills him with the spirit of understanding, he will be wise, and he "will reveal instruction in his teaching, and he will glory in the law of the Lord's covenant" (8). Finally, he will leave a recognized name because of his wisdom (9-10). Both in the hymn to the scribe and elsewhere in Ben Sira the wise man (who at least partly is identified with the scribe) is associated with the rulers and priests.[36] Scholars have disagreed

---

[35]Ben Sira uses a wisdom perspective to understand the rest of the Biblical tradition and incorporates into the role of the wise man the earlier roles of prophet and recipient of divine revelation.

[36] Burton Mack, *Wisdom and the Hebrew Epic* (Chicago, Univ. of Chicago Press) 89-107, demonstrates the links between the description of the scribe and the later descriptions of Israel's rulers, prophets and priests in chs. 44-50. Ben Sira includes a Hellenistic encomiastic motif both in ch. 39 and chs. 44-50. Clearly, though he cannot mention his own name, he includes himself and hopes that his book will make his wisdom and his fame remembered.

whether Ben Sira is himself a priest, especially in view of his glorification of Simon the priest in ch. 50.[37] The argument need not be settled to understand Ben Sira's teaching on the scribe. All groups had scribes, including the priests. If Ben Sira is not a priest, he is supportive of the Temple, priests and central Jewish government in Jerusalem and sees Jewish tradition and wisdom as stemming from traditional Yahwism. It is very likely that he was associated with the governing class, either as a teacher or some kind of official. Whether he was rich or poor, priest or layman, he identified with the governing class and saw wisdom (which included the Bible) as the key to life, government and the order of the world.

In Ben Sira the understanding of scribe has been widened so that it is almost equivalent to that of the wise man. This merging of roles will also be seen in the Letter of Aristeas below. The scribe is a wise man learned in scripture and traditional Jewish wisdom and the range of wisdom is great and varied. The meaning of all the terms in 39:1-3 cannot be pinned down exactly and is probably meant to be inclusive rather than precise.[38] While it is probable that Ben Sira is not proposing a total identification of wise man and scribe, he certainly sees little difference in their capabilities and characteristics. Scribes filled a certain social role, subordinate to the governing class, and represented the ideal learned Jew.

Ben Sira's scribal interests and authorial activities may derive from his being a teacher. His grandson, who translated his book from Hebrew to Greek, says in his preface that he was a teacher. Appended to the end of his book is a hymn (51:13-30) which mentions what is probably a school *(bet midrash)*. Since this hymn is found independently among the Dead Sea Scrolls in a version close to, but differing from the Greek.[39] it probably was

---

[37]H. Stadelmann, *Ben Sira als Schriftgelehrter* (Tübingen: Mohr, 1980) holds that Ben Sira was most probably a priest. J. Marböck, *Weisheit im Wandel.* (Bonn, Hanstein, 1971) and "Sir. 38, 23-39, 11: Der schriftgelehrte Weise: Ein Beitrag zu Gestalt und Werk Ben Siras," *La Sagesse de l'Ancien Testament,* ed. M. Gilbert (Gembloux: Duculot/ Leuven: Univ. Leuv., 1979) 306, holds that he is a layman.

[38]Marböck, "Weise," 311-314.

[39]It is one of a group of psalms of David in 11QPs, published in James A. Sanders, *The Psalms Scroll of Qumran Cave 11. Discoveries in the Judaean Desert* IV (Oxford: Clarendon, 1965) 79-85.

not original to Ben Sira and thus not a statement by him that he was a teacher.[40] Whether the hymn is by Ben Sira or not, if the hymn dates from the second century and if *bet midrash* is correctly understood as a school, it is the earliest explicit mention of a school in Palestinian Jewish literature and reflects either Ben Sira's historical social setting or a very early understanding of his role.

Ben Sira's picture of the ideal scribe was probably influenced by Greek social and educational ideals. Since Ben Sira wrote in the early second century, B.C.E., scholars have argued over Ben Sira's attitude toward Hellenism. Some have seen him as opposed to Hellenistic wisdom, but most have understood him to be promoting Jewish wisdom within a Hellenistic context and without general hostility to Greek ideas. Ben Sira is influenced by Greek practices and thought but remains centered within the Jewish tradition. For example, he shows the influence of Greek ideas by giving his name as author of the book (50:27), rather than remaining anonymous and attributing it pseudonymously to Solomon.[41] He also mentions writing several times and is the first author to say, within the course of his work, that he writes.[42]

Much more than in earlier works we can glimpse Ben Sira's understanding of the knowledge, role and setting which is to be associated with scribes. The scribe has comprehensive knowledge, like the wise man of Biblical literature, and fills many roles in the political life of the nation, as well as that of teacher and schoolmaster.

[40]Sanders and J. Haspecker, *Gottesfurcht hei Jesus Sirach* (Rome: PBI, 1967) 90, n. 7 argue that the peom is not original to Ben Sira. Stadelmann, *Ben Sira,* 30-33 defends its authenticity, but his arguments are strained. M. Hengel, *Judaism and Hellenism,* Philadelphia: Fortress, II, p. 89, n. 88, suggests that 11QPs has an earlier form of the prayer which Ben Sira has reshaped. The Cairo Geniza Ms. B version seems to be a retroversion from the Syriac version. The Greek is close to the Qumran version and more authentic.

[41]This is probably an important reason why the book was not accepted into the Hebrew canon.

[42]44:5 [in the Masada Hebrew text]; 42:7. The epilogue to Qohelet, by a later, Hellenistic editor of the work, says that there is too much making of books but Ben Sira refers to writing in the body of his text.

ENOCH

Enoch is referred to three times as a scribe in the Ethiopic Book of Enoch (1 Enoch). Since 1 Enoch is a composite of Enoch materials developed over two or three centuries, it is necessary to describe separately the two parts of Enoch from which the passages come. In the first section of 1 Enoch (1-36), which dates from before the Maccabean Revolt, Enoch is twice referred to as a scribe of righteousness (12:3-4; 15:1) and sent as a messenger to the Watchers, a group of angels who have sinned against God. His role in condemning the evil Watchers and announcing their punishment overlaps the role of prophet. At the beginning of the last part of 1 Enoch (92:1), the Epistle of Enoch, which dates from the latter part of the second century, B.C.E., Enoch appears as the scribe who has written this part of the book: "Written by Enoch the scribe—this complete wisdom teaching."[43] The writing of a wisdom book fits the activity normally assigned to scribes and is more comprehensible than the first two uses of the title scribe.

Though Enoch is not called a scribe in the Bible, the figure of Enoch in the apocalyptic books which make up 1 Enoch is a complex mixture of traditional elements. He is conceived of as a wise ancient who is the recipient of apocalyptic revelation and as a prophetic figure, since he communicates God's judgment and God's plan for the future. As a recipient of apocalyptic revelation he is associated with mantic wisdom and also with traditional wisdom, which in Enoch is transferred into an apocalyptic-eschatological context.[44] The opening verses of the last part of Enoch show that he is especially a teacher of righteousness and that the author of Enoch in the second century has associated this mythic figure with roles which are familiar to him, teacher, seer, tradent, and *writer*. Evidently all or some of these roles

---

[43]Translation from James VanderKam, *Enoch and the Growth of an Apocalyptic Tradition* (CBQMS 16; Washington; CBA, 1984) 173. Manuscript variants affect the translations of this section. E. Isaac in *Pseudepigrapha of the Old Testament* vol. 1, p. 73 translates the single manuscript he uses as "(Book) five, which is written by Enoch, the writer of all the signs of wisdom. . . . " The designation of Enoch as scribe also appears in the Aramaic fragments edited by J.T. Milik, *The Books of Enoch: Aramaic Fragments of Qumrân Cave 4* (Oxford: Clarendon, 1976) 262, and so it is original to the text and not an addition by the Ethiopic tradition.

[44]VanderKam, *Enoch*, 171-172.

were associated with scribes in the author's time.

F. Dexinger suggests that the author identifies himself with Enoch and was, like Enoch in the narrative, a scribe passing on Enoch traditions in writing and teaching his generation how to meet changes and challenges to Judaism.[45] J. Collins has suggested that the Enoch traditions are the products of "scribes who were distressed by the encroachments of Hellenism and the consequent erosion of traditional customs and aggravations of class divisions."[46] Whatever the precise situation and motive of the author of the last section of Enoch, he understood both himself and his hero Enoch to be scribes who are concerned with the (written) traditions and life of Judaism. Because of the literary form and perhaps because of the author's alienation from Jewish leadership, no mention is made of public roles for the scribe.

THE LETTER OF ARISTEAS

The Letter of Aristeas to Philocrates is a pseudonymous Greek Jewish composition, most probably from Alexandria in the latter part of the second century, B.C.E.[47] It is supposed to be an account of how the Egyptian king commissioned a Greek translation of the Hebrew Bible and of the discussions the seventy-two translators had with the king concerning kingship. The purpose of the narrative is to affirm the value of Jewish wisdom and its importance for Gentiles. It also affirms the excellence of the wise leaders found among the Jews and thus seeks to establish respect and acceptance for Judaism in the Hellenistic world. Most of the book is taken up with the wise discourse between the king and translators. The legendary story of the production of the translation, for which Aristeas is best known, is a minor part of the narrative.

The title "scribe" does not appear in Aristeas, but translating

---

[45] F.Dexinger, *Henochs Zehnwochenapokalypse und offene Probleme der Apocalyptikforschung* (SPB 29; Leiden: Brill, 1977) 149-150.

[46] John J. Collins, *The Apocalyptic Imagination* (New York: Crossroad, 1984) 63. See 58-59 also.

[47] George Nickelsburg, *Jewish Literature Between the Bible and the Mishnah* (Philadelphia: Fortress, 1981) 165-169.

the Bible is a scribal act and many attributes assigned to the translators are those assigned to high ranking or well born scribes in other texts.[48] The translators are described as "best" or "excellent" *(aristoi)*, a characteristic of aristocrats in Greece. They have distinguished parentage and "education" or "scholarship" *(paideia)* and they know both the literature of the Jews and of the Greeks. They have some specifically Greek accomplishments, including a talent for talking about the law (the ability to speak well was an essential Greek virtue for the educated person). They seek the "mean," an Aristotelian ideal of virtue, they are not uncouth, nor conceited in dealing with others and they can listen and comment appropriately. In addition, they are also qualified for embassies. While in Egypt on an embassy they discuss kingship with the king, a typical concern of both wisdom literature and Greek philosophy. All these charateristics are proper to the aristocracy and since they were "loved"[49] by Eleazar, the high priest, they were not subordinate servants, but equals to him in some sense.

The description of this group also fits the wisdom ideal of the scribe attached to the highest levels of the ruler's court and has much in common with the scribe as depicted in Ben Sira. The translators and the scribe are wise men who know the whole tradition, can function in international situations, and have the talent to be leaders, judges, and scholars. In the Hellenistic age the international ideal of the wise man endured in the Near East and Israel, both in Palestine and in the diaspora. Israel continued to adjust its idea of wise man to meet changing circumstances and the development of the Jewish tradition. The use of the term scribe in Ben Sira and its absence in Aristeas may reflect Palestinian and Diaspora usage. The Alexandrian Jewish community was led by educated, wealthy, high born people who are the model for the translators. Since the Jewish community had very limited independence and Jews were not Alexandrian citizens, the community may not have had an official role for scribes, in contrast to Jerusalem.

---

[48] Aristeas #120-127. See text and translation in *Aristeas to Philocrates,* ed. Moses Hadas (reprint New York: Ktav, 1973).

[49] A form of the verb *agapaō* is used.

SECOND BARUCH

2 Baruch is an apocalypse written after the destruction of the Temple in 70 C.E. The narrative is set at the time of the destruction of the first Temple, but the real interest of the author is the aftermath of the war with Rome. Baruch the scribe, from the Book of Jeremiah, becomes the community leader, both carrying out traditional scribal tasks of writing to the exiles and also receiving apocalyptic revelation and fulfilling a prophetic leadership role for the community. In 2 Baruch, in contrast to the Biblical Book of Jeremiah, Baruch's authority exceeds that of Jeremiah (2:1; 9:1-10:4) and the community looks to him for guidance and for knowledge of God's will in a time of crisis. When Baruch tells the people that he will soon depart, they fear that their one last link with God will be broken and that no one will be available to interpret Torah for them (46:3). It seems that the author and his community understand genuine leadership to be prophetic and scribal, involving both interpretation of the Bible and visionary contact with God.[50] Such an understanding of the scribal office fits well an apocalyptic group because apocalyptic literature has strong links with the wisdom tradition, both traditional and mantic. For example, Daniel, an archetypical apocalyptic seer, is a wise man and an official in Babylon.

Scribes in Josephus

Josephus uses scribe in the usual Greco-Roman way for officials at all levels from village to royal court.[51] He does not use the term for an organized social group, nor does he use it for groups especially devoted to the law, like the Pharisees. In the first half of the Antiquities, when Josephus is summarizing the Bible, he retains scribes where they appear as royal officials or as individuals (e.g., Baruch, Ezra). Josephus manifests his own

---

[50]G. Sayler, *Have the Promises Failed? A Literary Analysis of 2 Baruch* (SBLDS 72: Chico: Scholars, 1984) 115-117.

[51]For the range of meanings and roles associated with the Greek word scribe *(grammateus),* see F. Poland, "Technitai," *Paulys Wissowa,* 2 Ser, Vol 5A, col. 2534.

understanding of the role and social status of scribes when he adds scribes to the Biblical account or refers to them in the Greco-Roman period.

In his addition of scribes to the Biblical account Josephus understands scribes to be mid-level officials serving the king. For example, when the Israelites defeated the Philistines in battle in 1 Sam. 14:31-35, they began to kill animals and eat them without observing the laws for slaughter of animals. The Hebrew says someone ("they") told Saul about it; Josephus says that the scribes told him.[52] Scribes are community officials with access to the king and responsibility for supervising observance of the law. According to 1 Chr. 23:1-6 just before his death David organized the Levites according to tasks, with six thousand assigned to be officers ($\check{s}\bar{o}ter\hat{i}m$) and judges. Josephus translates officers as scribes, thus indicating that he understood them to be middle and low level government officials.[53] Scribes are also government record keepers. When David took a census of the people in 2 Sam. 24:1 he sent Joab and the commanders of the army to take the census. Josephus understood census taking as a scribal, not a military activity, so in his account Joab takes the chiefs of the tribes and the *scribes* with him.[54] In the story of Esther scribes are twice added to the story by Josephus as keepers of records. When the king cannot sleep, he has royal chronicles brought to him by his servants; in Josephus scribes bring out these records of the king.[55] In another passage the Hebrew list of government officials who help the Jews includes princes, satraps, governors and, literally, "doers of the king's work."[56] Josephus translates the vague Hebrew expression as scribes, using scribe as a title for a government official.

In two places Josephus refers to Temple scribes. In the first passage (Ez. 7:24) when the Persian king allows Ezra to return to Jerusalem he exempts from "tribute, custom or toll" the following groups: priests, Levites, singers, doorkeepers, Temple

---

[52]*Ant.* 6.6.4 (120).

[53]*Ant.* 7.14.7 (364). Josephus follows the LXX.

[54]*Ant.* 7.13.1 (319).

[55]Esther 6:1; *Ant.* 11.6.10 (248, 250).

[56]Esther 9:3. This phrase is usually translated as royal officials or king's stewards. *Ant.* 11.6.13 (287). Josephus follows the LXX.

servants and other servants of the house of God.The last two terms are repetitious and vague. In the Aramaic of the passage the temple servants are *netinayya,* a word drawn from the Hebrew of Ezra and probably meaning one given to the Temple. This group may have been a specific type of Temple functionary in the post-exilic period. The final category is a periphrastic expression which seems to include all others associated with the Temple. 1 Esdras, a second century B.C.E. Greek rewriting of Ezra-Nehemiah which was used by Josephus, translates the two terms as Temple servants *(hierodoulos)* and Temple functionaries *(pragmatikos).*[57] The second term is even more general in 1 Esdras' translation than in the Aramaic original. Josephus replaces 1 Esdras' unclear category, *pragmatikos,* with "scribes of the Temple."[58] Josephus clarified the text by inserting a group of Temple officials known to him when he was in Jerusalem.[59] Though their exact tasks are not specified, teaching, record keeping, preservation of the sacred traditions and ruling on points of law and custom are all possible.

Some scribes had low status and others very high status during the Herodian period. In one of the dynastic battles among the descendants of Herod, his sons Aristobolus and Alexander threatened to reduce Salome's family to servitude. Specifically, they threatened that the mothers of the family would weave at the loom with slave girls and the brothers would be village scribes.[60] Josephus notes that the threat against the brothers was a sarcastic reference to the careful education they had received. The passage implies that village scribe was a very low status occupation. The scribe was most probably a person who could read and write and knew the social and legal formalities well enough to write letters, contracts and petitions. Such a low level specialist might also have been a village official representing the government in small, local affairs.

At the other end of the spectrum was Diophantus, a scribe of Herod, who was alleged to have forged a letter and who was

---

[57] 1 Esd. 8:22. A *pragmatikos* can be a legal advisor or lawyer as well as many other things.

[58] *Ant.* 11.5.1 (128).

[59] See the Temple scribes in Antiochus III's letter, treated above.

[60] *War* 1.24.3 (479). The Greek is *komōn grammateis.*

eventually executed.[61] To have been able to plot and carry out a forgery he must have been a highly placed official close to Herod. Aristeus, a distinguished priest from Emmaus, was the scribe (secretary) of the council *(grammateus tēs boulēs)*, was killed with fifteen other eminent men during the seige in Jerusalem.[62] The council was the ruling body in Greek cities and the secretary was the administrator of the council and an important city official.[63] It is clear that Aristeus was picked for execution because he was a high official in Jerusalem.

Josephus mentions scribes in a number of places because they are common and accepted in his world. The functions and social status and power of scribes vary from high officials to lowly village functionaries. Literacy was crucial to their place and function in society, but their exact status depended on the ruler or governing class. Josephus does not present the scribes as a specific, distinct group with its own teachings like the Pharisees, Sadducees and Essenes. Rather, the scribes were a well known, accepted type of social actor who could hold varied roles and be accorded different social statuses.

TEACHERS OF THE LAW IN JOSEPHUS

Since the scribes are often seen as teachers of the law or as experts in its interpretation both by modern scholars and by ancient sources such as the New Testament and rabbinic literature and since Josephus does not use the category scribe for those learned in the law, a brief treatment of those learned in the law in Josephus is in order. Josephus often refers to learning in the law, especially when he is portraying Jews as a cultured, learned group with its own wisdom. His portrayal of the teachings of the Pharisees, Sadducees, Essenes and revolutionaries as philosophies has already been reviewed in chapter six. He calls the two teachers, Judas and Matthias, who directed their zealous young students to tear down the Roman symbols

---

[61] *War* 1.26.3 (529) and *Ant.* 16.10.4 (319).

[62] *War* 5.13.1 (532).

[63] See Acts 19:35 where the town scribe/clerk calls the assembly to order in a crisis.

by another good Greek term for a learned person, *sophistai*.[64] In the conclusion to the *Antiquities* Josephus acknowledges the distinction between Jewish and Greek learning, notes that Jews do not value Greek learning greatly and describes their criteria for Jewish learning as follows:

> They give credit for wisdom to those alone who have an exact knowledge of the laws *(nomima)* and who are capable of interpreting the meaning of the Holy Scriptures *(hierōn grammatōn)*. Consequently, though many have laboriously undertaken this training, scarcely two or three have succeeded, and have forthwith reaped the fruit of their labors.[65]

This description is an ideal and an exaggeration. Josephus, who is congratulating himself for having completed the *Antiquities,* is drawing the readers' attention to his own learning and certainly counts himself among the two or three who have succeeded in mastering the Jewish tradition, but in addressing his Greco-Roman audience Josephus does not use any technical term for the learned Jew and does not designate the learned person as a scribe.

Josephus' usage of the word scribe may reflect its meaning in the Greco-Roman world where it did not have the Palestinian Jewish connotation of one learned in the law, but simply referred to an official or more literally a student of Greek grammar. Writing in Hebrew in Palestine Ben Sira calls one learned in the law a scribe (*sôfēr*), a term which his grandson faithfully translates into the Greek *grammateus*. But in the Greek preface to the translation, the grandson, writing in Alexandria in the latter part of the second century, refers to both his audience and his grandfather as learned in the law, without any recourse to technical terms. Likewise, the Letter of Aristeas, which also probably comes from Alexandria, describes the learning of the seventy-two translators, but does not call them scribes or give them any title. 4 Maccabees, written in the diaspora, transforms

---

[64]See a discussion of this matter by G. Maier, "Die jüdischen Lehrer bei Josephus," *Josephus-Studien* (Festschrift O. Michel), eds. O. Betz, et al. (Göttingen: Vandenhoeck, 1974) 260-270. *War* 1.33.2 (648).

[65]*Ant.* 20.12.1 (264).

the scribe Eleazar into a learned priest. Ben Sira, 2 Maccabees and the synoptic gospels may reflect a Palestinian understanding of scribe as one learned in the Jewish law.[66]

Scribes in the New Testament as Jewish Leaders

More than in any other source the scribes are seen as a unified group in the New Testament, but this view may not be historically accurate. The synoptic gospel writers see the scribes as a unified group in opposition to Jesus but say very little about them. We shall briefly review the conclusions reached in chapters eight and nine and relate them to the material from our other sources.

In Mark the scribes are associated with Jerusalem and the chief priests as part of the government of Judaism. Though their roles are not specified, their close association with the chief priests means they functioned as high officials and advisors and that some attained membership in the governing class. The Markan scribes were dependent on the priests and derived their sustenance from the Temple. Even when scribes appeared in Galilee, they were identified a couple of times as coming from Jerusalem. Their teachings are referred to in an offhand way which suggests that they were recognized as authoritative teachers of Jewish law and custom. The scribes are thus typical members of the retainer class and part of the normal structure of society in an agrarian empire, as outlined in chapter three. Mark presents them as a unified, political group because for him their salient, unifying characteristic is opposition to Jesus. Actually, the scribes probably stand for a plethora of Jewish community officials (many of them scribes) who opposed Jesus' claim to authority and growing following.

For Matthew both the scribes and Pharisees had many interests in common and were the learned groups par excellence in Judaism. The scribes were connected both with village life and the leaders in Jerusalem and part of the middle leadership of Judaism. Matthew stresses scribes because he recognizes the

---

[66]See Stadelmann, *Ben Sira,* 257, n. 1 and 258.

role of Christian scribes in the new Christian community.[67] His quarrel is not with the role of scribes as learned guides of the community and guardians of the tradition, but the Jewish scribes' opposition to Jesus. It is very likely that Matthew's view of scribes as community leaders in the Galilean villages reflects more the situation of his church than conditions in Palestine before the war.

In Luke-Acts the scribes are not a very distinct group but are like the Pharisees in their belief in resurrection. The scribes are an appendage of the Pharisees for most of the gospel and at the time of Jesus' death the scribes are associated with the chief priests in Jerusalem, as they are in the other two synoptic gospels. In Acts the scribes continue to appear as learned leaders in Jerusalem, active in protecting Judaism. Luke also inserts a new category of leader, the lawyer. Lawyer replaces scribe in one instance and lawyers are similar to scribes and Pharisees. Luke adds no new evidence for first century Palestine. His understanding of the scribes is either vague (he conflates them with the Pharisees) or guided by the general functions of scribes in the Greco-Roman world.

The scribes presented in the synoptic gospels are best understood as bureaucrats and also as experts on Jewish life. They could have been low level officials and judges both in Jerusalem and in the towns and villages of the country. Mark, the most reliable of the gospels, which may reflect conditions in Palestine just before or after the war and most probably has traditions from the middle of the first century, locates scribes mainly in Jerusalem or says they are from Jerusalem. Only twice (2:6; 9:14) does he simply place them in Galilee. Their presence there is prima facie probable both as village scribes who write contracts and other documents and as low level government officials.[68] However, such functionaries would not have made a

---

[67]Christian scribes seem to be implied by 13:52 and 23:34. Scribes are opponents when they are joined to Pharisees. See R. Hümmel, *Die Auseinandersetzung zwischen Kirche und Judentum im Matthäusevangelium* (Munich: Kaiser, 1963) 17-18; van Tilborg, *Leaders,* 128-147; Hengel, *Studies in Mark,* 74-81, esp. 78-81.

[68]Sean Freyne, *Galilee from Alexander the Great to Hadrian 323 B.C.E. to 135 C.E.* (Wilmington: Glazier; Notre Dame: Notre Dame UP, 1980), ch. 8, theorizes that the scribal class from Jerusalem tried unsuccessfully to spread its interpretation of Jewish life to Galilee before the war and then engaged in a long, successful struggle after the war (cf.

coherent social class or organization opposed to Jesus, as the gospels understand them. The gospels testify most reliably to scribes connected to the government in Jerusalem where their role seems to be as associates of the priests both in judicial proceedings, enforcement of Jewish custom and law and on-going business in the Sanhedrin.[69] The gospel traditions about scribes may reflect the opposition of many scattered local officials to early Christian communities before and after the war, and perhaps opposition to Jesus also.

Scribe is used once in Paul's letters where he contrasts the wisdom of the world with the foolishness of the cross and claims that the cross is true wisdom. In the course of his attack, he cites scripture and then asks rhetorically "Where is the wise man *(sophos),* where is the scribe *(grammateus),* where is the debater *(suzētētēs)* of this age?" (1 Cor. 1:20). Paul seems to be referring to well known terms for educated intellectual leaders in the Greco-Roman world, of which scribe is one.

Scribes in Rabbinic Literature

Later rabbinic literature, the Mishnah, the Talmuds and various midrashic collections refer sporadically to the scribes *(sôferîm* in Hebrew), early authoritative teachers to whom a number of rulings and legal interpretations are attributed. Modern historical reconstructions of the development of Jewish law have usually identified the scribes as the Jewish scholars who had great influence on Judaism from the time of Ezra down to the time of the pairs in the second century. The scribes

---

esp. p. 328). The evidence for this is slim and the sociological and economic probability is small. The scribes in Jerusalem were supported by the chief priests and part of their government. Galilee was under the control of Herod Antipas; if any scribes were active there, they were his own and probably had a different agenda from Jerusalem. Scribal activities were intensely political and must not be imagined as the activities of popular lecturers or teachers in the modern world. For scribes as Levites and subordinate judicial officials as well as teachers and spiritual authorities, see D.R. Schwartz, "'Scribes and Pharisees, Hypocrites': Who were the Scribes?" *Zion* 50 (1985) 121-132.

[69]J. Neusner, *Evidence,* 118, thinks that the scribes in the first century were judges and administrators, subordinate to the supreme authority of the Romans. After 70 scribes as well as Pharisees and priests formed the core of teachers who became the rabbis. The Mishnah's scribal, priestly and Pharisaic interests reflect the diverse origins of the rabbis.

are also often identified as members of the Great Assembly, the (legendary) ruling body of Judaism during this period.[70] Scholars have differed concerning whether they were priests or not and when their influence ceased, as well as on the scope of their teachings. Some attribute certain anonymous teachings of the Mishnah to them, but no clear method exists for isolating these traditions. Lauterbach holds that they commented midrashically on Scripture and that the Mishnaic form is later, but this view has been challenged.[71] All these interpretations of the scribes have treated them as a cohesive body with a well defined agenda and independent power, but the evidence for this position is very weak.[72]

That the scribes were not an organized group with its own teaching can be seen in the rulings explicitly attributed to the scribes in rabbinic literature. Rules which are designated the "words of the scribes" (*divrē sôferîm*) are scattered in the sources and form no coherent body of teaching. In the Mishnah the scribes are used as the source for teachings which are thought to be ancient or for rulings which are not fully accepted or are of less authority then scripture. For example, the restrictions concerning eating the fruit of young trees are said to apply outside the land of Israel as well as inside as a matter of *halaka,* that is, Biblical law which is generally accepted as such in rabbinic teaching.[73] On the other hand, the restrictions concerning

[70]See Guttmann, *Judaism,* 7-9 for a summary of the usual reconstruction. J.Z. Lauterbach, *Rabbinic Essays* (repr. New York: Ktav, 1973) 27-29 and 163-194 has been influential on the development of the common view as has Epstein, *Mebo'ot,* 503-05, who speaks of the scribes in connection with the development of midrash in the pre-rabbinic period. See also Y. Gilat, "Soferim," *Encyclopedia Judaica* (Jerusalem: Keter, 1974) 15:79-81; also A.Demsky and Ed., "Scribe," 14:1041-1044 on the Biblical scribe and the Torah copyist.

[71]See Lauterbach in the previous note for the priority of midrash. He follows several earlier Jewish historians. The antiquity of both simple law and custom and interpreted scriptural law is affirmed by E.E. Urbach, "The Derasha as a Basis of the Halakha and the Problem of the Soferim,"[in Hebrew] *Tarbiz* 27 (1957-58) 166-182 and David Weiss Halivni, *Midrash, Mishnah and Gemara* (Cambridge: Harvard, 1986) 19-37.

[72]Urbach, "Derasha," comes closest to the truth in noting that the scribes were a group subordinate to the priests and elders who engaged in the scribal practices and types of interpretation common in the Greek world. However, he retrojects the rabbinic period into the first and second centuries B.C.E. and makes the scribes into universal educators of the people.

[73]m. Orlah 3:9.

growing diverse crops together are also binding outside the land of Israel, but only by authority of the "words of the scribes," which may mean a supposed ancient enactment or simple rabbinic teaching.[74] In view of the fact that other passages which refer to the words of the scribes seem to imply that the traditions derive from older and reliable authorities, this passage too probably invokes their authority, which is less than Scripture but greater than any recent rabbinic teacher.

The rabbis' desire to circumscribe the authority of the teachings of the scribes is most clear in m. Yadaim. When the transmission of uncleanness through the hands is being debated by R. Joshua and the sages, R. Joshua tries to argue by analogy from the laws concerning the transmission of uncleanness to the hands from the Torah scroll. This rule, which is unknown in the Bible, is attacked as insufficient ground for a legal argument.

> You may not judge (intepret) the words of Torah from the words of the scribes, nor the words of the scribes from the words or Torah, nor the words of the scribes from the words of the scribes. (m. Yadaim 3:2)

The sages desire to distinguish sharply the authority of the laws in Scripture from the teachings of the scribes and sharply circumscribe the authority of the latter.

Though the Mishnah circumscribes the authority of the teachings of the scribes, it does not condemn or annul it. In m. Sanhedrin, ch. 11 the Mishnah deals with those who deserve the penalty of strangling and especially those who misled the community. M. Sanhedrin 11:3 decrees that those who deny that one must observe some part of the words of the scribes are to be treated with greater stringency than those who deny that one must observe some point of Scriptural law. Denial of Scriptural law probably merits a less stringent punishment because it is obviously authoritative and so whoever denies it will be sum-

---

[74]For the latter, see Alan Avery-Peck, *Mishnah's Division of Agriculture: A History and Theology of Seder Zeraim* (BJS 79; Atlanta: Scholars, 1985) 336, who opts for the meaning rabbinic teaching. Avery-Peck places this law in the latest, Ushan stratum of the Mishnah and notes that it is unrelated to the preceding problems which unfold in the tractate.

marily rejected and pose no danger to the community and the authority of Scripture. But, a denial of authority to any words of the scribes is more dangerous to the community because it has more chance of drawing acceptance from other members of the community and undermining the rabbinic teaching authority.

Most of the passages in Mishnah which mention the words of the scribes are concerned with purity. Certain rules which are concerned with instruments susceptible to uncleanness and which seem to defy the general principles of uncleanness are attributed to the scribes by Rabbi Joshua, who comments: "A new thing did the scribes innovate and I have nothing to answer" (m. Kelim 13:7). Joshua seems to mean that he cannot answer those who object to these teachings of the scribes but at the same time his attribution of these teachings concerning odd cases to the scribes is an effort to ground them on early authority. Secondary matters are also attributed to the scribes in m. Yebamoth 2:3-4 where certain marriages between closely related relatives are said to have been forbidden by an ordinance (*mitzwāh*) and other, secondary degrees of union, which are less important and more debatable, forbidden by the words of the scribes (2:4).[75]

The words or teachings of the scribes can function as a general category for classifying differing types of rules. In m. Parah 11:5-6 reference is made to a class of unclean person, those who require immersion according to "the words of the scribes." In 11:6 this category of person is combined with another, those who require immersion according to "the words of Torah." Clearly the authors of the Mishnah distinguished laws of differing authority according to their origin in Scripture or in early teaching. The category of laws deriving from the words of the scribes also appears in m. Tohorot 4:7 which lists a number of cases of uncleanness which are in doubt because of uncertainty concerning whether they occurred in the public or private domain. These doubtful cases, which the sages (*ḥakāmîm*) declared clean, include the category of rules based on the "words of the scribes." Note that the words of the scribes and the teaching of the sages are here distinguished.

The authority of the scribes is less obvious and well established than that of the Bible, as can be seen in the preceding mishnaic

---

[75]Further comments on these teachings of the scribes are contained in m. Yeb. 9:3.

passages. The references to the scribes in the Tosefta are similar to those in Mishnah where they are used as a source for certain teachings. Later talmudic literature also mentions the scribes from time to time, sometimes in a way congruent with the passages cited above and sometimes with other meanings. Scribe, in the talmudic lexicon, can refer to a copyist who produced Torah scrolls,[76] to a literate person who writes letters and documents, and to a teacher and interpreter of scripture.[77] In addition, the teachings of the scribes can function as they do in the Mishnah, as an ancient source of authority for Jewish traditions.

The figure of the scribe in rabbinic literature is consistent with scribes in other literature. However, the historical role assigned the *sôferîm* in passing on part of the legal tradition and the implication that they were a cohesive "rabbinic-like" group fits the later rabbinic view of its own origins rather than the known historical facts.

The Roman Community

Some of the diaspora literature reviewed earlier suggested that scribe was not used for the Jew learned in the law. One other body of evidence from the diaspora needs to be assessed. The Greek title scribe *(grammateus)* appears over twenty times in the inscriptions from the Jewish community in Rome.[78] The Roman community had at least eleven separate congregations from the first century B.C.E. to the fourth C.E. Scribe or secretary of the congregation is the second most common title, after *archōn* ("leader," "president").[79] The limited evidence of the inscriptions shows that the scribe was not the leader of the congregation, but a subordinate official, probably the keeper of records and writer of marriage contracts and similar documents. Misspellings in an inscription by a scribe suggests that the

---

[76]The post-Mishnaic tractate "Soferim" is addressed to such copyists.

[77]Halivni, *Midrash,* 18-19; Epstein, *Mebo'ot,* 503, nn. 17, 18.

[78]See H.J. Leon, *The Jews of Rome* (Philadelphia: Jewish Publication Society, 1960) ch. 8.

[79]Leon, *Jews,* 183.

average scribe was not greatly learned.[80] Since there probably would not have been enough work as a maker of scrolls and contracts to keep a scribe busy full time, the role of community scribe would have been a part time occupation often filled by a person with a minimal training. The slim evidence gathered by Leon fits the Greco-Roman pattern, which was alive in some Jewish communities of the Roman Empire. The scribe was a literate person who might not be greatly educated and who fulfilled limited but essential functions in the community.

Summary

Since the evidence for scribes in Judaism is sparse and scattered, the role of the scribe in the Near East has been used to provide a cultural context for understanding the references to scribes in the New Testament and Jewish literature. The title scribe covers many roles in society and can be used of individuals in several social classes and contexts. In Jewish society scribes are found working for the king and the Temple. Such scribes may have been drawn from the priests and Levites, as well as the people. Scribes who held high office were probably drawn from the aristocracy or at least prominent families.[81] Scribes were found in the bureaucracy in great numbers, in villages and also among groups such as the Pharisees. Scribes had an effect on the preservation of prophecy, wisdom writing and the Pentateuch and overlapped circles which had priestly, apocalyptic, and wisdom orientations. In the talmudic period the roles of wise man and of scribe (in the broad sense) were assimilated to the title of rabbi (though scribes as specialized technicians were also recognized).

Scribes do not seem to have formed a unified class or organization, though groups of scribes might be characterized as belonging to a given class and status and at times scribes may have had organizations of which we have no evidence. In

---

[80]Leon, *Jews,* 184-85 and Inscr. 102 (p. 278).

[81]LeMoyne, *Sadducéens,* 352-354, says that the Sadducees probably had their own scribes.

general, the evidence we have supports the idea that most scribes were dependent on the wealthy governing class both for their training and employment. The technical competence required of even a copyist demands a period of freedom from work and the aid of a teacher, both of which can only be provided by an individual or institution with wealth. The government and wealthy land owners needed literate individuals to keep records, collect taxes, serve as officials and judges and engage in correspondence and thus needed continually to train a small number of people as scribes. Sociologically most of them would have been retainers, that is, people who had left the peasantry but did not have an independent place and power in society.

The socially lowest type of scribe would have been the village scribe who was little more than a copyist who knew how to draw up letters and legal documents. The village scribe might also have been a low level administrator reporting to the authorities, keeping records and carrying on communication between the government and people. Such a scribe might have instructed some youngsters in writing and reading, but he was most probably not a learned teacher or highly educated keeper of the cultural traditions.

Most scribes, including those pictured in the gospels, were middle level officials. They were the agents of the central government and probably served in various bureaucratic posts. Their position gave them some power and influence, but they were subordinate to and dependent on the priests and leading families in Jerusalem and Herod Antipas in Galilee during the time of Jesus. Reconstructions of scribes as an independent class which challenged the priests for power and led Jews in new social and religious directions give no thought to the economic and political sources of this hypothetical group's power. Surely the highly learned and most talented among the scribes had influence and some achieved power in Jewish society, but the economic basis for the government was taxes and the taxes were collected by the Hasmonean high priests at the Temple and then by Herod and the Romans, as well as the Temple authorities. It is to these social leaders that scribes would have been attached.

The highest level of scribe may have come from or joined the governing class. High officials and governmental counsellors, those at the center of the government, would have achieved great influence and some power. They would also have been responsible for keeping central records, for writing international correspondence and for the education of talented successors. Such training, experience and activity at the top of the government would have been the prerogative of relatively few of the scribes. Many of them were probably drawn from the priests or leading families and, though possessing the skills of scribes, not called by that name, but by the more prestigous category of priest, notable, etc.

Scribes associated with the central governing class would most likely have been thoroughly educated in law, cultural traditions, history and all aspects of religion. It is such a scribe, learned in all aspects of Judaism, that Ben Sira pictures in chapter thirty-nine. Ben Sira's scribe and his successors were those who edited and shaped the Biblical traditions and also, like Ben Sira, produced original works for themselves, for their patrons, or for the Temple and governmental authorities in order to implement social programs, protect the culture or adapt the tradition to new circumstances. On occasion they also produced works of protest to counteract social trends and dangers.

We cannot know from the texts whether any rabbinic claims concerning the teachings of the scribes can be securely attributed to scribes in any period. Nor do we learn from the Mishnah anything about what kind of group these scribes might have been nor what their social roles, influence and power might have been. As was pointed out at the beginning of the chapter, reconstructions of the role of scribes have usually presumed that they were a lay phenomenon alongside the priestly institution which gradually attained power over Jewish society during the Hellenistic period. However, no evidence for such a development is available and the sociological probabilities argue that scribes would have been dependent on those in power. Scribes do not seem to be a coherent social group with a set membershp, but rather a class of literate individuals drawn from many parts of society who filled many social roles and were attached to all parts of society from the village to the palace and Temple. The modern historical reconstruction of the scribes as learned teachers and leaders in the post-exilic period, based on many passages of rabbinic literature and some New Testament passages, is probably correct for some scribes at some times. In all cases, however, the scribes must be contextualized among other social groups and their power and influence integrated into the whole picture of Jewish society. They must not be treated as an autonomous group with its own power and continuous agenda. Scribes were varied in background and allegiance and were individuals filling a social role in different contexts rather than a unified political and religious force.

12

The Place of the Pharisees in Jewish Society

Data on the Pharisees is so sparse and difficult to evaluate that any historical reconstruction must remain incomplete and uncomfortably hypothetical. Many attempts have harmonized very different and contradictory sources and others have placed great weight on single texts and minor details; the results have been very speculative. The historical context of the Pharisees in the Roman empire and sociological structure of that kind of society will provide boundaries and guidance for this reconstruction. Though an infinite variety of concrete social arrangements are possible, many of them unique, sociological categories and theories will provide a framework for understanding what the Pharisees may have been. This summary chapter will review the results of the previous chapters, address problems raised there, and take account of some other relevant evidence. Special emphasis will be placed on the type of group the Pharisees were and their geographical location.

The position of the Pharisees in Hasmonean and Herodian society must be kept firmly in perspective, despite the emphasis on them in rabbinic literature and the New Testament. They were one small group among many, some of which had names and endured and others of which were just nameless, temporary coalitions, factions and movements. Josephus bears witness to the complex social organization and strife during the Greco-Roman period, as do the New Testament and rabbinic traditions to a lesser extent. In both the pre-exilic and post-exilic periods Judaism changed constantly and significantly in response to the empires surrounding and often controlling it. In the Hasmonean and Herodian periods the Pharisees were one, but only one, well known group. characterized by a distinctive way of living Judaism and constant social involvement.

That political and factional strife was normal in the Greco-Roman period can be seen in Qumran literature. Since we have no literature directly from the Pharisees and since scholars have claimed that Qumran literature alludes to the Pharisees, a brief review of certain Qumran texts will enlarge our understanding of the Pharisees and their setting. Qumran literature is filled with polemics and invective which bear witness to the social, political and religious strife among Jewish groups during the Hasmonean period. The wicked priest, the man of lies, the man of scorn, the spouter of lies, the lion of wrath and the seekers after smooth things are only some of the adversaries condemned for a variety of crimes by the Qumran literature. Though the allusions to the Qumran community's opponents, which are contained in the pesharim to Habakkuk, Nahum, Psalm 37 and other documents, are very difficult to correlate with history, they testify to the political and religious strife at the inception of the Qumran community in the second century B.C.E. (probably under Jonathan or Simon) and also under Alexander Jannaeus, to whose reign the Pesher Nahum certainly refers.[1]

Pesher Nahum refers to two Greek kings, Antiochus and Demetrius, who have been convincingly identified with Antiochus IV Epiphanes (175-164 B.C.E.) and Demetrius III Eukairos (95-88 B.C.E.), and refers to the lion of wrath who crucified his opponents, that is, Alexander Jannaeus.[2] Though the allusions are symbolic and the punishments of the adversaries couched in Biblical and eschatological terms, the impression of social and political conflict inside and outside the Jewish

---

[1]For two recent and judicious reviews of scholarship, see Devorah Dimat, "Qumran Sectarian Literature," *Jewish Writings of the Second Temple Period,* ed. Michael Stone (Assen: van Gorcum; Philadelphia: Fortress, 1984) 483-550, esp. 508-513 and 542-547; Geza Vermes, *The Dead Sea Scrolls: Qumran in Perspective* (Cleveland: Collins-World, 1978) 150-154. For the *pesharim* see Maurya Horgan, *Pesharim: Qumran Interpretations of Biblical Books* (CBQMS 8; Washington: Catholic Biblical Assn, 1979) 158-191.

[2]See ch. 5 on Josephus' *Ant.* 13.14.2 (379-383). Note that the opponents are not identified as Pharisees. The Pharisees later take vengeance on those who supported the crucifixions so they must have been allies in opposing Alexander Jannaeus.

community fits the account of the period written by Josephus. Pesher Nahum also speaks of two groups of opponents, metaphorically designated Ephraim and Manasseh, as well as another group, the "seekers after smooth things."[3] The "seekers after smooth things" have been identified with the Pharisees and "Ephraim" and "Manasseh" with the Pharisees and Sadducees.

According to Pesher Nahum, Ephraim was crucified by Alexander Jannaeus, an act which the Qumran community probably approved.[4] The identification of the "seekers after smooth things"[5] and "Ephraim" with the Pharisees is common in the literature, but hardly certain.[6] The eight hundred opponents crucified by Jannaeus are not called Pharisees by Josephus (see ch. 5) and the opponents of Jannaeus in Josephus and the pesharim need not be identified with one of the three schools of thought listed by Josephus.[7] The metaphoric designation "seekers after smooth things" suggests that the Qumran community found their opponents too accommodating to changes in Jewish society, either because they twisted the meaning of the law (Is. 30:10) or allied themselves too closely with non-Jewish authorities and practices. The use of various epithets connected to "lie" and "falsehood" suggests that the community disagreed with its opponents on many points of interpretation and practice. Since the Qumran group had left Jerusalem, the "seekers after smooth things" were probably still

---

[3] *Dôršê ḥalāqôt. Ḥalāqôt* means smooth things, flattery and falsehood in Hebrew. Is. 30:10 contrasts true prophecy with the smooth things and delusions desired by rebellious Israelites who will not listen to the Torah of the Lord. Daniel 11:32 says that Antiochus Epiphanes will seduce by flatteries (*ḥalāqôt*) those who act wickedly against the covenant. The Qumran expression may refer to those who seek modes of interpreting and living Judaism more in accord with the Hellenistic world or just in contradiction to the Qumran interpretations of the law.

[4] 4QpNah 3-4.i.7. See Y. Yadin, "Pesher Nahum (4QpNahum) Reconsidered," *Israel Exploration Journal* 21 (1971) 1-12, who reinterprets the text on the basis of the Temple Scroll. His interpretation is affirmed by Joseph Fitzmyer, "Crucifixion in Ancient Palestine, Qumran Literature and the New Testament," *CBQ* 40 (1978) 493-513.

[5] 4QpNah 3-4.i.2, 7; ii. 2, 4; iii. 3, 6-7; 4QpIsa c 23.ii.10; 1QH 2:15, 32; CD 1:18.

[6] Dimat, "Qumran," 511-512; Horgan, *Pesharim,* 161. Frank M. Cross, *The Ancient Library of Qumran* (Garden City: Doubleday, 1961) 123, n. 25 is more cautious.

[7] Manasseh is linked to the Sadducees because Pesher Nahum (3-4.iii.9) says that "rivers" (Nahum 3:8) refers to "the gr[ea]t ones of Manasseh, the honored ones of the [city, who suppo]rt M[anasseh] (Horgan's translation). But the great and honored members of the community were not necessarily Sadducees.

there and active in Palestinian political struggles in a way the Qumran community did not approve. The Qumran polemics against their opponents testify to the diversity and conflicts in Jewish society but not that their opponents were Pharisees.

This brief review of the Qumran literature's allusions to its opponents is consistent with Josephus' depiction of the Hasmonean period. As the Hasmonean family struggled to establish and legitimate its rule in Palestine, it faced opposition from other groups desiring power, such as priestly families it had displaced in Jerusalem, traditional social elements which did not recognize its authority and surrounding peoples ready to take advantage of weakness. The Hasmoneans constantly strove to build support for their rule through alliances, coalitions, war and persuasion.[8] The changing political fortunes of the Pharisees, as well as Essenes and Sadducees, depicted in Josephus and Qumran literature fit this historical process very well.

Group Types

In Part Two the Pharisees were compared to various types of ancient and modern groups. While reviewing systematically all the evidence, several general characteristics of all groups must be kept in mind. First, groups like the Pharisees, who existed for two centuries, change over time, sometimes significantly. Their social activities, effectiveness and inner relations vary greatly according to political, cultural, economic and social circumstances. Second, groups often have several functions and roles at once and thus can legitimately be placed in several categories. For example, modern labor unions are economic advocacy groups, political interest groups and social fellowship associations simultaneously. A professional association may be a scientific research group, a lobby and a fellowship group. Third, individuals belong to many groups and must distribute their commitment, time, energy, activity, roles and functions among them. Consequently, the boundaries of groups and people's identification with groups is often less definitive and significant

---

[8]For example, 1 Maccabees is pro-Hasmonean propaganda and 2 Maccabees is anti-Hasmonean.

for life than they appear to be when formally listed. People intensify or diminish their involvements with groups, all the while remaining members in good standing.[9] How actively a person participates as a member of a group depends on the web of commitments, social relations and circumstances which provides the context for decisions.

The Pharisees most probably fulfilled many group roles in Jewish society. The discussion of the Pharisees as a group will concentrate on their communal activities and functions in society rather than on a static list of group characteristics.

POLITICAL INTEREST GROUP

The Pharisees in Josephus' narrative functioned as a political interest group which had its own goals for society and constantly engaged in political activity to achieve them, even though it did not always succeed (see chs. 5-6). They generally did not have direct power as a group and were not as a whole members of the governing class. They were a literate, corporate, voluntary association which constantly sought influence with the governing class. As such they belonged to the retainer class, a group of people above the peasants and other lower classes but dependent on the governing class and ruler for their place in society. They were found in Jerusalem and they probably fulfilled administrative or bureaucratic functions in society at certain times. In each era of Jewish history from the Hasmonean period until the destruction of the Temple they were present and struggling to gain access to power and to influence society.

REVIVAL OR REFORM

The Pharisees' association probably functioned as a social movement organization seeking to change society.[10] The social,

---

[9]Some theorists subordinate groups to networks. Group membership is a mode of categorizing one's very complex and overlapping social relationships which are better understood as a network. See L. Holy, "Groups," in *The Social Science Encyclopedia*, 346.

[10]Henri Taifel, *Differentiation between Social Groups: Studies in the Social Psychology of Intergroup Relations* (London/New York: Academic, 1978) 28-46. See

political and economic situation of Palestinian Jews underwent a number of upheavals in the Greco-Roman period which demanded adaptation of Jewish customs and a reinterpretation of the Jewish identity fashioned by the Biblical tradition. In addition, the Hasmoneans and the governing class changed Israel into a small, militarily active Hellenistic kingdom and took control of political and economic resources in order to control society. The Pharisees probably sought a new, communal commitment to a strict Jewish way of life based on adherence to the covenant. If they did so, they sought to capitalize on popular sentiment for rededication to or reform of Judaism. Such popular sentiment can produce a social movement which seeks reform, but a long lasting, complex campaign for reform or renewal requires the formation of a social movement organization which aims at promoting or resisting change in society at large.

SOCIAL RELATIONS NETWORK

The Pharisees' position in society was part of a complex network of relationships and depended heavily on circumstances, on strong patrons and loyal clients and on the cultivation of influence and alliances in society. Josephus' descriptions of the Pharisees contend that they cultivated harmonious relations with all, had great respect for their traditions and elders and consequently, had a large following for their attractive way of life,[11] but give no reasons for this behavior. Possibly the Pharisees, most of whom did not have hereditary ties to positions of power, stressed internal and external social relations to build up their own group and win it favor and influence with others.[12] Their social status was not stable like that of hereditary or traditional leaders (priests, village elders, etc.) so they had constantly to recruit new members and compete for influence with

also John D. McCarthy and Mayer N. Zald, "Resource Mobilization and Social Movements: A Partial Theory," *American Journal of Sociology* 82 (1977) 1212-1219, esp. 1217-1219.

[11]See ch. 6.

[12]That their struggle for power and influence was a group struggle is shown by the absence of names of Pharisaic leaders in most cases.

those in power.[13] This view of the Pharisees is borne out by the gospels according to which the Pharisees were recognized leaders and competed with Jesus and his followers and others for influence among the people. The Pharisees' beliefs and behavior as Jews were different enough from those of Jesus and the early Christians, as well as other Jewish groups, to provoke disputes and factional competition and conflict. Their appearance in the gospels indicates that they were established and influential in Jewish society and were looked on favorably by at least some of the population.

Unfortunately the lack of information about the Pharisees prevents a detailed analysis of all the social relations which bound them to all the other groups and classes in society.[14] Since personal relationships were as important as large scale hereditary and class categories, the Pharisees' status and influence probably depended greatly on their network of supporters and allies. Such networks constantly changed and had to be maintained with great effort and skill. The network of relationships which bound together people in villages and towns included kinship, friendship, patronage and debts of honor. People had dozens of personal and corporate relationships which defined their place in society and their own self-concept and identity. They belonged simultaneously to a major class in society, a kinship group and a territorial group (this usually included religion), to sub-groups within their class and perhaps to voluntary associations. In addition, their activities might have made them parts of coalitions and factions in the struggle for power or income. The Pharisees, scribes and followers of Jesus all belonged to groups which cut across the major classes of society. Interactions between people in all these relationships usually involved several roles at once with many mutual obligations.[15] The Pharisees were not a simple group with a limited,

---

[13]Instability is typical of status based on achieved, rather than legally or socially ascribed, prestige. One's status is always at risk from newcomers or from declining achievement. Even hereditary or traditionally ascribed status could be lost and had to be buttressed by achieved status. See ch. 4 and also C. Wolf, "Status," in *Social Science Encyclopedia,* 825-826.

[14]See ch. 4 for the significant elements of networks.

[15]Differing social commitments probably contributed to the conflicts in the early Christian communities recounted in Acts 6 and the Pauline letters. Though faith in Jesus

concrete goal but a long lasting, well connected, voluntary, corporate organization which sought to influence Jewish society and entered into many mutual relationships to accomplish their aims.

SOCIAL ROLES

A major question unanswered by the sources concerns the daily activities of the Pharisees and the source of their livelihood. The older theory that they were urban artisans is very unlikely because artisans were poor, uneducated and uninfluential. The more common theory that the Pharisees were a lay scribal movement, a group of religious scholars and intellectuals who displaced the traditional leaders and gained great authority over the community is likewise very unlikely.[16] Though some Pharisees were part of the governing class, most Pharisees were subordinate officials, bureaucrats, judges and educators. They are best understood as retainers who were literate servants of the governing class and had a program for Jewish society and influence with the people and their patrons. When the opportunity arose, they sought power over society. This means that their organization cannot be viewed as a monastic like community or withdrawn sect which demands primary and total commitment from every member. It is most likely that Pharisees were bound together by certain beliefs and practices (to be reviewed below) and by endeavors to influence social change.

How much did being a Pharisee demand? Concretely, a person was not primarily a Pharisee. A member of the Pharisees retained his family and territorial allegiances, his roles in society and occupation, his friends and network of associates. In some way not revealed in the sources he committed himself to be a Pharisee and this commitment with its particular understanding of the Jewish covenant and Jewish life guided many of his

---

and his way of life was supposed to be primary and determinative, many other family and social demands and norms beset the members of the Christian communities.

[16]See most recently, Rivkin, *Hidden Revolution,* 211-251. This theory, held by many, was popularized in the English speaking world by Jacob Lauterbach, "The Pharisees and Their Teachings," *HUCA* 6 (1929) 69-139, reprinted in *Rabbinic Essays,* 87-162. See esp. 77ff/97ff.

endeavors and claimed a part of his time, energy and resources. The Pharisaic movement has some characteristics in common with Greek schools of thought and must have educated its members to some degree. This view of the Pharisees, admittedly hypothetical due to lack of evidence, is consistent with what the sources tell us of the Pharisees, including the information given by Saul the Pharisee. In addition, the fact that the Pharisees' life was complexly interwoven with Jewish society may explain why Josephus has much to say about the very different, alluring and exotic Essenes, and little to say about the more ordinary Pharisees.

SECT

Several scholars have argued that political oppression under Herod and the Romans forced the Pharisees out of the political sphere and prompted them to become a sect-like table fellowship group.[17] While such a change in Pharisaic activity is possible, it seems less likely both historically and sociologically. The choice between political or sectarian activity is not necessary since an ancient group like the Pharisees would necessarily be involved in all aspects of social life, political and religious. Though Herod and the Romans did tighten control on the traditional Jewish leaders who survived the Hasmonean period, neither destroyed or reformed in a major way traditional leadership, but manipulated it for their purposes. Even if the Pharisees had reduced political influence and involvement, they were still active and interested in the whole of Jewish society.

Neusner has most often argued that the legal agenda of the Pharisees, centered around food laws and festivals, bespeaks a sectarian table fellowship which was not part of the political struggle of first century Palestine.[18] However, Neusner has also

[17]See chs. 6 and 10, esp. Smith, "Palestinian Judaism," followed by Neusner, *From Politics to Piety*. Lee Levine, "On the Political Involvement of the Pharisees under Herod and the Procurators," [in Hebrew] *Cathedra* 8 (1978), 12-28, esp. 18-20 and 24-26, offers further arguments that the Pharisees were predominantly non-political from the Herodian period on. All allow for political activity by some Pharisees.

[18]Jacob Neusner, "The Fellowship *(Haburah)* in the Second Jewish Commonwealth," *HTR* 53 (1960) 125-142; *Rabbinic Traditions,* 3:304-306; *From Politics to Piety,* 81-96;

noted that this identification is hypothetical because the group who developed the early agenda of the Mishnah is not certainly known for a number of reasons.[19]

Caution is appropriate, for reconstruction of the Pharisees from stories of the pre-destruction sages and from the early stages of the mishnaic tradition is hazardous. Though the traditions which stem from the early first century mostly concern ritual purity, agricultural tithes and sabbath observance, they do not prove that the Pharisees at that period were turned inward. First, since the traditions to be preserved in the Mishnah were selected by the post-destruction rabbis, their selection and narrow scope may reflect their interests rather than the traditions and interests of the Pharisees before the destruction. Second, the emphasis on intra community relations is consistent both with the descriptions Josephus gives of the Pharisees and with their lessened, but not terminated, political influence after the Hasmonean period. Third, sects throughout history have been politically and socially involved with change in society and protest against the status quo as often as they have been withdrawn from society.[20] The classic distinction between sect and cult should be maintained in which sects have greater (negative) social involvement and cults much more tenuous social relations both within the group and with society at large. Fourth, the stress on purity rules as boundary creating mechanisms is typical of minority groups who are striving to keep their identity and bring about change in a strong society.

If the Pharisees are a sect according to Wilson's categories, they best fit the *reformist* type which is a group which seeks gradual, divinely revealed alterations in the world.[21] This type of sect engages in political and social activities similar to those of the Pharisees. Wilson characterizes reformist sects as "objectivist" because they seek change in the world, not just in individuals or in a person's relations with the world. A reformist sect differs from the three other objectivist types of sect, the revolutionist

"Two Pictures of the Pharisees: Philosophical Circle or Eating Club," *AnThRev* 64 (1982) 525-538; "Three Pictures."

[19]See ch. 10; Neusner, *Evidence,* 50, 70-71.

[20]See the discussion of Wilson's typology in ch. 4.

[21]See the end of ch. 4 and Wilson, *Magic,* 23-26 and 38-49 for these categories.

which awaits destruction of the social order by divine forces (apocalyptic groups), the introversionist which withdraws from the world into a purified community (the Qumran community) and the utopian which seeks to reconstruct the world according to divine principles without revolution. However, these types are not hermetically sealed off from one another. A group may have more than one response to the world at the same time, that is, it may overlap two or three of these categories. It may also change over time and even cease to be a sect if social conditions change. Consequently, if the Pharisees are understood as a sect, they may have had introversionist tendencies, manifested in their purity regulations, without losing their involvement or desire for involvement in political society. These introversionist tendencies may have been more pronounced in the first century, C.E. than in the previous two. They may also have had revolutionist tendencies connected to their apocalyptic beliefs, tendencies also seen at Qumran.

Since this study has stressed the political and social activities of the Pharisees, what gain can be made by characterizing them as a sect rather than as a political interest group? The problem concerns both correct classification and idiomatic usage of terms. Sect commonly connotes a withdrawn religious group and politics suggests pragmatism, self interest and ad hoc compromise. Both of these meanings are inappropriate for the first century. Sects in Wilson's analysis involve more than social activity for change; they are characterized by a vigorous inner life and operate as self-select, intermittently operative communities.[22] Though the sources tell us little about the Pharisees' inner community life, they do indicate that they had one. Concerning political involvement, some European political parties and groups, which have a detailed program for society undergirded by social and political theory and sustained by an intellectual tradition, provide a rough analogy to the Pharisees better than American political parties, which have no intellectual tradition nor consistent platform and are more like coalitions of powerful and influential people seeking power.[23]

---

[22]Wilson, *Magic,* 32.

[23]Both Rivkin, *Hidden Revolution* and J. Bowker, *Jesus and the Pharisees* (Cambridge: Cambridge UP, 1973) make the intellectual and scholastic tradition the

SCHOOL

The nature of Greek schools and other associations was treated at the end of chapter six. A brief review of that discussion will help identify the Pharisees. The sources presume that the Pharisees were educated but they do not say how or how much. Josephus presents them as reputedly accurate interpreters of the Jewish tradition, a claim which implies that all learned their own traditions and some were highly educated. In the gospels they are informed and subtle adversaries of Jesus, a role which implies familiarity with tradition and custom. But the gospels may reflect later Jewish leaders who opposed the early Christian community. The rabbinic sources which portray the Pharisees as learned rabbis are retrojecting second and third century Judaism into the first century. It is perhaps more probable to imagine the Pharisees as learned leaders of the people, but so little is known about Jewish education in the pre-rabbinic period that the Pharisees' educational system and level cannot be certainly known.[24] Their education may have been carried out informally under the sponsorship of a patron or institutionally.

The Pharisees may profitably be compared to Hellenistic philosophical schools or schools of thought if the analogy is cautiously and loosely applied. They had a program of reform for Jewish life, a particular interpretation of Jewish tradition and a definable and sometimes controversial outlook on fundamental matters crucial to Judaism.[25] But, the Pharisees as depicted by Josephus acted as a political interest group and thus went beyond the activities of many Greek schools. The designation school (of thought) is appropriate as long as this expres-

---

core of the Pharisaic movement. While this element is present and important, movements, sects and other social groups originate from a desire to act on conviction in a certain way. An intellectual tradition or a particular way of looking at the world develops in conjunction with social and political involvement. To see the Pharisees mainly as scholars is to abstract them from society.

[24]See Anthony J. Saldarini, "School," *Harper's Bible Dictionary*, ed. Paul J. Achtemeier (San Francisco: Harper, 1985) 912-913.

[25]If some Pharisaic literature had survived, it would give guidance in this area. It is possible that they did not write an extensive literature, either for theological, social or political reasons, But it is equally possible that their literature was destroyed or lost, just as the Essenes' was until the chance discovery of the Dead Sea Scrolls in 1947.

sion is not understood to refer to an exclusively academic and theoretical association.

FACTIONS

The first century "Houses" of Hillel and Shammai, so important in the development of Jewish law and life after 70, are best understood as factions which became institutionalized after the deaths of their leaders. These and other factions, which carved out their own ways of living Judaism to preserve their identities as Jews, thrived in the first century when Judaism was subordinate to Rome. Hillel and Shammai, along with Judas the founder of the fourth philosophy, Jesus the preacher of the kingdom of God and his followers, and others easily gathered modest groups of enthusiastic followers who strove to convince other Jews to join them and sought influence and power over social policy. In the late first century and early second century the leaders of the rabbinic movement probably did the same. Internally, the Pharisees had their own vision of how society should be but rabbinic literature indicates that they had many disagreements within their small and diverse movement. Just how they were organized is not completely clear, but their endurance in society for over two centuries and their eventual emergence as a power in Jewish society during the second and third centuries argues to a coherent program and determined policy developed over time and most probably with many variations and factional disputes along the way.

BELIEFS AND TEACHINGS

The accounts of the Pharisees' beliefs in Josephus and the gleanings available in rabbinic literature and the New Testament provide incomplete information which is difficult to interpret. According to Josephus, who wishes to relate the Jewish schools of thought to Greek philosophy, they affirmed the influence of divine activity on human life, the joint effect of human freedom and fate, and reward and punishment in the afterlife. Josephus' contrast of the positions of the three schools of thought probably derives from their eschatology and apocalyptic expectations.

The Sadducees pictured humans as independent and distant from God both in life and after it; the Pharisees pictured God and humans as in a close relationship both in this life and the next. The Pharisees probably held positions on eschatology, divine providence and human responsibility which were different enough from traditional Jewish teachings and attitudes to require some positive commitment and explicit defense, However, we have too little of second Temple literature to specify the nuances of Pharisaic teaching in contrast to other groups.[26]

The rabbinic laws and stories which can be somewhat reliably dated to the first century (see ch. 10) show that the Pharisees had a strong interest in tithing, ritual purity and sabbath observance and not much of an interest in civil laws and regulations for the Temple worship. The New Testament also shows that the Pharisees had unique interpretations of these matters and sought to promote their observance and defend their validity against challenge by Jesus and his early followers. In the Greco-Roman period the Pharisees, Qumran community, priests and other groups vitally interested in the struggle to live Jewish life in the Roman empire had differing ideas concerning agricultural, sexual and food laws. Serious differences in the understanding of Jewish covenant and commitment to God, people and land separated these groups and factions within Judaism. Implicit in these programs for living Judaism were profound judgments concerning the meaning of Judaism and its place in the larger world where it was politically subordinate.

The purity rules, which seem so arcane to modern westerners, regularized life and separated that which was normal and life giving from that which was abnormal or ambiguous and so a threat to normal life. Such a set of categories and rules excluded that which is foreign or strange; their usefulness against the attraction and influence of the Romans and Hellenistic culture is obvious.[27] Purity and tithing rules separated the Pharisees,

[26]The explosion of study on Jewish ("intertestamental") literature of the second Temple period has shown that the teachings in Palestinian Judaism were multiple and diverse. In addition, apocrypha and pseudepigrapha previously assigned to the Pharisees and Sadducees are really indicative of the presence of other groups.

[27]See Mary Douglas, *Purity* and *Symbols* for purity rules as boundary setting mechanisms and for the necessity of such boundaries in groups which do not control society and must protect themselves from assimilation.

Sadducees and Essenes, all of whom affirmed the Biblical rules and had a distinctive interpretation of them in daily life, from one another and from the followers of Jesus as well as from numerous other messianic, apocalyptic, political and reformist groups.

Galilean Pharisees?

The synoptic gospels place the Pharisees mostly in Galilee and hardly at all in Jerusalem. Josephus and the Gospel of John associate them with the governing class in Jerusalem. Rabbinic literature places the pre-destruction sages in Jerusalem and has little to say about Galilee. The historical reliability of the Galilean tradition which derives from Mark and his sources is questionable. Bultmann argued that most of the dispute stories originally lacked the Pharisees as adversaries and M. Smith has tried to show that all lacked them.[28] Bultmann is correct that the tradition tends to add Pharisees to many stories and gradually sees them as the adversaries of Jesus par excellence. However, the contention that the early church put the Pharisees in all the Galilean disputes or moved disputes with the Pharisees from a Judean to a Galilean location lacks cogency.

The traditions used in Mark (written in the mid-60's or early 70's) date from at least the middle of the first century and were edited and ordered by the author of Mark to serve his own purposes. We do not know where the traditions were fashioned previously to Mark, in Jerusalem, Galilee, or Syria. If they were formed in Jerusalem, the disputes may reflect the early community's conflicts with the Pharisees in Jerusalem. However, even if this is the case, it is very unlikely that the early followers of Jesus would have placed Pharisees in Galilee if their presence there would be manifestly contrary to the first century situation. That the Jerusalem Pharisees were transposed to Galilee in Mark or his sources is rendered less probable by the care with which the passion narrative, one of the earliest traditions in the

---

[28]Bultmann, *History,* 52-54 and Smith, *Magician,* 153-157 cited in ch. 8. Smith thinks that the original sources had "scribes" in many cases and that Pharisees were added later to fit the experience of the early Christian community.

gospel, keeps the Pharisees separate from the governing class in Jerusalem. All early Christian traditions assume and affirm that Jesus was a Galilean and that he worked there. The disputes with his opponents, including the Pharisees, are deeply embedded in the tradition and reflect the struggles of his life. Granted that the disputes have been refined and reworked to fit the later needs of the Christian community and that Pharisees are often added to the narrative in Matthew, Luke and John, and perhaps to the Markan narrative as well, the presence of the Pharisees in a number of pre-destruction Christian traditions about Galilee argues that the presence of Pharisees was not improbable and that Jesus' opposition may have included Pharisees.[29]

The Pharisees do not appear as residents of Galilee in Josephus. Three Pharisees are sent to Galilee from Jerusalem as part of the delegation to remove Josephus as commander during the revolution.[30] However, Josephus concentrates on events and people at the center of Judaism in Jerusalem in his works and never gives a complete account of the officials and groups who made up Jewish society. If the Pharisees were a minor presence in Galilee, they might easily have gone unmentioned in the *War* and *Antiquities* and even in the *Life* which recounts Josephus' exploits in Galilee. Their absence in Josephus' accounts of Galilee does suggest that they were not one of the leading political, social or religious forces there.

Paul's identification of himself as a Pharisee to the Philippians in eastern Macedonia implies that the Pharisees were known and probably active outside Judea and Jerusalem. His letters suggest that his sphere of activity, including persecution of early Christians, was Palestine and southern Syria. He was known by reputation to the Judean followers of Jesus as a persecutor. Paul says that after the revelation of Jesus to him, he did not go up to Jerusalem, but to "Arabia," which refers to the Nabatean kingdom in the Syrian desert, and then returned to Damascus.[31]

---

[29]See Freyne, *Galilee,* 320-323 for a similar conclusion. Freyne mounts a number of arguments for Pharisaic presence in Galilee in ch. 8.

[30]*Life;* see ch. 5.

[31]Gal. 1:16-17. Only Acts says that he was on his way to Damascus when he had his vision of Jesus. Galatians' phrase "and then I returned to Damascus" suggests that Paul had been in Damascus when he had his revelation.

After becoming a follower of Jesus Paul seems to have made his base in northern Syria at Antioch. Antioch was not far from Paul's place of origin (according to Acts), Tarsus in Cilicia, which was at the pass leading into the interior of Asia Minor. Paul may have come into contact with Pharisaism in Cilicia or Syria. The evidence is tenuous, but if Pharisaism was known and influential outside of Judea, the most likely sphere of influence would be Jewish communities in the Semitic areas to the north, including Galilee, the Damascus area to the northeast, the rest of southern Syria and greater Syria beyond.

To affirm that the Pharisees were present in Galilee is not to affirm that they were in charge, or even a dominant force there. The Pharisees and Jesus were both minor social forces who had similar interests, sought to influence the people in similar ways and so were likely opponents. If the Pharisees were present in Galilee, they were not part of the governing class, nor were they part of the traditional leadership of Galilee. They were a recognized and established social group, but only one among many in Palestinian society. The Pharisees must be fitted into the social and political situation there which was complex and very different from that in Jerusalem. Thus a brief treatment of the political and social organization of Galilee will help to put both the Pharisees and their opponent Jesus in perspective.

GALILEE

Galilee is often stereotyped as Galilee of the gentiles (Is. 8:23 [Heb.]) where Jewish influence was diminished. Such characterizations have usually been based on the misconception that normative Judaism dominated most of Palestine and thus Galilee was abnormal. Galilee, like Perea, had a large Jewish population alongside a substantial non-Jewish population and was ruled by a Jewish king, Antipas, son of Herod the Great. Recent archaeological research has shown conclusively that Galilee had its own distinctive material culture with significant differences between upper and lower Galilee. Politically, Galilee and Jerusalem had different rulers from the death of Herod (4 B.C.E.) until the death of Agrippa I (44 C.E.), when the Roman procurators took direct control. Herod Antipas, like his father before him, had his own officials to keep order and collect taxes. The struggle to control Galilee and the conflicts among the aristocratic factions and people form the backdrop of much of Josephus' *War* and *Life*. None of these Galilean leaders were under the power of the chief priests or leading families in Jerusalem, and as the attempt to remove Josephus showed (ch. 5), they resisted Jerusalem's authority.

Galilee was divided into several administrative and taxation districts whose boundaries changed with political events.[32] Sepphoris and Tiberias (built by Antipas) were the two most influential cities and administrative centers in lower Galilee during the first century.[33] A variety of local officials watched over and administered the villages and towns. The presence and power of such officials explain the appearance of the Herodians and other officials of Herod in the gospels, the political execution of John the Baptist and the threats to Jesus in Galilee. All of these arrangements were standard in the Hellenistic world and show how peripheral both Pharisees and Jerusalem priests would be to the indigenous leadership.[34]

Galilee had a distinctive piety and other cultural variations in comparison with Judea and Jerusalem. Though the descriptions of Galilean piety have been based partly on uncritical methods and sometimes exaggerated,[35] the Temple and priesthood surely played a lesser role in Galilee than in Judea. The rabbinic sources, which usually exaggerate the sages' control and influence over society, have few traditions about their presence in Galilee before the war.[36] Freyne has argued for some Pharisaic influence

[32]For the five districts and councils *(synedria)* set up by Gabinius in 57-55, see *War* 1.8.5 (170) and *Ant.* 14.5.4 (91). For later toparchies and districts, see the summary in Schürer, Vermes, Millar, *History*, 2:184-198.

[33]See Schürer, Vermes, Millar, *History,* 2:172-182.

[34]See Freyne, *Galilee,* ch. 3. Mk 6:21 and Luke 8:3, 24:10 mention officials of Herod Antipas' court. Josephus' accounts of the war in Galilee mention numerous Galilean groups and offices with power and influence.

[35]Büchler, *Jewish-Palestinian Piety,* ch. 2; Geza Vermes, *Jesus the Jew* (London: Collins, 1973), chs. 2-3.

[36]A talmudic authority, 'Ulla, claimed that Johanan ben Zakkai lived in Galilee eighteen years and was only called upon to decide two cases (j. Shab. 16:8 [15d end]). Though such an isolated statement cannot be historically verified, it and other passages show that rabbinic traditions associated the sages with Palestine and Judea until after the Bar Kosiba war. Freyne, *Galilee,* 315, takes the substance of the story as historical

on Galilee before the wars, but his arguments, based on a few passages in Josephus and some rabbinic texts of doubtful worth, are tenuous.[37] The recent claims by Oppenheimer that the Pharisees had a great influence on Galilee are based on an uncritical use of rabbinic literature and have been ably refuted by Michael Goodman.[38] Even in the second century the rabbis were not the local administrators, but subordinate to the traditional leaders of Galilee.[39] On the other hand, Vermes sets up too sharp a dichotomy between Pharisaic piety and Galilean piety when he says that the Pharisees could not have been in Galilee disputing with Jesus because they were scholarly disputants and Jesus was a popular holy man.[40]

The evidence is too ambiguous to permit a certain conclusion concerning the Pharisees' presence in Galilee. If they were there, they were a minor and probably relatively new social force, struggling to influence people toward their way of life. This would explain why they were in constant conflict with Jesus and other proponents of traditional piety different from their own.

SOCIAL ROLES IN GALILEE

If some Pharisees lived in Galilee, what might their roles and activities have been? There is little reliable evidence for this in the gospels or rabbinic literature. The Pharisees have been pictured as religious professionals or a religious elite, but these categories fit modern social structure in which the religious establishment is separate from the political and commercial spheres of life. The

---

but says that Johanan went to Galilee as a representative of Jerusalem scribalism, not Pharisaism.

[37]Freyne, *Galilee,* 309-323.

[38]A. Oppenheimer, *The 'Am Ha-Aretz. A Study in the Social History of the Jewish People in the Hellenistic-Roman Period* (Leiden: Brill, 1977), reviewed by M. Goodman, *JJS* 31 (1980) 248-249. In his own study, *State,* 93-118, Goodman argues that the rabbis struggled from 132 on to establish their ways of living Judaism against Galilean customs. They succeeded only in the third and fourth centuries.

[39]Goodman, *State,* 119-133. For an excellent review of the difficulties in establishing the social status of the rabbis (and Pharisees) see Cohen, "Historical Settings," 49-50. He points out that rabbinic literature testifies to tensions between local aristocrats and administrators and the insurgent rabbis.

[40]G. Vermes, *Jesus and the World of Judaism* (Philadelphia: Fortress, 1983) 30-32.

proper question, to which there is no definitive answer, is: For whom did they work? Where did they get their livelihood? The later rabbinic picture of rabbi artisans does not fit this period.[41] The Pharisees could only have worked for the governing class, which controlled the wealth of the society; specifically in the first century, this was the Temple leadership in so far as it was represented in Galilee, Herod Antipas' government, or landowners. The Pharisees' stress on tithing and priestly piety for the laity could have been attractive to the Jerusalem authorities who desired to collect tithes from all Jews in Palestine and who could have met resistance from Jews in Galilee, outside their political control. This kind of activity would continue their role, clearly seen in Josephus, as retainers of the Jerusalem authorities. If the Pharisees in Galilee were representatives of the Jerusalem leadership, it would explain their small numbers in Galilee, their lack of mention in other sources and their absence from accounts of indigenous Galilean society and leadership. It would also explain their hostility to Jesus and their willingness to form coalitions with the Herodians to oppose him.

It is possible that the officials and retainers of Herod Antipas supported and encouraged the Pharisees and that they served some functions in the government of Galilee. Since the Pharisees were supporters of an ordered Jewish society and of observance of Jewish law, their goals would have been harmonious with those of Antipas, who desired to keep his predominantly Jewish kingdom in good order. The Pharisees' emphasis on tithing and practices which promoted Jewish identity could be used to promote loyalty to a Jewish king who kept Galilee peaceful and provided a buffer between Galilee and the Roman empire.

Finally, the Pharisees could have been supported by the wealthy landowners who found the Pharisaic understanding of Judaism a support for Galilean society. But traditional leaders do not usually share power or form alliances unless there is a need.[42] Since Galilee was relatively peaceful and prosperous

---

[41] See ch. 3. Even in the talmudic period, it is clear that rabbis came from many economic classes and supported themselves in various ways.

[42] Luke portrays the Pharisees as wealthy, established patrons who are failing in their role as protectors of the people and exploiting them (see ch. 9) but his view of the Pharisees in Galilean society does not seem to be based on accurate, firsthand knowledge.

until 44 C.E., when the Roman procurators took direct control and relations with the government deteriorated, it is unlikely that the landowners would have allied themselves with the Pharisees as a protest against oppression. In the end, whether the Pharisees were present in Galilee and what their roles there might have been remain uncertain and obscure.

13

The Sadducees and Jewish Leadership

Though the Sadducees appeared, mostly along with the Pharisees, in Josephus, the New Testament and rabbinic literature, the sources give so little information about the Sadducees that great care and restraint is needed in characterizing them. Most treatments of the Sadducees and the first century assume that all the chief priests and other leaders of Judaism in Jerusalem were Sadducees.[1] However, Josephus does not say that all Jewish leaders were Sadducees, but only that those who were Sadducees came from the governing class. It is likely that a very small number of the governing class were Sadducees.

Because Josephus describes the Sadducees along with the

---

[1]LeMoyne, *Sadducéens*, 11-26, reviews previous literature. LeMoyne's book covers all aspects of the Sadducees, analyzing the texts and providing a reasonable and cautious synthesis. He is sometimes too uncritical in his use of rabbinic sources. Aside from entries in standard reference works, another synthesis with bibliography can be found in G. Baumbach, "Der sadduzäische Konservativismus," *Literatur und Religion des Frühjudentums,* eds. J. Maier and J. Schreiner (Würzburg: Echter, 1973) 201-213; also by the same author "Das Sadduzäerverstandnis bei Josephus Flavius und im Neuen Testament," *Kairos* 13 (1971) 17-37, where he holds that the Sadducees were the majority of the Sadokite priests who remained in Jerusalem and did not go to Egypt or Qumran. See the more recent study by E. Bammel, "Sadducäer und Sadokiden," *Ephemerides theologicae lovanienses* 55 (1979) 107-115 who thinks that the designation Sadducee was first used by priests brought in from Egypt and Babylon by Herod in order to counter Hasmonean influence on the priesthood. V.Eppstein, "When and How the Sadducees Were Excommunicated," *JBL* 85 (1966) 213-224, uses rabbinic sources uncritically without regard to date. Levine, "Political Conflicts," 74-79, argues very speculatively that the Sadducees were a military group who came to power under John Hyrcanus. They were priests who were also involved with diplomacy. Thanks are also due to Gary Porton of the University of Illinois at Champaign-Urbana for making available two unpublished papers on the Sadducees.

Pharisees and Essenes, most commentators have taken the Sadducees, like the Pharisees and Essenes, to be a sect-like group. However, sects and sect-like groups are by definition in reaction against the establishment or majority social position. If the Sadducees were from the governing class, as Josephus says, they were probably not a protest group in the proper sense, but a small group with particular ideas about how some parts of Jewish life ought to be lived and specific beliefs to go along with those practices.

The task of reconstructing the Sadducees from the sources is daunting and in many respects impossible. Josephus mentions one individual Sadducee; he describes the Sadducees as a group only in contrast to the Pharisees and Essenes. Since Josephus bends history to suit his purposes, his descriptions of the Sadducees cannot be taken at face value. The gospels and Acts mention the Sadducees only a very few times. They agree with Josephus that the Sadducees do not believe in resurrection, that they are to be contrasted with the Pharisees and that they are connected with the Jerusalem leadership. Beyond this they tell us little.

The Sadducees are mentioned only a relatively few times in rabbinic literature and these references are scattered in various collections from different periods. Thus, the historical reliability of all these passages is suspect.[2] When the Sadducees appear in the Mishnah and Tosefta, they are disputing with the Pharisees over some practice or teaching. Since the rabbinic authors saw themselves as heirs of the Pharisees, the Sadducees are always bested in argument.

JOSEPHUS

Josephus describes the Sadducees along with the Pharisees and Essenes on several occasions. Only once does he refer to an individual Sadducee, Ananus the high priest.[3] Ananus fits the descriptions given elsewhere of the Sadducees, that they are

---

[2]See LeMoyne, *Sadducéens,* 321-27 and passim for critical problems.

[3]*Ant.* 20.9.1 (199-203). In two places Ananus' name is followed by the term *Sadouki* (*War* 2.17.10 (251); 2.21.7 (628). In each case he appears in a list of people who are

from the highest level of society and that they are stern in their administration of justice. The descriptions of the Sadducees are not objective and are very incomplete. In each case the Sadducees are described in conscious contrast to the Pharisees and Essenes and none of the descriptions is extensive because Josephus is more interested in the Essenes in the *War* and the Pharisees in the *Antiquities* than he is in the Sadducees.

Josephus places the Sadducees within the governing class, an understanding of them which is consistent with everything else he says about them. The views attributed to them, rejection of the new belief in afterlife and the new customs being developed by the Pharisees, are characteristic of any dominant class. They wish to retain the status quo and keep the focus on the nation (and potential kingdom) of Israel in this world, not in the next. Their views of providence, as presented by Josephus, may reflect a post-exilic view of God as very transcendent and far from the affairs of the Jewish nation (which had lost its king and independence). They are seen as nasty and arrogant because they have and exercise power and because they compete with each other for power.

It must be emphasized again that Josephus does not say that all the priests or Jewish leaders were Sadducees, only that the Sadducees were drawn from that (presumably much larger) group. The Sadducees seem to have been an established, but minor, group in Judaism. As such they served Josephus' purpose of presenting Judaism as possessing respectable and old philosophies in the Hellenistic mold. Just how organized the Sadducees were is left unsaid in all the sources. Since they came from the dominant class and reflected the established ways of Judaism, probably one's commitment to and participation in the Sadducees could be of low intensity.

NEW TESTAMENT

The relatively few references to the Sadducees in the New Testament generally agree with the view of them found in

---

identified as the son of X. Thus, *Sadouki* means "son of Sadok" (a good high priestly name), not "Sadducee."

Josephus. Because affirmation of Jesus' resurrection was central for Christians, the characteristic of the Sadducees which most strongly impressed them was the Sadducees' rejection of life after death. The single controversy with them in Mark (ch. 12, with parallels in Matthew and Luke) and the argument between the Pharisees and Sadducees provoked by Paul in the Sanhedrin (Acts 23) all depend on the denial of resurrection. Matthew links the Sadducees with the Pharisees in opposition to Jesus, a coalition which is possible on a temporary and limited basis. In Acts they are associated with the chief priests and temple authorities (4:1; 5:17) and the Sanhedrin (ch. 23) as opponents of the early followers of Jesus.

RABBINIC LITERATURE

The Sadducees appear mostly as opponents of the Pharisees and always as adversaries of the authors of rabbinic literature. They are not legitimate participants in the numerous debates which go on among the sages, but an outside group to be refuted and scorned. The talmuds sometimes reach the point of not accepting them as legitimate Jews. In rabbinic literature, especially in the Tosefta, the Sadducees are identified with or closely associated with the Boethusians, a group even less well known than the Sadducees. It seems that the rabbinic authors had a clear sense of the Sadducees as opponents who differed on some essential points of practice and belief, but no precise and consistent knowledge of what those differences were.

In the earliest sources, the Mishnah and Tosefta, the Sadducees differ from the Pharisees and tannaitic authors especially concerning ritual purity and sabbath observance. The disagreements are typical mishnaic disputes and concern limited points of behavior and interpretation, some public and some private. An additional couple of cases concern civil law. No fundamental disagreements over hermeneutic principles for interpreting Scripture or the relationship of customary interpretation to the written canon appear, nor does a comprehensive picture of the Saducean position emerge from these few disputes.

The Mishnah and Tosefta refute the views of the Sadducees rather than present a fair picture of their positions. The later sources, especially the Babylonian Talmud, paint the Sadducees in even more lurid colors and suggest in places that they were not really Jews, but heretics. Such is certainly not historically true, but the result of a later defense of rabbinic authority and its way of life. In general, little reliable historical information is preserved in or recoverable from the rabbinic sources.

Conclusion

Though the evidence concerning the Sadducees is sparse, both Josephus, the New Testament and rabbinic literature assume that the Sadducees were an established and well recognized group of first century Jews. They take them for granted and Josephus claims that they were respected (though with limited influence) within Jewish society and culture.

Some scholars have held that the Sadducees were the Hellenized, aristocratic leadership of Judaism, but the sources give no evidence that the Sadducees were Hellenized in any special way.[4] (All Jewish society, thought and literature had been affected by the Hellenistic empire and its Hellenized successor, the Roman empire to some extent.)[5] It is certain that the chief priests and leaders of the dominant families cooperated with the Romans and sought to keep the peace and the status quo, upon which their power and prosperity were built. The Romans, for their part, were noted for developing and patronizing provincial elites.[6] While the chief priests protected the Jewish way of life, they were neither reformers nor revolutionaries.[7] If the Sadducees were drawn mainly from the governing class and aristocrats in Jerusalem, as Josephus and his interpreters suggest,[8] then the Sadducees may have been a movement reacting against the assimilationist tendencies of some leaders. The balance between

[4]LeMoyne, *Sadducéens*, 334-335; 350-352.

[5]Elias Bickerman, *From Ezra to the Last of the Maccabees* (NY: Schocken, 1962); Hengel, *Judaism and Hellenism.*

[6]Nicolas Purcell, Ch. 23, "The Arts of Government," *The Oxford History of the Classical World,* eds J. Boardman et al. (Oxford/New York: OUP, 1986) 569.

[7]Horsley, "High Priests."

[8]LeMoyne, *Sadducéens*, 342-344; 349-350.

accommodating a foreign power and protecting a cultural tradition is difficult if not impossible to maintain and it is likely that disagreements in the governing class would have spawned groups and movements with different understandings of Judaism. As Josephus pictures them, the Sadducees had a body of teaching and a way of life which was intensely Jewish but different from that of the Pharisees and Essenes.

We know little about the specific characteristics of the Sadducees. Standard treatments of the Sadducees often differentiate them from the Pharisees on the basis of their insistence on literal interpretation of Scripture and their rejection of the oral Torah. Neither criterion is explicit or implicit in the sources and both are misleading. When one examines ancient Biblical interpretation, both that which is designated literal and that which is more elaborate, all the interpretations are far from what contemporary scholars consider literal. In fact, every group for which we have evidence turned to the individual words, sentences and fundamental ideas of the Bible in order to justify and also develop its way of life and all expanded on them in order to link their ideas with Scripture.

The explicit doctrine or teaching about the oral Torah in contrast to the written Torah does not appear until the third century, C.E., though the idea is implicit earlier.[9] But oral Torah is of limited value as a category because in a sense, all Jews had their own oral Torah. That is, each locale and probably each sub-group or social class had its own customs and specific rules for how to live Judaism. These laws and customs had developed over decades and centuries and were common to all groups. The Pharisees and later the rabbis promoted a certain version of such rules with an underlying vision of the Jewish way of life. Josephus' characterization of the Sadducees, that they accept no observance apart from the laws, serves to contrast them with the Pharisees. Thus it means simply that they observed the Biblical laws as they interpreted them and that they rejected the Pharisaic interpretation. It does not say that the Sadducees had great hermeneutical differences with the Pharisees but only that the Sadducees were not Pharisees and so they rejected Pharisaic

---

[9]Peter Schäfer, "Das 'Dogma' von der mündlichen Torah," in *Studien zur Geschichte und Theologie des rabbinischen Judentums* (Leiden: Brill, 1978) 153-197.

teaching. In this the Sadducees (and Pharisees) were like all other Jewish groups, each of which had its own traditions, social and religious goals and laws.[10] That the Sadducees were more traditional and the Pharisees more innovative makes it appear that one interpreted Scripture and the other did not, that one accepted a new body of law and the other did not. In fact, post-exilic Judaism had already engaged in massive adaptation of traditional Jewish life to new circumstances and the Sadducees as part of that Judaism had a distinctive interpretation of many parts of Jewish life.

The testimony of all the sources that the Sadducees did not believe in resurrection, afterlife and judgment fits the other things we know about them and is historically reliable and convincing. The Sadducees' belief is the traditional Biblical view; ideas of resurrection, immortality and afterlife entered Judaism in the second century B.C.E. and only gradually dominated Judaism over the next four or five centuries.[11] If Sadducees were predominantly from the governing class, which tends to be very conservative in a traditional society, it is probable that they did not accept the new innovation of resurrection. Their rejection of life after death and judgment also explains Josephus' classification of them (in Greek terms) as stressing free will and denying fate. Though as Jews they certainly believed in God's covenant and care for Israel, they did not believe in his apocalyptic intervention in world history and so could be presented as denying fate and stressing human control over life. In addition, the rejection of the new belief in afterlife and the new customs being developed by the Pharisees, is characteristic of any dominant class. The Sadducees probably wished to retain the status quo and keep the focus on the nation (and potential kingdom) of Israel in this world, not in the next. As was noted above their views of providence, as presented by Josephus, may reflect a post-exilic view of God as very transcendent and far from the affairs of the Jewish nation (which had lost its king and

---

[10]LeMoyne, *Sadducées,* 372-379.

[11]See George W.E. Nickelsburg, *Resurrection, Immortality, and Eternal Life in Intertestamental Judaism* (HThSt 26; Cambridge: HUP, 1972). Mishnah Sanhedrin 10:1, from about 200 C.E. still has a stricture against those who deny resurrection of the dead; later talmudic comments on this passage speak not of those who deny resurrection of the dead, but who deny that it can be proved from Scripture.

independence). We know little more about their beliefs and customs. They most probably had a different style and sense of the whole than the Pharisees. To the outside observer the differences would have appeared as minor, but within the community such differences typically produce fierce conflicts over control and influence, such as those reflected in the sources.

The Sadducees are often characterized as a sect by scholars. If they were a tightly organized protest group against the mode of the Jewish life fostered by the high priest and most powerful members of Jewish society, then the designation sect would fit. However, we have no direct proof that this was so nor do the sources suggest this. If they merely represented a mode of living Judaism popular among the governing class, they then are too highly placed to be a real sect, that is, a group which is in reaction against the dominant force in society and which claims to be the true heir to the tradition as did the Qumran Essenes. Our analysis of the Sadducees would be helped by some knowledge of their inner organization, the intensity and exclusivity of commitment required and the rules governing their activities, but we lack all such information.[12]

HISTORY

The history of the Sadducees is equally obscure. The Sadducees appear in Josephus during the Hasmonean period along with the Pharisees when John Hyrcanus switched his allegiance from the Pharisees to the Sadducees. The only rabbinic text which deals with the origins of the Sadducees is a paragraph in the Fathers According to Rabbi Nathan.[13] This passage, which is taken as historical by LeMoyne,[14] is most probably a later rabbinic explanation for the presence of Sadducees and Boethusians in rabbinic traditions and for the interchange of their names. Sadok and Boethus are said to have been disciples

---

[12]LeMoyne, *Sadducéens,* 331.

[13]Abot de Rabbi Nathan, Version A, ch. 5 and Version B, ch. 10. For translations and notes see J. Goldin, *The Fathers According to Rabbi Nathan* (Yale Judaica Series 10; New Haven: Yale, 1955) 39 and Anthony J. Saldarini, *The Fathers According to Rabbi Nathan (Abot de Rabbi Nathan) Version B* (SJLA 11; Leiden: Brill, 1975) 85-86.

[14]LeMoyne, *Sadducéens,* 113-119.

of Antigonus of Soko, the enigmatic figure who appears between Simon the Just, the last of the men of the Great Assembly, and the first of the pairs of leaders identified by the rabbis as their intellectual ancestors and leaders of Pharisaism.[15] The attachment of the founders of the Sadducees and Boethusians to Antigonus deprives them of legitimacy and establishes them as original opponents of the Pharisees. The Sadducees and Essenes were not derived from the Great Assembly, the legendary source of authority in the early second Temple period, nor were they derived from the rabbinic pairs who are mentioned a number of times in rabbinic literature, but rather they were disciples of the most obscure of the members of the chain of tradition, Antigonus, to whom is attributed an enigmatic saying concerning reward for obedience to God. The association of Sadducees and Boethusians with the disciples of Antigonus is also governed by the appropriateness of Antigonus' saying for the dispute between the Sadducees and the sages concerning life after death, judgment and reward and punishment. Antigonus' saying is:

> Antigonus of Soko took over from Simeon the Righteous. He used to say: Be not like slaves who serve their master for the sake of their allowance; be rather like slaves who serve their master with no thought of an allowance—and let the fear of heaven be upon you.[16]

The disciples of the disciples of Saddok and Boethus are said to have examined the saying of Antigonus and determined that it implied no afterlife.[17] These disciples then withdrew and formed

---

[15]Abot 1:3.

[16]See E. Bickerman, "The Maxim of Antigonus of Socho," *HTR* 44 (1951) 127-151 for the original meaning of the saying.

[17]Finkelstein, *The Pharisees,* 153-154 holds that the saying was originally a denial of afterlife. The version of the saying cited in the Fathers According to Rabbi Nathan adds a clause that turns the saying into an affirmation of reward after death. In Version A it says "And let the fear of Heaven be upon you, *so that your reward may be doubled in the age to come.*" Version B Says, "And let the fear of Heaven be upon you, *and you will receive a reward, both in this world and the world to come, as if you had done (it yourself)."*

two sects.[18] This version of their origin assumes that belief in afterlife was already established in Judaism in the second century B.C.E. and that a couple of generations later (around 100 B.C.E., when Josephus indicates that the Pharisees and Sadducees were in conflict) two groups of disciples became heretics. This is a highly tendentious account of the situation. That the break became sharp during the reign of either John Hyrcanus or Alexander Jannaeus is very likely and that they disagreed concerning life after death is certain. However, the Sadducees just continued with traditional Jewish beliefs and resisted innovation by the Pharisees and others.

The history of the Sadducees is as uncertain as their origins. Versions of their history vary according to whether scholars identify the Sadducees with the high priest and leaders, how they evaluate the reliability of rabbinic sources and Josephus, and whether they consider them to be a political party or religious sect.[19] Most reconstructions see second Temple society in simple terms, with a few groups vying for power. This simplification is based on a naive reading of the sources. Neither the priests nor the aristocracy enjoyed serene dominance during the Greco-Roman period.

One cannot speak of the priests as a unified group, much less identify the Sadducees with them. When the Hasmonean family became dominant in Jerusalem after the war against Antiochus IV and when Jonathan later became high priest and was succeeded by Simon and his descendants, the priestly class was thrown into confusion. Even before the war various factions had fought for control and the high priesthood had changed hands. In the Hasmonean takeover the traditional high priestly families lost power and influence. The Hasmoneans did not easily succeed in establishing their power; Josephus' account of this period

---

[18]"Withdrew" or "separated" *(prš)* is a technical word for sect-like organizations which break off from dominant groups. It is also the root from which the Pharisees' name is taken. Version A has "withdrew from Torah," a more sharp judgment which probably reflects later editing by talmudic authors who saw the Sadducees as heretics. The word for sect in Version A is *peraṣôt* (literally, "breaches," as in breaches in a defense wall) and in Version B *mišpaḥôt* (families), perhaps reflecting the belief that these groups were composed of priestly "families."

[19]For a fairly critical and judicious review of the evidence, see LeMoyne, *Sadducéens*, 381-399.

shows a number of struggles and intrigues. 1 Maccabees, which is a pro-Hasmonean account of the war from about 100 B.C.E., tries to connect the Hasmoneans with the Sadokite line and Phineas (1 Macc. 2:54) in order to establish their legitimacy. In the Herodian period various priestly families had their members appointed high priest, with Herod choosing high priests who would enhance his power or at least not be a threat to it. After the death of Herod high priests changed to reflect the vagaries of Jewish politics and Roman policies.

The aristocracy cannot be viewed as a static group during the Greco-Roman period either. Hasmonean struggles over succession, the Roman dominance of Jerusalem, political turmoil during and after Herod's reign and the long path to the great war against Rome all produced a myriad of political coalitions, alliances and disputes. The sources for this period give only a glimpse at the waxing and waning fortunes of numerous individuals and families among the Jewish elite as well as insurgent groups among the people and emerging leaders. Consequently, the social and political situation in the governing class, among whom we must number most of the Sadducees, was complex and changing. The situation was further influenced by the members of the priesthood and the retainer class, including the Pharisees, scribes and other officials.

Glossary of Sociological Terms

[Words in **bold letters** are defined in this glossary.]

Achieved Status: membership or **Status** based on the activities of the person and the effects produced on social relationships by those activities.

Artisan Class: Those skilled in the crafts necessary for society. Most were limited to the goods they could produce with their own labor and, like the peasants, lacked power and wealth.

Ascriptive Status: an assigned group membership or social **Status,** role, or place within that group based on birth or thrust on one by an outside force, such as a political entity or a culture.

Class System: a hierarch of **Classes** ranked in terms of some single criterion, such as politics, property, occupation, heredity.

Class: the place of a group or person in society based on economic criteria, according to Weber's classic definition. Class is often associated with power, as in Lenski's theory used in this book, and overlaps status and party. A wider and more common definition of class is a large body of persons who occupy a position in a social hierarchy by reason of their manifesting similarity of valued objective criteria, such as kinship, power, achievements, possessions, etc. See **Status** and **Party.**

Coalition: a temporary alliance of distinct parties for a limited purpose, in which the resources used by the coalition remain linked to its original members. A coalition is temporary and not the primary identity of the members.

The nature of the commitment and the wider goals of each member may vary considerably.

Commitment: One of Parsons' **Generalized Symbolic Media** of interaction. Generalized commitments, seen in cultural patterns and motivations, underlie the concrete relationships which bind the members of a society together and can be used to motivate people to action.

Conflict Theory: the sociological theory that society consists of conflicting forces and competing interests; the effort to understand all social activity as the result of conflicting needs, desires and goals. Conflict theory is often opposed to **Functionalism** which stresses organic unity among social roles and activities ordered to the well being of society as a whole.

Corporate Group: a discrete, multi-member aggregate having property, aims and duties which inhere in the group as such, and are distinct from those of its individual members. Each member has rights and duties with respect to the group. All members are bound together by virtue of their shared membership in the group and by their common obligation to protect its interests and fulfill its obligations.

Faction: a type of **Coalition** recruited personally according to structurally diverse principles by or on behalf of a person. Factions tend to be characterized by unstable membership, uncertain duration, personalistic leadership, a lack of formal organization, and a greater concern for power and spoils than ideology or policy.

Formal Group: an organization with procedures for mobilizing and coordinating the efforts of various, usually specialized, subgroups or individuals in the pursuit of joint objectives.

Functionalism: the sociological theory that all human action contributes to human living and specifically human society. The effort to understand the part that each type of action and each social group or role plays in producing and sustaining society as an organic unity.

Generalized Symbolic Media: Talcott Parsons' four generalized symbolic media of interaction are four types of "power" (in the general sense) used in social relations among individuals. They are **Power** (in the proper sense), **Influence,** money and **Commitment.** See also **Wealth.**

Governing Class: A small class which served the ruler and had control of most of the power and wealth in ancient society.

Group: in its most general definition, any collectivity of humans. More specifically, any collectivity bound by principles of membership and a set of rights and duties. See **Formal Group** for most social groups.

Honor (and **Shame**): Honor and shame define one's public standing and one's personal self image which is dependent on that public standing. Honor and shame are the two poles of a social evaluation based on the type of personality considered ideal in a society. The evaluation is sanctioned by public opinion and also derives from the person's self-image and self-evaluation. Honor is especially the preoccupation of individuals in small scale, exclusive, face-to-face societies where standing and prestige are dependent on people, not on impersonal offices.

Influence: One of Parsons' **Generalized Symbolic Media** of interaction. The influential person is considered to be a reliable source of information or judgment concerning that information and thus is able to have an impact on the judgment and action of others.

Interest Group: one of the most common types of voluntary association, organized on the basis of distinctive concerns, needs, desires or goals shared by the members, with the goal of fostering those shared interests.

Involuntary Group: collectivities into which people are born or which impose themselves upon people such as kin groups, political communities, social classes and castes.

Lower Classes: Peasants, Artisans, unclean and expendable classes who formed the bulk of society in antiquity and were characterized by a lack of **Power** and **Wealth**.

Movement: social activity which is very diffuse and lacks almost all organization. See **Social Movement** and **Social Movement Organization.**

Network: a set of social relationships among individuals and groups of people, specifying the relationships as simple or multiplex (involving more than one role), one directional or mutual, evaluating them by importance and worth, frequency and duration of contact and describing them according to structural features such as its size, density, the degree of closeness of connection, clustering and intermediaries.

Non-Corporate Group: a collectivity, such as a **Movement, Coalition, Faction,** usually lacking fixed structure and held together by temporary and narrow common interests. It cannot by right claim the resources of the members and has a less clear identity than stable **Corporate Groups.**

Party: the place of a person or group in society based on political power. See **Class** and **Status**

Peasant Class: Those who produced food either on their own land or that of others. Production was usually limited to subsistence plus the excess required to pay taxes to the **Upper Classes** and thus peasants usually lacked **Wealth** and **Power.**

Political Interest Group: a collectivity which seeks to convert its interests into public law or gain control over social behavior. This category includes modern pressure groups.

Power: One of Parsons' **Generalized Symbolic Media** of interaction; the generalized capacity to secure the performance of binding obligations by members of an organization when the obligations are legitimized with reference to their bearing on the collective goals and when there is enforcement by negative sanctions against recalcitrance.

Retainer Class: Those who served the neeeds of the ruler and **Governing Class,** including soldiers, bureaucratic government officials, educators, religious leaders. They shared the life of the governing class to some extent, but had no independent base of power or wealth (in contrast to the modern middle class).

Sect: a religiously based group which is either actively involved against society or withdrawn in reaction to it. Such groups are often political forces. In its classical Christian definition sect is contrasted with the dominant religious force, church.

Shame: see **Honor.**

Social Movement Organization: a complex, or formal, organization which identifies its goals with the preferences of a **Social Movement** or a counter movement and attempts to implement those goals. A social movement organization is, therefore, a **Voluntary, Corporate Group** similar to the **Political Interest Group.** See **Movement** and **Social Movement.**

Social Movement: an effort by a large number of people to solve collectively a problem that they feel they have in common, such as promoting or resisting change in society. See **Social Movement Organization.**

Status: the place of a group or person in society based on one's legal standing and prestige. Emphasis may be placed on relational or on positional structural elements which determine status. See **Class** and **Party.**

Upper Classes: The ruling classes (according to Lenski), including the ruler, **Governing Class,** priests, merchants, and **Retainers.** This relatively small group controlled the excess production of the **Peasants** and other **Lower Classes.**

Voluntary Corporate Group: a collection of people with permanent existence, recruited on recognized principles, with common interest and rules (norms) fixing rights and duties of the members in relation to one another and to these interests.

Voluntary Group: a collectivity organized for the pursuit of one interest or of several interests in common. See **Voluntary Corporate Group.**

Wealth: physical resources which can be used to maintain life, achieve one's purposes and gain power over others. In antiquity wealth was usually tied to productive land and was dependent on the acquisition and maintenance of **Power.** In modern times, by contrast, wealth in the form of money is often the path to power.

Subject Index

Author Index

Index of Ancient Sources

BIBLE

APOCRYPHA AND PSEUDEPIGRAPHA

JOSEPHUS

PHILO
Legatio ad Gaium

RABBINIC LITERATURE MISHNAH

TOSEFTA

PALESTINIAN TALMUD

BABYLONIAN TALMUD

OTHER LITERATURE

About the Author

ANTHONY J. SALDARINI is Associate Professor in the Department of Theology at Boston College. He earned his Ph.D. from the Department of Near Eastern Languages and Literature at Yale University. He co-translated, along with Daniel Harrington, SJ, *Targum Jonathan of the Former Prophets* (volume 10 of *The Aramaic Bible* series).